D0203672

THE HAWTHORNES

The story of seven generations of
an American family

THE HAWTHORNES

By Vernon Loggins

GREENWOOD PRESS, PUBLISHERS
NEW YORK   1968

Copyright 1951
COLUMBIA UNIVERSITY PRESS, NEW YORK
Reprinted with the permission of Columbia University Press.

CS 71
.H4
1968

First Greenwood reprinting, 1968
LIBRARY OF CONGRESS catalogue card number: 69-10121

INDIANA-
PURDUE
LIBRARY

WITHDRAWN

FORT WAYNE

Printed in the United States of America

TO ELOÏSE PARKHURST-HUGUENIN

ACKNOWLEDGMENTS

FOR expertly directing me during my many weeks of gathering Hawthorne material in Salem, I thank Miss Florence M. Osborne, the Essex Institute librarian.

I wrote *The Hawthornes* at the MacDowell Colony, Peterborough, New Hampshire. During each of the three summers devoted to the labors I used the Veltin Studio, which was used from 1919 to 1934 by Edwin Arlington Robinson. For the beautiful privilege of working where this great poet once worked, as well as for many other privileges granted me at the Colony, I thank Mrs. Edward MacDowell and her colleagues on the managerial staff.

I thank those who read the manuscript and made suggestions for improvement. They are Mrs. Helene G. Baer, Mrs. Leonora Brennecke, Mr. Bruce Carpenter, Miss Mabel Daniels, Mrs. Inez Perrin Day, Miss Ruth Dougan, Mr. Joseph A. Duffy, Dr. Abraham Flexner, Miss Muriel E. Kern, Miss Henrietta Mason, Mrs. Eloïse Parkhurst-Huguenin, Mrs. J. C. Shlan, Mrs. Leonora Speyer, Miss Margaret Widdemer, and Mr. Thurman Wilkins.

VERNON LOGGINS

Columbia University
March 4, 1951

CONTENTS

THE HAWTHORNES

MAJOR WILLIAM HATHORNE, 1607–1681
Jehovah in the wrath of His vengeance is scowling upon you!

COLONEL JOHN HATHORNE, 1641–1717
Did Mr. Burroughs bring you any of the poppets of his wives to stick pins into?

CAPTAIN JOSEPH HATHORNE, 1692–1762
I give to my wife Sarah my silver tankard with an H marked on it.

CAPTAIN DANIEL HATHORNE, 1731–1796
My boys, she means to fight us!

CAPTAIN NATHANIEL HATHORNE, 1775–1808
This Night we saw the North Star, which I think is a great pleasure to a homeward Bound Mariner after a Long Voyage to India.

NATHANIEL HAWTHORNE, 1804–1864
Life is made up of marble and mud.

MOTHER M. ALPHONSA LATHROP, O.S.D., 1851–1926
As St. Thomas Aquinas says, the greatest value of a gift is the love there is in it.

THE OLD HOME

HAWTHORN HILL, a picturesque height overlooking the village of Bray in the English shire of Berks, gots its name, says tradition, from a hawthorn tree which once upon a time crowned its crest. In turn, tradition adds, it provided a surname for the husbandman who tilled its slopes and the fields adjacent. Authoritative records show that at the beginning of the sixteenth century the Hawthornes of Bray, from whom the Hawthornes of Salem in Massachusetts were descended, dwelt in the neighborhood of Hawthorn Hill.

They were humble yeomen. Yet it is likely that they already held in common one possession which many a rich proud Berkshire aristocrat was in time to covet. It was their family legend, a tale telling of a supposed Hawthorne who lived long before the sixteenth century. His story as reconstructed from two varying versions here follows.

He grew up to be a tiller of the soil, this early Hawthorne, like his father and grandfather. But when he took a wife and begot sons and daughters he enlarged the house he had inherited from his forebears and turned it into an inn. The rude stone structure, with three or four chambers for travelers and a watertight roof of thatch, stood at the foot of Hawthorn Hill, hard by the ancient road which twisted and turned between London and Oxford. The establishment, known soon throughout the valley of the Thames as the Woodman, bore a sign showing a green-coated forester, axe raised, about to chop into the trunk of a great gray oak.

The innkeeper was a man of kind heart, and above all

hospitable. He showed such generosity to his guests that they abused him and kept him poor. His wife, given to nagging, sometimes called him a fool.

One night he dreamed a dream. In it a Presence, in the form of a comely woman, appeared before him and announced that if he would go and wait on London Bridge at noon on a specified day he would hear of a means to better his condition. He awoke, and dismissed the dream from his mind. But a few nights later he dreamed it again, with the same detail. Then one night the following week he dreamed the dream a third time.

On getting out of bed at dawn the next morning he suddenly realized that this was the day when the Presence had admonished him to repair to London Bridge. Long before the autumn sun had filled the valley with light he was astride the best of his horses galloping eastward on the crooked river road.

A few minutes before noon he walked into the gloom of London Bridge, in appearance a tunnel through buildings of stone. On the steps of the chapel that marked the center he found a place to stand and wait. It seemed to him that all London was going towards Southwark, and all Southwark towards London. As he smelled the odorous pedestrians and felt his ears crack from the clatter of horseshoes striking cobblestones, he began to think that his wife was right, that surely he was a fool.

Then a Citizen of London, well-dressed and pompous of mien, came up to the innkeeper and abruptly engaged him in conversation. The man from the country stated freely why he was waiting on London Bridge. And he was on the point of telling where he had come from when the Citizen broke in and said, "Nonsense! I myself once dreamed that if I'd dig under the tree which tops Hawthorn Hill I'd find a treasure. I'd never been told of Hawthorn Hill, nor had any of my friends. Was I going to search all the isle of England for a place heard about only in my sleep? Not I, my man. I'm too wise to put trust in dreams. You had better learn a lesson from me and depart from here before somebody takes you for an idle fellow and gets you into trouble."

With a smile of superiority the Citizen turned from the chapel steps and joined the stream of pedestrians headed for the London side of the river. The innkeeper for a moment stood fixed with amazement. Then, again in control of himself, he jostled his way as rapidly as possible to the Southwark bank, where he had left his horse in the care of a hostler.

He was far up the Thames on his return to Bray before he could think of anything except the possibility of treasure buried on Hawthorn Hill. "How did it get there?" he heard himself ask aloud. Then other questions flashed into his consciousness. What was the source of the supernatural power directing him? Was the Presence he had seen in the dream good or evil? Was he being tempted into one of the Devil's snares? Should he interpret the statement of the Citizen as a warning rather than a revelation? The more he pondered these problems the more perturbed he became. Yet all the while he urged on his tired mount.

It was past midnight when he got back to his inn. He was relieved to see that every window was dark, and he himself unsaddled and fed the horse. Without considering that he too needed refreshment, he procured a spade and climbed to the top of the hill. First he made sure that no human being could be watching. Then, near the trunk of the hawthorn tree, he began to dig, eagerly and audaciously.

He had made a hole three feet wide and three feet deep when his spade struck something solid. His heart beating fast, he loosed the soil crusted round the object, drew it up, and saw in the light of the moon that it was a lidded iron pot about eighteen inches high and twelve inches in diameter. The thing was heavy, and in his excitement he let it slip from his hands. When it struck the ground and turned over, the lid slid off, and out rolled a mass of coinlike discs. The innkeeper quickly scooped them back into the pot, unable to tell in the dimness the quality of the metal.

Hoping wildly that it might at least be silver, he grabbed up the pot, ran down the hill, and entered the great hall of the inn through a side door. There were still flames in the fireplace, and in the light the innkeeper saw that the discs really were coins, all alike—and of gold!

On each were stamped undecipherable characters and a head not English. The money all together filled half the pot, on the outside of which, where the circumference was greatest, ran an inscription, also undecipherable.

The innkeeper was about to waken his wife, children, servants, and any travelers who might be guests for the night. He wished to assemble them all in the great hall and shout, "I'm a rich man! I'm a rich man!" But, after reflecting a moment, he locked the pot of gold in a bronze chest, which was so ponderous that no gang of thieves could budge it without making a great noise.

With the key safe in the purse he always kept securely fastened to a waistband tied next to his naked skin, he ate and drank, then went upstairs, and was soon stretched out in bed beside his sleeping wife.

But he knew no rest that night. In snatches of slumber he repeatedly saw the crowd on London Bridge break into a dance of demons and the Citizen turn into a creature with horns and tail and cloven feet. More than once he sat up suddenly, sure that a band of outlaws from Windsor Forest had forced open the inn and were stirring about in the great hall. Again and again he fancied that his wife, whom he loved and trusted in spite of her shrewishness, was trying to remove from his waistband the purse which held the key to the chest. Each time he awoke and saw that she was sleeping in innocence, he was overcome with remorse.

For a week his nights became more nightmarish. The days, when his strange experience was his one thought, were equally tormenting. He reasoned that if he told his wife what was hidden in the bronze chest she might also come under the sway of a hellish power. He was even unable to bring himself to go to the Bray church and open up his heart in the confessional. What prevented him from coming out with the truth in the hearing of a man of God? Of all the questions that weighed upon the innkeeper this was the heaviest. His only answer was that the treasure must be the Devil's. Still when he dreamed at night that burglars were in the great hall to cart away the heavy chest he invariably woke up grabbing for his weapons.

On the ninth afternoon following the discovery of the gold he had trading to do at the fair in Maidenhead. When dark came he joined a number of his friends at a Maidenhead tavern, hoping that much ale, a good supper, and an evening of conviviality would help rid his mind of the awful worries.

When he got back to his inn that night he at least felt bolder. The hour was late. His wife and all the household had been long in bed. Heedless of the racket he was making, he tossed logs on the fire. Then he opened the chest, took out the pot of gold, and set it on the mantel where everybody would be bound to see it. At last he had decided to share with the whole world the truth about the treasure, whatever the truth might be.

Just as he stepped back from the mantel he heard a knock at the front door and the call in a sharp masculine voice, "Ho, landlord!" He who a moment before had been bold was now petrified with terror. The only traveler arriving at the inn at this hour would be the Devil. The innkeeper had been harboring the Fiend's gold, and the time had come for him to sign away God's claim to his immortal soul. Like stone he stood, as the knocking and calling grew louder and more insistent.

Then he saw his wife, a heavy shawl thrown over her nightdress, descending the stairs.

"You here, husband?" she asked in surprise. "Why haven't you admitted the knocker? Are we so rich that we can afford to turn travelers away?"

The innkeeper could neither speak nor move. He could only gaze while his wife unbarred the big door and swung it open.

Two young holy men entered, wearing the vestments of clerks of Oxford. One was no more than twenty, while the other was perhaps twenty-five. As they rushed to warm themselves at the fire, the innkeeper's wife closed the door behind them and went to rouse servants to care for their horses and to bring food and prepare beds.

"You're hard to waken, landlord," said the older clerk. "You made us fear we were not going to benefit from this warmth. We've ridden from Oxford since sundown, and the night is bitter for October."

Soon there was an air of cheer before the fire. Servants had drawn up a table, and were bringing in meat and drink. The clerks were eating and chatting. The innkeeper was punching the logs to make them burn more brightly, while his wife, aware of the garb she had on, was keeping herself in the background.

All at once the innkeeper saw that she had her eyes on the money pot, and then the clerks turned their eyes in the same direction.

"That's a curious vessel, landlord," said the older. "I've never seen its like before."

The innkeeper—from whom all fears had vanished—

picked up the pot and placed it on the table where the guests were eating. Then he removed the lid and began to sift the golden coins through his fingers. A servant, aghast at what he saw, ran to summon other servants and all the older children. Soon fifteen or twenty persons, most of whom wore nightcaps and had blankets wrapped about their bodies, were gathered in the great hall listening to the innkeeper relate his story. He began with a description of the dream in which the Presence first appeared, and told everything, not omitting his suspicion of his wife.

"This gold was coined by the Romans," said the older of the clerks, when the innkeeper finished his story. "It was placed in this pot and buried in the earth a thousand years ago. The writing indicates the value, and the head is that of one of the late emperors."

"And look at what we have here," said the younger clerk, scanning the inscription on the outside of the pot. "Translated into the language of England the Latin says,

'Beneath the place where this pot stood,
There is another twice as good.'

Let's ascend the hill and dig more, landlord. Maybe we'll triple your riches."

The group in great excitement lighted torches, and, holding them high, walked rapidly to the summit of Hawthorn Hill, the innkeeper with a clerk on each side of him leading the way. They found the spade in the hole where the innkeeper had left it the week before, and at a command from him the strongest of the servants began to dig. A cold east wind was lashing the branches of the hawthorn tree and tossing here and there the tassels on nightcaps, but all were watching the hole too intently to think of discomfort.

As they expected, the digger unearthed a second pot, just three feet below the place where the first had been found.

The two vessels were alike, except that the second bore no writing and was filled with coins right up to the brim.

"You say you own this hill, landlord?" asked the older clerk.

"Yes, Father. It's in the middle of my parcel of acres."

"Then the treasures are yours, by all rights moral and legal. In the way in which you've gained such wealth I see the workings of some Heavenly Being who loves you. I may even say that this miraculous manifestation has the marks of a service of the Mother of God. Perhaps She was impressed with your generosity to wayworn wanderers and wished to reward you. We must never question the methods of the Blessed Virgin. She, and not the Adversary whom She trod upon when he was a Serpent, is the Ingenious One."

The next day the innkeeper renamed the inn the Money Pot, took down the sign showing the green-coated forester, and hung in its place the Roman vessel bearing the inscription. With his wife no longer inclined to nag, he lived the remainder of his many years in great happiness. Out of his abundant riches he donated large sums to Holy Church, gave with his own hands to the poor of Bray, dowered his daughters well, for his oldest son and heir set his acres and houses in order, bought a new farm for each of his younger sons, and as landlord of the Money Pot granted always the same hearty welcome to travelers who had sovereigns in their pockets and to travelers who had only farthings.

Such, in matter, was the legend of the Hawthornes as it appears to have been related in Berkshire before the Reformation. A native of Bray, whose family had intermarried with the Hawthorne family, brought the story to Maryland in the middle of the seventeenth century. In the version he passed on to his descendants the Roman Catholic detail was an essential element of the plot. A Berkshire antiquarian, who published a synopsis in 1861, followed a version in

which the references to the confessional and the Blessed
Virgin were omitted.

The American ancestor of the Hawthornes of Salem gave
the name Hawthorn Hill to a height rising on one of his
grants of land. In his Puritan code the telling of idle tales
was listed among the sins. He must have seen godliness in
the family legend he had brought from the Old World.
For there can hardly be a doubt that the story, changed
to meet Puritan standards, was kept alive by oral tradition
among the Hawthornes of Salem until the most eminent of
them all, the romancer Nathaniel Hawthorne, made use
of it in "An Old Woman's Tale," printed originally in the
Salem *Gazette* for December 21, 1830.

The romancer's earliest definitely identified direct ancestor
was Thomas Hawthorne of East Oakley in the hundred of
Bray, born about the time of the discovery of America.
He was a yeoman, holding a field near Hawthorn Hill, and
was unable to write his name. Before the end of his life he
saw the established church in England changed from Roman
Catholic to Anglican. But he, an ignorant plowman, could
have had little understanding of the significance of the
Reformation.

Nor could his son and heir, the second Thomas Hawthorne, born about 1520. He too was an illiterate yeoman.
For many years of his life he was a parishioner of the Bray
priest who stuck to his flock while the English church under
Henry VIII, Edward VI, bloody Mary, and Queen Bess
shifted back and forth from Catholic to Protestant and who
replied upon being called a turncoat, "Not so! Not so! For
I have always kept my principle, which is this, to live and
die the vicar of Bray." The second Thomas Hawthorne
probably saw nothing irregular in the attitude of this kind
and genial spiritual adviser. Certainly the yeoman never

guessed that one day the priest's easy conscience would be made the subject of humorous ballads. Perhaps to this particular Hawthorne the Reformation meant no more than witnessing the excruciating deaths of Berkshire's several martyrs.

The eldest son and heir of the second Thomas was the first William. It was during his lifetime that the preferred spelling for the family name came to be Hathorne. Born about 1543, he was in his middle teens when Elizabeth came to the throne, in his middle forties when the Spanish Armada was destroyed, at the end of his fifties when James VI of Scotland became James I of England, in his early sixties when the colony of Jamestown was established in Virginia, and in his late seventies when the Pilgrims settled at Plymouth in New England. He lived to see the beginning of the reign of Charles I.

Like his father and grandfather, he died a yeoman. But he was more ambitious and aggressive. He knew how to read and write. Besides, he belonged to an age in which men of his class had the opportunity to accumulate wealth and rise in the world. He enlarged and improved the farm he had inherited in Bray. Then, through his marriage, in 1570, to Anne Perkins, he became the owner of a farm equally extensive and valuable in the adjacent hundred of Binfield. At different periods in his life he held under lease other lands, including two beautiful fields at Water Oakley on the Thames. In addition to as much as a hundred and fifty arable acres and two substantial stone dwellings, he possessed a bakehouse, a washhouse, a milkhouse, an applehouse, a millhouse, and a carthouse. He had horses, oxen, cows, sheep, goats, pigs, poultry, and bees. Among his sundry belongings were a Bible and other books, painted tapestrylike wall hangings, a halberd, a sword, a musket, and silver plate, including eighteen spoons.

From 1600 to 1602 he was one of the wardens of Bray church. He perhaps went there from time to time to read from Foxe's *Book of Martyrs*, a black letter copy of which was kept chained to a desk at the west end of the south aisle. During his latter years he heard from the Bray pulpit sermons denouncing dissenters, especially the stubborn critical group known as Puritans. At one time he was a trustee of a church charity.

He and his wife Anne won a new respect for the name Hathorne. In their endeavor to raise their offspring to the level of the gentry they were in great measure successful. Each of their three daughters was married into a good family, and the younger of their two sons became the lord of a manor.

This younger son, Master Hathorne, Gent., born about 1578, was the first member of the family to be christened Nathaniel. He must have been precocious, handsome, and gallant. For it was through his two marriages that he became identified with the gentry. His first wife saw her ancestral Staverton Manor pass, by devious exchange, into the hands of William Laud, who, before he became Archbishop of Canterbury, deeded it to the municipality of Reading, his native town, for the support of a charity hospital. Her brother, claiming the rights of cousin and heir, brought action for the return of the property to his family, and in the prolonged litigation which followed was supported by her husband. Before the case was finally settled in favor of Laud, she was dead and Nathaniel Hathorne was married to another gentlewoman. Among his possessions at the time of his death was the manor of South Braham in Somersetshire. His will was proved July 29, 1654. He left no sons.

His brother, two or three years his senior, was the second William Hathorne. About 1605 this William married a good

and capable but illiterate woman, known only by her
Christian name Sarah. While he was ambitious for several
of the children she bore to him, he himself was satisfied to
live his life as a yeoman.

But since he was an eldest son, he was the inheritor of
his father's lands, and they were extensive enough to raise
him above the station of ordinary yeomanry. Until 1608,
when his first child was near the age of two, he lived with
his parents in Bray. In that year he moved to the Binfield
farm, which had belonged to his mother's family.

Here his sons and daughters grew up—in the dwelling
which all of them were to remember as home. There were
a hall and a parlor, each with a fireplace, and there were
chambers above. On the floors downstairs were green rugs;
and the furnishings included a round table fitted with a
drawer, a cupboard provided with a cloth which had blue
at the ends, a big chest which was for the exclusive use of
the master of the house, another chest of elm, a great joined
chair, a low leather chair, and many joined stools. There
were big andirons, and brass candlesticks. On the hall table
at which the family ate were silver spoons and pewter bowls
and platters. In the upstairs chamber used by the father and
mother there was a great feather bed fitted with green
valanced sea curtains, sheets, blankets, pillows, and pillow
cases of holland or homespun linen. Here and there in the
field in which the stone house stood were the numerous
outbuildings where the children, when they grew big
enough, helped at shearing sheep, weaving the clothes they
wore, milking cows and goats, grinding grain, and pressing
apples for cider.

Though they were trained in the manners of gentlefolk,
they were never allowed to forget that their father was a
yeoman. The daughters learned how to cook, sew, make
beds, and clean a house. The sons mastered all that was to be

known in England at that time about the art of husbandry. They could fertilize soil and keep it productive. They knew how to grow and harvest wheat, barley, oats, and grasses for hay. They could raise vegetables, keep an orchard healthy, and care for bees. They were taught how to breed horses and cattle, how to fatten and slaughter pigs, and how to preserve meat with salt or spices.

Servants, bonded for a term of years, performed the hardest labors of the farm. While yeoman Hathorne was obliged to bow to many, there were those who bowed to him. To distinguish one class from another and to give each its due was a lesson his children learned early and carefully.

On Sundays they went with their father and mother to the Binfield church, where the preaching they heard was as contentious as the preaching the older William Hathorne was hearing at Bray. The vicars of the two parishes, determined to keep Berkshire the stronghold of conformity which it had become, grew more and more violent in their attacks upon dissenters as the years passed. The Hathorne children were taught to believe that a Puritan was blind to truth, dead to virtue, and unspeakably traitorous. The oldest and brightest of the brood, the third William Hathorne, born in Bray towards the end of 1606 or near the beginning of 1607, was deeply interested in these arguments in defense of unqualified conformity.

He was a boy of extraordinary intelligence, quick in grasping knowledge, yet deliberative in weighing its practical value. His parents, encouraged perhaps by his grandfather in Bray and his uncle, Master Nathaniel Hathorne of South Braham, saw that he was given an education exceptional for one of his class. Wherever it was received, it fitted him to appear before the world for the rest of his life as an unmistakable English gentleman.

His earnestness, and especially his concern over matters

religious, must have amazed at times his father and mother. His brothers and sisters doubtless looked upon him with awe—and with annoyance, for he was surely always telling them what they should or should not do. Though he might have lost their affection, he kept their respect. He knew intuitively how to be politic. There are hints that he made Spenser's *Faerie Queene* a sort of guide, and it is certain that Sir Philip Sidney's *Arcadia* was among his favorite books.

It seems that when young William was nineteen or twenty, shortly after the death of his grandfather Hathorne, he spent some time in the town of Dorchester, not far from his uncle Nathaniel's estate in Somersetshire. If he was actually in Dorchester, he could have heard there the preaching of the Reverend John White, one of the Puritan clergymen whom the vicar of Binfield was denouncing. The Puritans, Mr. White insisted, had no desire to leave the established church. Their goal, he declared, was to carry on reformation until they had freed the Church of England from the last trace of Roman Catholicism. He emphasized the Calvinistic doctrine of the sovereignty of God as expressed in the Thirty-nine Articles. But in his interpretation of this belief he was more explicit than the vicar of Binfield. Mr. White asserted that those whom God had elected for salvation must make manifest their election by piety and good works. A man's prime duty, he argued, was to live a good life and thus show that his will *could* be one with God's. Mr. White was not merely a priest officiating at prescribed ceremonies. He was a teacher training his parishioners in a code of behavior. In his sermons he spoke often of the plans which he and other Puritans had under way for establishing in the wilderness of the New World a colony of such Church of England communicants as were willing to submit themselves and their all to the laws revealed in the Old and New Testaments.

Whether by the Reverend John White in Dorchester or some other clergyman in some other place, the third William Hathorne was instructed in the tenets and aims of the Puritans. As to the results of the lessons he received, there need be no speculation. By the time the young man was twenty-one he had gone through the experience which the Puritans called conversion. He was convinced that he had been destined to be numbered among the elect of God. Henceforth he was in God's hands. It was the will of Heaven, he believed, that he should join the colony about which Mr. White was speaking and in the New World help in creating, at last upon earth, a Divine State. The power of this will as it seethed in his heart the rebellious young convert could never have surmised.

There must have been consternation in his Binfield home when he announced his conversion. His father and mother could have had only the slightest comprehension of the spiritual force inherent in Puritanism. Like their ancestors, they were content to follow as they could the teachings of their vicar. The strange driving determination they saw in their son was a phenomenon before which they could do no more than cower. The great hope of their lives had no doubt been that William would tread in the steps of his uncle Nathaniel and become a worthy landed gentleman. But if his mind was made up to turn from a commendable course in England and go on this mad adventure to America, they, as English parents, were ready to help him.

Witnessing his departure would be like witnessing his death. But losing him was only one of the sacrifices which Puritanism was to exact from the second William Hathorne and his wife Sarah. Among their son's young Puritan friends was Richard Davenport, a native of Dorsetshire and a zealous disciple of the Reverend John White. The youth, a professional soldier, had pledged himself to become a member of the proposed Puritan colony which was being sponsored by the recently formed Company of the Massachusetts Bay in New England. It is probable that while waiting to be called upon to fulfill his pledge he visited William in Binfield. Anyway it is certain that about this time he met the youngest Hathorne daughter, Elizabeth, not yet fourteen, and that he fell victim to her charms and won her heart. With the dominating William on hand to plead for the lovers, the father and mother gave their consent to an engagement, though they knew that once they saw the girl leave for America she would be out of their lives forever.

Sooner than Richard Davenport expected, he received a summons from the Massachusetts Bay Company to report at Weymouth. From there, late in June, 1628, he sailed in the ship *Abigail* with a number of colonizers headed by John Endecott, also a disciple of the Reverend John White. The destination decided upon was the harbor of Naumkeag, about forty miles up the New England coast from Plymouth. Mr. Endecott, a gentleman nearing middle age, carried his wife with him. But to risk the life of a bride of fourteen on such an adventure was, to Elizabeth Hathorne's parents, altogether unthinkable. The girl, supported by the promise that if her fiancé was unable to return to England for the marriage she could go to him at the time her brother William sailed, stayed in Binfield. When a letter from Naumkeag announced that Mrs. Endecott had failed to survive the fierceness of the New England winter, Elizabeth, who was training herself to be a Puritan wife, no doubt concluded that Providence had had a hand in postponing her marriage until Richard could provide a warm shelter.

Arrangements were made whereby William was given

a money settlement in lieu of his patrimony. Then, following instructions received from the Massachusetts Bay Company, the Hathorne parents saw that their son and daughter were equipped with sufficient clothing to last for at least four years. For William there had to be knit stockings, Norwich garters, shirts, doublets and hose of leather provided with hooks and eyes, waistcoats of green cotton wool bound with red tape, leather girdles, felt hats with steeple crowns and brims lined with leather, gloves of sheepskin and calf and kid, linen handkerchiefs, and buckles for hats and shoes. Elizabeth needed dresses of various weights of woolen in many colors, skirts to be worn with a farthingale, tight-fitting bodices, stomachers, white linen collars, a ruff or two, white caps, and high-crowned felt hats with brims protruding forward and backward. Both had to be provided with leather to be made into shoes as need might arise, and both required sea chests, mats to place under beds aboard ship, rugs, blankets, sheets, bolsters of Scotch ticking filled with wool, and linen for towels and tablecloths and napkins. Certain foods would have to be taken, such as oatmeal, dried pease, and biscuits. Crannies in packed sea chests, said the instructions, should be filled with little bags of flower, vegetable, and herb seeds.

Young William Hathorne, a Puritan on the eve of a crusade, seems still to have been dissatisfied with what his father and mother were doing in his behalf. It appears that he persuaded them to turn over to him his brother John, a boy of no more than twelve and possibly only nine. The orphaned children taken to Plymouth in the *Mayflower* had stood the rigors of the climate better than the men and women. The Reverend Francis Higginson, who had arrived in Naumkeag in the summer of 1629, had written, "Little children here by the setting of corn may earn much more than their maintenance." Mr. Higginson had also said, in speaking of lobsters, "The least boy in the plantation may catch and eat what he will of them." If arrangements were made for little John Hathorne to accompany his brother and sister to the New World, papers of indenture were drawn up binding him to work for William until he was seventeen or eighteen. William in turn agreed to pay the ship captain's bill for the boy, to feed and clothe him, to teach him husbandry and a little reading and writing, and to give him two suits of clothes and maybe a Bible at the end of his term of indenture.

The Massachusetts Bay Company did things slowly. It was at least the spring of 1630 and possibly as late as the summer of 1633 before the day finally arrived when the Hathorne father and mother saw their home forever broken up. William, Elizabeth, and perhaps little John set out for some port to embark for the Massachusetts Bay country. The numerous printed accounts of voyages to the New World, designed to encourage migration, passed over hardships. But William and Sarah Hathorne knew that their departing children would have to draw upon all their strength to survive the ordeal that lay ahead of them. The ship, of not more than three hundred tons, would be jammed with every type of human being, the filthy and odorous predominating. There would probably be goats and pigs and half a dozen cows on board. For ballast the ship would carry the bricks and hardware so greatly needed by the colonists in building shelters. There would be stretches of stormy days when every creature would have to remain below decks, where there was no provision for sanitation and the stench was suffocating. If the ship was fortunate enough to have a chirurgeon, he would be kept busy looking after the sick. There might be an epidemic, such as the smallpox which had struck the *Talbot* in 1629 and had claimed within two days one of the Reverend Mr. Higginson's little daughters. There would certainly be those afflicted with the dreaded scurvy before the end of the two or three months' voyage. The destination was a forest meeting the sea, a forest teeming with savages. Yet in such a place the Divine State upon earth about which William and Elizabeth had talked with such fervor was supposed to rise. The older William Hathorne and his wife Sarah, like many another father and mother in England whose offspring had been touched by the Puritan urge, could only bid their children goodbye and pray for their survival. Even if they were not called upon to give up John at this time, they saw him leave to join William in the New World a few years later.

Of their own religious and political affiliations during the troublous decades which followed the break-up of their family circle there can be only speculation. The probability is that they were true to the traditions of English yeomanry and lived by the principle which had satisfied the celebrated vicar of Bray. On that July day in 1647 when Charles I in the custody of a guard from Cromwell's army arrived at the Greyhound Inn in Maidenhead for a meeting with his children after several years of forced separation, William and Sarah Hathorne might have been among the thousands who decked the houses on High Street with green boughs and strewed the thoroughfare with flowers, shouting all the while, "God save the King!" When later, after the execution of Charles, William and Sarah Hathorne went into the Bray church and saw that the royal arms on the rood screen had been replaced with the arms of the Commonwealth, they probably prayed, "Long live the Protector!"

It is certain that the father and mother gave their wonted attention to practical affairs between 1630 and 1650. They saw their two daughters left in England married into the gentry, one into the Berkshire family which was soon to provide a countess for the Earl of Stirling. They saw that two of the sons left at home were settled on the ancestral lands. There could have been little correspondence with the children in America. When the father made his will he wondered whether John was still alive. William was bequeathed £100, Elizabeth £40, and John £20, "if not dead."

The second William Hathorne, like his brother the first Nathaniel, lived into the 1650's. His wife, buried in the Binfield churchyard September 8, 1655, survived him by four years. He was a great-grandson of the first Thomas Hawthorne and the romancer's great-great-great-great-grandfather.

GOD'S STATE

THE CLAIM has been made that young William Hathorne arrived in Naumkeag harbor on the *Arbella* on June 12, 1630. It is certain that this ship at that time brought Governor John Winthrop, Sir Richard Saltonstall, Lady Arbella Johnson, her husband Isaac Johnson, Thomas Dudley, his daughter Anne, and her husband Simon Bradstreet. William Hathorne was to be closely associated with several of these notables in the venture of establishing God's State upon earth. But the claim that he sailed for Naumkeag in their company is not supported by the available records. It can only be said that he and Elizabeth and John possibly reached New England as early as the summer of 1630, possibly on the *Arbella,* and that the older brother and sister arrived—on the same ship, states a sworn deposition— not later than the end of 1633 and the younger brother before 1642.

William's first obligation in the New World was to see Elizabeth wedded to Richard Davenport. The house to which the groom took his bride was a roughhewn dirt-floor wooden structure, situated on Naumkeag's main east-west trail. The roof was solidly thatched, and there was a stone fireplace, with trees to turn into logs growing right at the door. The Reverend Mr. Higginson had said, "All Europe is not able to afford to make so great fires as New England." Richard as well as every other settler had been puzzled at first by the problem of lights. Then one night someone visited an Indian wigwam, and afterwards Mr. Higginson had written, "Yea, our pine trees, that are most plentiful of all wood, doth allow us plenty of candles, which are very useful in a house, and they are such candles as the Indians burn, having no other, and they are nothing else but wood of the pine tree cloven into two little slices, something thin, which are so full of the moisture of turpentine and pitch, that they burn as clear as a torch." Richard had found out that the quantity of game to be hunted in the vicinity of Naumkeag far surpassed what he had hunted in England. For a time he had missed greatly the leavened bread he had known in the Old World, but he had learned to like the hard flat loaves made from the flour of Indian corn. In England herrings had been caught only to be eaten, but here they were so plentiful that they were used to fertilize the corn patches. Richard and other settlers had learned from the Indians that such a method of enriching the soil was expedient, and they called it "fishing the fields."

There were exciting experiences for Richard to relate to Elizabeth and William. The red men in Massachusetts Bay had so far been only carefree, curious, and childlike. The troublesome persons had been the English settlers who had preceded Mr. Endecott. There had been an accounting with the notorious Thomas Morton and his followers at Merry Mount, the loafers who, in the words of Governor Bradford of Plymouth, had "set up a Maypole, drinking and dancing about it many days together, inciting Indian women for their consorts, dancing and frisking together and worse practices." Richard Davenport, a trained soldier, must have been in the company when Mr. Endecott with a group of helpers journeyed the twenty miles south to Merry Mount, ordered the Maypole chopped down, and in strong words commanded Morton and his outlaws to mend their ways. Then there had been difficulties with Roger Conant and the adventurers he led, all of whom were now referred to as the "old planters." They had found neither Plymouth nor

Cape Ann to their liking, and had settled in Naumkeag, two years before the coming of Endecott. Tactful negotiation had been required, but now Conant was satisfied, and showed promise of becoming a man of importance in the colony.

Richard did not need to mention his privations and disappointments. His anxious eyes, hard face, rough hands, and knotty muscles bespoke the suffering he had endured. The first winter, when there was a great scarcity of food, had been a long horrifying ordeal. He had seen many, in addition to Mrs. Endecott, give up and die.

The following summer two ministers had come, Mr. Higginson and the Reverend Samuel Skelton, filling the settlers anew with Puritan fervor, reviving courage. The church the clergymen had organized was an independent Christian body. So grave had grown the oppression of Puritans under Charles I and Laud that a connection with the Church of England had not even been considered. Though nominally in fellowship with the Separatist congregation at Plymouth, the Naumkeag congregation was an entity unto itself. In the spring of 1630 Richard had seen the beloved Mr. Higginson succumb to the New World hardships. Since then Mr. Skelton had borne alone the burden of spiritual leadership in the settlement. The church was responsible for the laws, and was introducing radical innovations. A recent ruling had made marriage a civil agreement rather than a sacrament. Richard Davenport and Elizabeth Hathorne had been united in matrimony by a magistrate, probably Mr. Endecott.

Richard had heard much talk about suitable substitutes for original place names. For certain towns decisions had at last been reached. Naumkeag was now Salem—the Hebrew word meaning *peace*. Shawmut was now Boston, Agawam was Ipswich, and Mattapannock had become Dorchester.

In the town last named, William Hathorne chose to make his home. Most of the settlers had been parishioners of Mr. White in Dorchester, England, and had begun to arrive in the summer of 1630—in so low a state of health that Samuel Fuller, a chirurgeon, had come up from Plymouth "to let some twenty of them blood." Once among them, William Hathorne lost no time in obtaining a grant of land. But before he could profit by this privilege he had to become a member of the church, which the settlers had organized as an independent congregation while waiting aboard ship in Weymouth harbor to set sail for New England.

Accepted as a planter, with possibly his young brother to help at the labors and perhaps also an adult servant or two, William Hathorne began to fell trees. His dwelling at the start could scarcely have been as sturdy as Davenport's in Salem, a town more advanced than Dorchester. William was lucky if his home was a dugout, or a wigwamlike hut, with a stick-and-mud chimney. In summer he was molested by strange flies and insects, and was constantly on the lookout for wild cats, panthers, and other animals which some swore they had seen in the forests, lions, serpentlike monsters with two heads, and great beasts, called molkes, as big as oxen. He slew many poisonous reptiles—copperheads and rattlesnakes, talk of which in England had turned more than one timid Puritan from thought of migrating to the Massachusetts Bay country. In winter there were wolves for him to guard against, as there had been in Berkshire. On days when great drifts of snow forced him to remain shut in his hut he learned the meaning of hunger. Perhaps—like one of his neighbors, who kept a diary—he found himself at these times of isolation conjuring up the image of cracked Indian corn boiled in sea water.

Neither fatigue from labor, nor apprehension of danger,

nor weakness from hunger could erase from his mind another image—that of God's State rising here in the wilderness. With each new ordeal of denial and suffering his will to do his part in bringing this great dream into reality grew stronger.

While he felt the fullest sympathy for the energetic settlers who shared his confidence, he had only contempt for the soft who threatened to become parasites. In his boyhood he had paid little attention to the stocks and whipping post he had seen in Holyport and other Berkshire towns. Here in Massachusetts Bay there had been no delay in setting up these machines of torture, mainly for the correction of idlers and triflers. William Hathorne rejoiced when he saw a victim under punishment. Only the severe discipline decided upon by the church authorities, who during the first years of Dorchester were magistrates as well as spiritual leaders, could fit this town to stand as a unit in the Divine State.

In Bray and Binfield the outlaws of Windsor Forest had been called the Devil's children. In New England, as Hathorne and many other Puritans believed, were creatures out of hell still more heinous—the red men. A few years before the arrival of the English a plague had swept away thousands of them. But for this Providence worked by a God whose face was shining upon the Puritans the savages would now be strong enough to attack the white settlements and exterminate every man, woman, and child. The red fiends might appear naïve and mildly amusing, and they might possess a wisdom from which the colonists were profiting. Still they walked the woods in shiftlessness, paying homage in their way to their father the Devil. In England, and even here, there were those who argued that the Indians should be compensated for the lands which the Massachusetts Bay Company was granting to the worthy. Pay wealth to the offspring of Satan for acres created by God? No idea, as Hathorne understood things, could be more absurd. He saw eye to eye with the Puritan leaders who declared, "The earth is the Lord's and the fullness thereof; to the saints is the earth given; we are the saints."

By the spring of 1634 the Dorchester authorities had concluded that young William Hathorne was a colonist of exceptional worth. On May 14 in that year, when he was twenty-seven, he took the oath as a freeman. This formality, implying his dutifulness as a church member and his promise as a leader, meant that he had become a member of the Massachusetts Bay Company and was a direct guardian of the charter which John Winthrop had brought to New England in defiance of all precedent. As a freeman William Hathorne was also a member of the General Court, which, according to provisions in the charter, not only passed laws but constituted a tribunal of justice. This body, as it existed in May, 1634, included all freemen in the colony, headed by the governor, the deputy governor, and the councilors, known as assistants.

But at the end of 1634 the General Court was changed into a representative body. Under the new system a town instead of sending all its freemen to a scheduled meeting sent two, called deputies. William Hathorne and a neighbor much older were the first elected to stand for Dorchester.

It was also in 1634 that Dorchester abandoned the direct rule of the church over secular local affairs and laid the groundwork for the type of town government which was to prevail in New England. Among the first selectmen chosen was William Hathorne, and one of the first duties which devolved upon him was to determine the damage done to the growing corn belonging to one settler by the pigs belonging to another.

In or prior to this year 1634 he was married. Only the Christian name of his wife, the name Ann, is known. There is reason to believe that she was born Ann Smith, of Wokeingham in Berkshire, and that she became engaged to William Hathorne in England and followed him to the New World, as his sister Elizabeth followed Richard Davenport. There is also reason to believe that Ann Hathorne was a native of Maidstone in Kent and had a sister in that place, Lydia Banks, who at one time gave William Hathorne power of attorney to act for her in a transaction involving her claim to certain Massachusetts Bay property.

The first child of William and Ann Hathorne, a daughter, was born early in March, 1635. She was christened Sarah, for the mother of William. He was too devoted to old family traditions to choose one of the new-fashioned Puritan names for his daughter. Among the children of his more up-to-date diarist neighbor were Experience, Waitstill, Preserved, Hopestill, Thanks, Desire, and Supply.

On May 6, 1635, two months after the birth of his first child, William Hathorne, listed in the records with the gentleman's title "Mr.," made his initial appearance as a deputy at a meeting of the General Court. The session was held at New Town, soon to become the seat of Harvard College and to be renamed Cambridge. An important case considered was a suit involving the ship *Thunder*, and among the arbitrators appointed to effect a settlement were Mr. Hathorne and the Reverend Roger Williams of Salem, both of whom were voted the power to examine witnesses under oath.

Young Mr. Hathorne was a gentleman of prominence in Dorchester. Yet at the end of 1636 he disposed of his lands there and departed for Salem. He perhaps traveled the twenty miles on horseback, his wife with her little daughter in her arms on a pillion behind him. His pigs, goats, and whatever household goods he had accumulated were probably in the meantime carried by boat, while his cows and oxen were driven overland by a servant, maybe his brother John. Dorchester, then only six years old, was undergoing a change. Many of the original settlers, seeking more fertile farms, were leaving to found the town of Windsor in the Connecticut Valley. New arrivals from England were taking their places. Shortly before Mr. Hathorne's departure the church was reorganized, with the Reverend Richard Mather, progenitor of the celebrated Mather family, named the minister. Still these facts throw little light on William Hathorne's reasons for moving to Salem. It is possible, as certain historians have suggested, that he was drawn there by a wise man who recognized his great promise, the Reverend Hugh Peter. It could be that his motive was nothing more than his desire to be near the Davenports.

They too had a little daughter, several months older than William's and Ann's. The child was called Truecross. But the parents had had a good reason for adopting this fashionable name. Richard was also now a freeman, classed among the larger Salem planters, often entrusted with the correction of unruly servants and with the responsibility of seeing that herdsmen observed the regulations when driving cattle to and from the town Common. But Salem knew him best as Ensign Davenport, standard-bearer of the trainband, which included all adult males in the town except invalids, cripples, ministers, and magistrates. When the ensign was on the drill field with his men on an afternoon in the autumn of 1634, John Endecott appeared on the scene, grabbed the standard, and with his sword cut from it the section containing the St. George's cross, which to him was a symbol of popery. About this time the Davenport daughter was born. In commemoration of Endecott's act of Puritan defiance her father gave her the name Truecross.

But the incident was not closed. Before the end of 1634 rumors reached Boston that Charles I was demanding the return of the charter and that Laud, now Archbishop of Canterbury, was planning to choose special commissioners to rule the colony. Governor Dudley and his advisers, who had no intention of either surrendering the charter or submitting to Laud, realized that an act which could be interpreted in England as treason had to be investigated with at least the semblance of great sternness. So Ensign Davenport was brought before the General Court with what was left of the standard and commanded to explain the mutilation. Endecott, who was present, assumed full responsibility. A committee was appointed to study the case, and—at that first session of the General Court which Hathorne attended —Salem's impetuous foe of popery was admonished and an order was issued barring him from holding any office in the colony for the duration of a year.

All this was now in the past, and Mr. Endecott, Salem's most important lay personage, was in greater esteem than ever before. The people loved to talk of his daring deed, which most of them considered heroic. The story of the exploit was already on its way into Puritan folklore. In the meantime little Truecross Davenport had grown big enough to babble her name.

The Hathornes while waiting to get a place of their own probably stayed with the Davenports, who had made of their dwelling one of the town's "fair houses." It was among the earliest of Salem's buildings which were to endure— the building which was to pass from the Davenports to the Corwins and, after several transformations, become celebrated as the "witch house."

The trail on which it fronted was being referred to as

the main street. On the opposite side of this thoroughfare, about an eighth of a mile eastward, the people had built the meetinghouse, which was physically as well as spiritually the town's heart. Yet it was only a small crude clapboard edifice. Passing it on the west, crossing the main street and forming a square, was the wide road which extended from the arm of the bay known as the South River to the arm called the North River. Towards the upper end of this road, on the east side, was located Mr. Endecott's "fair house." Towards the lower end, on the west side, was the dwelling which until the preceding January had been occupied by the Reverend Roger Williams.

It was the home from which the great defender of individualism fled into the snow-filled forest to receive succor from his friends the Indians when he learned that constables from Boston were on the way to Salem to arrest him and send him back to England. Since his arrival in the New World— in January, 1631—he had been an object of attack, first in Boston, then in Salem, then in Plymouth, and again in Salem. The promoters of God's State, where every man must think as the church prescribed, could only interpret Williams' doctrine of the right of the individual to liberty of conscience as heresy. The people of Salem, led by Endecott, stood by Williams, and paid as the price of their loyalty a portion of the town territory. Fearful of other sacrifices which the enemies of their beloved minister might demand, Endecott and his colleagues, including Richard Davenport, at last yielded. In September, 1635, Williams was ordered by the General Court to quit the colony within six weeks. He stayed twice that long before plunging into the forest to join the Indians, whose language he had learned while at Plymouth and whose lawful ownership of the Massachusetts Bay lands he defended to the last. Under their protection he made his way southward, to found Rhode Island

and show that a Puritan could be tolerant and merciful as well as bigoted and cruel.

Mr. Hathorne, who had voted for the banishment of the Reverend Roger Williams, had been in Salem only a few days when the town council granted him a farm of two hundred acres under the condition, wrote Mr. Endecott in the record, that he transfer his church membership from Dorchester to Salem. That matter was attended to without delay, and William Hathorne became the possessor, early in 1637, of a tract of land several miles to the northwest, in the section which was beginning to be called Salem Village. On the farm was a crude residence, and here Mr. Hathorne installed his wife and child and set to work to make improvements. There was also on the land a lofty mound, from the summit of which the owner could see to the east the open ocean and to the west, on a fair afternoon, the crest of Monadnock, seventy-five miles away, deep in the unexplored territory of the red men. Soon everybody was calling the mound Hathorne Hill.

The year Mr. Hathorne was establishing himself in Salem, 1637, was the year of the Antinomian controversy, instigated by Mrs. Anne Hutchinson, of Boston. If the church had adopted the doctrine she preached, the doctrine which contends that salvation is a matter of spiritual illumination and depends in no way upon good works, the history of New England would have been different and William Hathorne, to whom public discipline was becoming more and more a chief concern, would have had little opportunity to render the service for which he was best fitted. He was no longer in the General Court, and had no direct part in the trial and condemnation of Mrs. Hutchinson. But, as all his later activity was to indicate, he thanked God when her enemies triumphed and sentenced her to banishment. He probably never met her in person. But he was well acquainted with her chief defender, twenty-three-year-old Governor Henry Vane, who was soon to return to England and inherit his father's title and lands.

In 1637 came another crisis for God's State, an ordeal the founders had feared from the beginning, conflict on a wide scale with the Devil's children, the Indians. The struggle, known as the Pequot War, was bloody. Second in command of the contingent of soldiers sent by Salem was Richard Davenport, raised to the rank of lieutenant. In a swamp fight on the Connecticut shore of Long Island Sound an arrow pierced his shoulder. He fell in a swoon, and was rescued just in time to prevent capture. Three weeks later he was able to lead an expedition to the village of Quinni-piac, which was to become New Haven. But for the aid of the banished Roger Williams, who persuaded his power-ful friends the Narragansetts to remain neutral, the conflict could have resulted in the slaughter of most of the whites in New England. As it turned out Massachusetts Bay and Plymouth, standing together as allies, won such a decisive victory that for almost forty years there was to be peace in New England between the white men and the red.

The Puritans contended that since they were God's saints they had the right to exercise vengeance in their own way. So they marched the hordes of Pequot captives to seaport towns, and shipped great numbers to the West Indies to be sold into slavery. One, a girl branded + 111 — on the belly, was claimed as property by Lieutenant Davenport. Mr. Ha-thorne was among the able-bodied younger men who re-mained in Salem to guard against any uprising of Indians in the vicinity. When several who lived near his farm were suspected of complicity in shooting one of his cows, the General Court ordered all their goods seized and held until they paid reparation and revealed the identity of the shooter.

In the autumn of 1637, in compliance with another order

of the General Court, the people of Massachusetts Bay celebrated a day of thanksgiving—a day when they expressed gratitude to God for the defeat of the Pequots, for the safe return of a majority of the soldiers, and for the victories of the foes of Roman Catholicism in the wars in Germany. William Hathorne had special reason on this occasion for being thankful to God. While Lieutenant Davenport was away fighting the Pequots, his seat in the General Court had been filled by his brother-in-law. Moreover Mr. Hathorne had been appointed to serve as an assistant magistrate at a quarterly court to be held in Salem, and he had been chosen one of the town's selectmen. After less than a year in his new home he was more a personage than he had been in Dorchester. He was rapidly rising to the position where he could serve God as he felt God desired.

Four years on his Salem Village farm were enough to convince him that living in a place so remote was most impracticable. Every day or two some official duty required his presence in the town center. He solved the problem by obtaining a grant to a smaller farm a mile southwest of the meetinghouse and erecting on the property a sturdy two-story residence. This place, known as the Mill Pond farm, was to remain his favorite home. Still he had no notion of selling the land on which rose beautiful Hathorne Hill. He was now the owner and manager of two farms instead of one.

At last he was a close neighbor of the Davenports. The little sons and daughters of the brothers-in-law probably played together every day except the Sabbath, running back and forth between the two homes. On several occasions Hathorne and Davenport were called upon to collaborate in public tasks. They served jointly in determining boundary lines between towns, in surveying highways from one settlement to another, in looking after the construction of bridges, and in appraising lands and other properties. But Davenport's real interest all the while was in affairs military, and Hathorne, getting close to the people in his capacity as a magistrate, was thinking most about public discipline.

In 1639 the General Court included him among the commissioners who were assigned the weighty task of drawing up a code of laws for the colony. It turned out that this work, the *Body of Liberties*, was done independently by the Reverend Nathaniel Ward. When the task was completed, in 1641, Mr. Hathorne was one of the three scribes appointed to supply authentic copies for each of the Massachusetts Bay towns. He knew the Bible, on which it was in the main based. In performing the grave duties which awaited him he was to follow it to the letter.

Already under its influence, he employed his voluble oratory in an attempt to convince the General Court that definite penalties should be fixed for such crimes as swearing and lying. The younger deputies supported his stand. But the assistants and older deputies—led by Winthrop, whose dictatorial ambitions Hathorne had had the courage to oppose at every opportunity—expressed blunt disapproval. The Reverend John Cotton, when told of Hathorne's "insurgent" speeches, preached a sermon of rebuke. This enabled Winthrop to get Hathorne suspended from the General Court. But after a few months he was back, dominated, with all his godliness, by his desire for revenge.

His chance came in 1643 when the General Court took up the matter of an organization designed to look out for the common defense of all New England. Both Winthrop and Hathorne were on the committee appointed to discuss plans with committees from other colonies. When the various representatives assembled, they decided that the organization should be known as the New England Confederation and should be made up of two delegates each from Massachusetts Bay, Plymouth, Connecticut, and New Haven. Rhode Island, under control of the heretic Roger Williams, was of course excluded. The General Court then had to choose the two Massachuetts Bay delegates. As Hathorne expected, Winthrop urged that only men of years of experience in public life should be considered for a mission of such serious importance. A vote was taken, and the two elected were William Hathorne and Simon Bradstreet, both in their thirties. There was little for Winthrop to do except speak slightingly of Hathorne in his journal.

On September 5, 1644, Mr. Hathorne reported with Mr. Bradstreet in Hartford for the first meeting of the New England Confederation. Earlier in 1644 Mr. Hathorne was excused by the General Court from duty with his home trainband because of "the many country occasions in which he was implied." Before the year was ended the deputies to the General Court were made a separate governing body, corresponding to England's House of Commons. The first chosen to act as presiding officer was William Hathorne, who was given the title of speaker.

The year 1644 was also important in the life of his brother-in-law. Looked upon as the most promising among the young military men in the commonwealth, Richard Davenport, on November 13, was raised to the rank of captain and appointed by the General Court to command the colony's chief fortress, The Castle, on an island in Boston harbor. He at once left Salem for this post, and in the years to come his family and the Hathornes were to cross paths infrequently.

He was scarcely settled at The Castle when his influence began to be felt. Lax militia officers throughout the colony were replaced by firmer men. Captain William Trask, who had been so long in command of the Salem trainband that he had grown indifferent to his responsibilities, was retired on the pretext that his home was too far away from the arsenal. Though Hathorne had been excused from military duty, he was named to succeed Trask. With the appointment came his commission as a captain.

It was at this time that his brother John Hathorne was made a freeman, when scarcely more than forty men of Salem had been honored with that privilege. As early as 1642, when he was twenty-one, John, it is certain, was in the town, married to a woman named Sarah. He was by then a member of the church and grantee of fifty acres of land "towards the Great River." A few weeks before his admission to the body of freemen he was appointed to "walk forth in time of God's worship to take notice of such as lie about the meetinghouse without attending the words or ordinances, or that lie at home or in the fields without giving good account thereof." John Hathorne was a strange choice for such an assignment. He himself was more disposed to "lie in the fields" than to "walk forth." How he ever passed the rigid test required by the ministers and elders for membership in the church is a mystery. Without the influence of his distinguished brother he would never have become a freeman. Rarely did a scribe show him the respect due a gentleman and list his name with the title "Mr." Captain Hathorne was to wish that his young brother, however serviceable in the past, had remained in Berkshire. John Hathorne was not created to be a citizen of God's State.

Since the coming of Richard Davenport in Endecott's company in 1628, Massachusetts Bay had been undergoing continuous change. More immigrants had thronged in than were to come in all the years down to the time of the American Revolution. But the convening of the Long Parliament in 1640 and then the outbreak of civil war in 1642 had inspired within the Puritans in England the will to stay at home and fight. Their duty as they now saw it was not to evade such oppressors as Charles I and Archbishop Laud but to defeat them in battle and bring them to justice. By 1644 ships from the Old World were arriving in New England harbors loaded only with merchandise.

The anxious founding years in Massachusetts Bay were at an end. Boston, the capital, was already a little city. There were four well-organized counties, the most northern and eastern being Essex, with Salem the shire town and Ipswich the next in population and importance. Salem, representative of the larger towns in the colony, embraced in 1646 the districts which were to become Beverly, Danvers, Peabody, Manchester, part of Marblehead, Wenham, Topsfield, and part of Middleton. The town contained all together about three thousand men, women, and children. The majority lived on farms. In the town center, Salem peninsula, there were probably seven or eight hundred, including farmers who wished to dwell in the vicinity of the meetinghouse, many fishermen, craftsmen of all sorts, a few shipbuilders, a few shopkeepers, and perhaps as many as a dozen keepers of ordinaries. Attached to the wealthier households, both on the farms and in the town center, were indentured servants; and there were thirty or forty Negro slaves. All this heterogeneous Salem was a typical unit in God's State.

At the head in the New Jerusalem were the ministers, custodians of the truth as revealed in the Old and New Testaments. Next to them stood the high secular officers, among whom Captain Hathorne was now an important figure. The only superior power which these two classes respected was divine power, that of the Three in One—Jehovah, King Jesus, and the Holy Ghost. As for King Charles I, an ocean three thousand miles wide separated him from New England, and safe in Boston was the charter he had granted, which, as interpreted, gave the ministers and their immediate agents the right to do whatever they pleased. During the first sixteen years of the colony they simply circumvented any threatened royal interference. Now, in 1644, with the forces of Parliament in the ascendant in England, they felt secure. Below them in the social order came the freemen of little consequence, like John Hathorne, and then the people of various degrees, down to the miserable blacks most recently brought from Africa and sold in open market.

The whole population had to be fitted into the theocratic pattern. All had been born totally depraved, the ministers taught, and only a very small minority had been foredoomed to be redeemed by Christ's passion and death. Yet the many who would burn in hell throughout eternity must live as if they would spend the hereafter singing psalms in heaven. Each and every one had to be drawn from evil courses and forced into paths of godliness.

According to the *Body of Liberties*, a sin was a crime, punishable as a crime. Captain Hathorne, endowed with the power of magistrate in Essex County, was much more than a trial judge. He was an arbiter of conduct, a moral adviser, a confessor, and a conciliator. He was a director of the police, and, above all, a prosecutor with informers ever moving among the people in search of criminals. One brought before him had to plead his own case. In God's State, where the magistrates were regarded infallible, no defense counsel was allowed. The *Body of Liberties* specifically forbade one to receive payment for defending another at a court trial.

As long as John Endecott lived in Salem, until 1655, he was chief Essex County magistrate and Hathorne was one of several assisting magistrates. In such capacity Hathorne served thirteen years, twice as long as any other. Then after Endecott's removal to Boston, Hathorne occupied first place on the Essex County bench. Up until the time when the fall of the Puritan government in England made it necessary for the leaders of God's State to give less attention to the development of moral perfection Hathorne had served sixteen years as a member of the Salem body of selectmen, which exercised minor judicial functions, and an equal period as a representative to the General Court, which was originally as much judicial as legislative and always heard appeals. Of all the lay arbiters of Puritan behavior, of all the civil officials of Massachusetts Bay who strove to keep the fear of God in the people's hearts, William Hathorne was perhaps the most experienced. Certainly no other was more conscientious. Seeing that those about him devoted themselves exclusively to good deeds, was, he felt, the work of all works which God had placed him upon earth to do, and mightier and mightier grew his will to do it well. By 1644 he was becoming the most dreaded personage in Essex County. "Go to Mr. Hathorne!" one would say in a dispute. Then, after he was appointed commander of the Salem trainband, the expression was, "Go to the Captain!" After his promotion in rank ten years later it was, "Go to the Major!" The faithful magistrate manifested no concern over his notoriety, and all the while grew more exacting in his determination to compel the people to live godly lives.

The colonists had been so carefully investigated before they were permitted to sail from England that Massachusetts Bay was remarkably free of such criminals as thieves and burglars. Still informers succeeded in finding a number in Essex County who had forgotten their fear of God, listened to the promptings of the Devil, and broken the commandment, "Thou shalt not steal." Mr. Hathorne assisted in the conviction of a man who had filched "soap to wash his shirts" and of another who had pilfered "half a cheese, a cake, and some

milk." The punishment for petty crimes of this kind as prescribed in the *Body of Liberties* was the restitution to the
proper owner of twice the value of the goods stolen, a whipping, and perhaps the obligation of wearing the letter T on
the outer clothing for a month or more. But the man who
stole heavily faced a heavy penalty. Once Mr. Hathorne and
his fellow magistrates ordered a constable to cut off a convicted burglar's ear and brand the letter B on his forehead.

One of the most obvious acts of dishonesty which Mr.
Hathorne had to judge was committed by his brother John,
who in 1650 sold what property he had in Salem, opened an
ordinary in Malden, and then after less than a year sold out
a second time and moved to Lynn to open another ordinary.
He had been there only a few months when he was brought
to court on a charge of forgery. He openly admitted that
the accusation was true, and was sentenced to pay a fine of
£50, to read a confession of repentance at the Lynn meetinghouse at the conclusion of exercises on the next Lord's
day, and then appear before the General Court in Boston
and defend his right to remain a freeman. The confession he
read must have shown extraordinary contrition. For when
his case was taken up by the General Court his fine was miti-
gated and the recommendation for his dismissal from the
body of freemen was dropped. "He's a Hathorne, a brother
of the Captain!" malcontents in Lynn must have said.

The keepers of ordinaries who secured licenses to draw
beer, wine, and strong waters were numerous. Shopkeepers
also had this privilege. Still the cases of drunkenness which
Mr. Hathorne was called to pass upon were comparatively
few. Offenders were usually given light punishment. A
Salem drunkard was ordered to wear for a time the letter
D on his breast. Several habitual tipplers were committed to
petty officers of the trainband for correction. One man was
brought before the magistrates on the charge of serving so

much drink at a gathering of neighbors at his home that men and women alike got tipsy. A witness, prodded by Mr. Hathorne, said, "They drank so much they couldn't tell ink from liquor." The generous neighbor was only admonished, and none of his drinking guests were apprehended. Another host was less fortunate. At a corn husking at his house "divers persons drank and became drunk." Because he failed to report the crime, he was sentenced to pay a fine.

Mr. Hathorne had to listen to accounts of brawls and fights. One offender was fined ten shillings when it was proved that he struck a neighbor "with a block called a dead man's eye and broke his head through that the blood came forth." A woman was fined the same amount for attacking another woman and calling her a "lousy slut."

At least one case of brawling which came before Mr. Hathorne terminated in tragedy. At the first court at which he sat as a magistrate Dorothy Talby was tried for "frequent laying hands on her husband to the danger of his life and contemning the authority of the court." She was found guilty, and was sentenced to be tied to a post, "to be loosed only to come to the place of God's worship." The next year she was again tried for "misdemeanors against her husband," and was ordered whipped. Later, as she claimed, she was told in a vision that she must slay not only her husband but also her children. And she succeeded in murdering a little daughter before she was apprehended. This time she was brought to trial before the court of assistants in Boston, and, for obeying this horrible command of Satan, was sentenced to be hanged.

But the Devil had not driven to insanity all the troubled married women who were brought before Mr. Hathorne. Katherine Pacy appeared with her husband Nicholas, who charged that she persisted in refusing to fulfill her duties as a wife. Her story was that Nicholas, knowing well what he was doing, had stolen her from Mark Vermans, to whom she was engaged. Now she was so beset with scruples over her unfaithfulness to Mark that she was unable to bring herself to yield her virginity to Nicholas. Mr. Hathorne "labored" with the young woman and made her see that she was committing a crime in "denying conjugal respects unto her husband." As for Nicholas, the court ordered him to stand before the Salem congregation the next Lord's day and read a confession of repentance, probably penned by Mr. Hathorne.

The godly Captain was even more severe in judging another troubler of hearts, Robert Cocker, who had "betrothed himself too securely with one maiden, and then contracted with another." The court commanded him to repair to the whipping post for a flogging of thirty stripes and then pay £5 to Thomas King, who had married the jilted maiden.

Before Mr. Hathorne and his associates on the bench were done with a case of domestic brawling, sometimes referred to as "combustion between husband and wife," it was likely to involve other crimes. Richard Prey could never have realized what he was letting himself in for when he submitted to arrest and appeared before Mr. Hathorne. Witnesses testified that he had called his wife "a jade and roundhead," had wished "a plague and pox on her," had sworn "by his faith and cud's buds" that he would beat her twenty times a day or master her, at supper one night "had taken his porridge dish and thrown it at her," on another occasion had "kicked her against the wall," and when told by a neighbor one day that the Captain could tame stouter hearts than his had replied, "I don't care for the court. Even if I knew they were going to hang me I'd break my wife's will. If ever I have trouble about abusing her, I'll cripple her and make her sit on a stool, and there I'll keep her." He was fined ten shillings for swearing, ten for cursing, twenty for beating his wife, and forty for contempt of court. If he failed to raise the money to pay the fines, he was "to be whipped at the iron works."

Mr. Hathorne tried many accused of fornication. Couples with babies born too soon after marriage came before him again and again. Besides, there were plenty of women of "whorish carriage" in Essex County and plenty of willing males to make trouble. One girl, accused of fornication with four men, confessed her guilt to Mr. Hathorne and his colleagues. They sentenced her to be whipped at once. But when she revealed that she had "sore breasts and boils her punishment was respited until next lecture day." For bearing a bastard, Katherine Black, a Negro girl, was sentenced to pay a fine of fifty shillings or receive a whipping. Another Negro girl convicted of fornication was not given the chance to save herself from corporal punishment.

Adultery, rape, sodomy, and bestiality, all listed in the *Body of Liberties* among the capital crimes, did not come under the jurisdiction of the Essex County quarterly court. But a considerable number at the order of Mr. Hathorne found themselves sitting in the stocks or tied to the whipping post for other irregularities related to amorousness. Philandering, "wanton dalliance," lascivious speech, kissing, and manifesting in any way "unclean" desire were crimes which Mr. Hathorne had to judge.

But in his presence one had to be careful in accusing another of private wrongdoing, always difficult to prove. Reuben Cuppie, for example, brought Richard Pitfold into court for a preliminary hearing on a charge of bestiality. Mr. Hathorne found the charge false, "which had it been true would have cost Pitfold his life." So Cuppie was sentenced to be whipped, and was also required to pay an indemnity to

Pitfold and the constable's charges for administering the flogging. Mr. Hathorne himself saw the stripes inflicted and the money paid.

On another occasion he sentenced Cuppie to be whipped for "running away to the eastward from his wife great with child, for stealing and blasphemy, lying, and swearing." Two witnesses testified that they had heard Cuppie say, "No, I don't go to meeting. The paring of my nails and a chip are as acceptable to God as the day of thanksgiving."

Another false accuser, one of Mr. Endecott's servant girls, learned to her sorrow what it meant to bring a criminal charge against a member of an important family. She claimed that her master's son, Zerubbabel, had got her with child, while Mr. Hathorne and his colleagues were sure that another man was the father of her unborn bastard. She testified that Zerubbabel had "teased" her while she was at her work of lacemaking and that she had said to him, "I'm not your common bawd." Asked by one of the magistrates, probably Mr. Hathorne, why she had not complained to the youth's father, the girl replied that she had considered doing so and had sought the advice of another woman. This person had said to her, "I know thy condition, alas, poor wench! For Zerubbabel has also insulted me. His father won't help." The girl, found guilty of defamation, was whipped and required to wear pinned to her cap a paper bearing the inscription, A SLANDERER OF MR. ZERUBBABEL ENDECOTT.

The face of the Almighty was shining upon New England during the years Cromwell was in the seat of power in London. Still Mr. Hathorne, with all his faith and force of will, must have felt at times that he was making little progress in his endeavors to render the people of Essex County fit subjects of Jesus, the King in God's State. Perhaps such crimes as theft and vagrancy were on the wane. But criticism of church and government was increasing. Among the people there were discontent and a growing tendency to express protest.

Satan was at work in their midst, Mr. Hathorne no doubt concluded; and he was all the more firmly convinced when he heard evidence in which hints of witchcraft turned up. One individual, on trial for absenting himself from meeting, was surely in the habit of praying to Beelzebub. For it was proved that the man had said in speaking of the ministers and magistrates, "These are the brethren. The Divil scald them!" A woman brought to court for brawling came under dark suspicion when a witness testified that she had called her spouse "the gurly gutted Divil." Another woman, on trial for defamation, admitted saying that Goody James was an old witch, that she was seen in a boat sailing towards Boston and at the same time in her yard in Salem. In the strange experiences of John Bradstreet, Mr. Hathorne and his associates on the bench at first suspected diabolism. Brought to court for a preliminary hearing on the charge of having familiarity with evil spirits, Bradstreet declared that he had read a book of magic and that when a voice came to him asking what he wished to command he had answered, "Go make a bridge of sand over the sea, go make a ladder of sand up to heaven, and go to God and come down no more." This time the court was realistic: Bradstreet was not sent to Boston to be held on a charge of witchcraft, but was ordered whipped or fined for telling a lie. The hanging in Boston in 1656 of Mrs. Ann Hibbins, found to be a witch by the court of assistants, had a salutary effect throughout Massachusetts Bay.

For years the people were to think twice before uttering lightly any of the names by which the Prince of Darkness was known. They were taught that to avoid his hellish snares they must go regularly to meeting and heed well every word the ministers spoke. Yet for absence from God's worship or misbehavior while in attendance one after another was brought before Mr. Hathorne. Two men were fined for "hunting on the Lord's day and shooting a raccoon while the exercise was in progress, thus disturbing the congregation." Another was fined for "staying at home and brewing on the Lord's day," and another for "sailing from Gloucester harbor on the Sabbath, when the people were going to morning exercises, he having hay in his boat." Those convicted of "much sleeping on the Lord's day in time of exercise" were for the first offense admonished, but if they persisted in falling asleep during sermon they were fined or whipped. When a sleeper at meeting in Salem struck the tithingman who woke him up, Mr. Hathorne saw that the criminal was fined for two crimes.

Informers were forever on the lookout for critics of church and government. Case after case involving those who expressed dissatisfaction was heard by Mr. Hathorne. For "reproachful and unseemly speeches against the rule of the church" a Salem woman was ordered to sit in the stocks an hour and suffer a severe whipping the next lecture day. A woman of Gloucester, on trial in Salem, had said, according to witnesses, "If it were not for the law I'd never go to meeting, the teacher is so dead. He's better fitted to be a lady's chambermaid than a preacher." The woman was fined and ordered to confess repentance before the Gloucester congregation. Elizabeth Legg, of Marblehead, was heavily fined and required to rise and declare at meeting: "I do acknowledge that I did evil in speaking slightingly and scornfully of our minister Mr. Walton, and in particular in saying we could have a boy from the college preach better than Mr. Walton for half the wages." A man was whipped or fined for saying in regard to the minister of Lynn, "I'd as lief hear a dog bark as to hear Mr. Cobbett preach." A father and son of Lynn were both fined and commanded to read public confessions for "deriding such as sing in the congregation and terming them fools." A Salem woman, for "scoffing at church membership," was fined, and condemned by Mr. Hathorne and his colleagues as "very ignorant, sottish, and imperious."

With critics of the established order daring enough to speak out from time to time, the Massachusetts Bay authorities were never free of fears of heresy. They had showed the length to which they were willing to go in suppressing it when they banished to the forests Roger Williams and Mrs. Anne Hutchinson. But arguments in favor of liberty of conscience and Antinomianism had scarcely been hushed when protests against the practice of infant baptism began to be heard. One who opposed it and freely said so was Lady Deborah Moody, of Lynn, whom Winthrop pronounced "a wise and anciently religious woman." Mr. Hathorne took part in terrorizing her and her husband, Sir Henry, into seeking refuge among the Dutch on Long Island. Mr. Hathorne was also one of the magistrates who admonished the wife of William Bowditch, ancestor of the illustrious Bowditch family, for urging that only persons of full understanding should experience the sacrament of baptism. It was Mr. Hathorne's court which ordered a man of Lynn to read publicly a confession of penitence for saying, "They who stay at meeting when a child is being baptized worship the Devil." Mr. Hathorne concurred in fining a man of Salem for declaring, "Next year I'll be a member of the church and have my dog christened."

Salem's most noted woman heretic, Mary Oliver, was for twelve years in clash with Mr. Hathorne. Winthrop wrote of her, "For ability of speech and appearance of zeal and devotion she was far before Mrs. Hutchinson, and so the fitter instrument to have done hurt." Her eccentricities drew attention. She was frequently ill, and aroused pity. If Mr. Hathorne had shown less ingenuity in combating her, she might have won a sufficient number of sympathizers to create schism in God's State.

At the fourth court session at which Mr. Hathorne sat as a magistrate her husband, Thomas Oliver, a cordwainer, appeared as plaintiff in a case involving debt. At meeting a few months later, while Mr. Peter, the minister, was celebrating the sacrament of the Lord's Supper, Mrs. Oliver rose and asked permission to commune. Mr. Peter graciously informed her that since she had not been received into the church she would have to be denied a place at God's Table. She proceeded to plead for the privilege, claiming eloquently that it was her right as a Christian. Mr. Endecott, once again the victim of sudden anger, broke into her speech and let her know that he was on the point of commanding a constable to eject her from the meetinghouse. Silenced by the threat, she sat down, and the Communion service was continued. But Mr. Peter had scarcely pronounced the benediction when Mrs. Oliver was arrested and placed in the custody of the marshals who were to take her to the Boston jail. Openly guilty of the crime of disturbing the most holy of the church ordinances, she could be tried only by the colony's highest court.

Though the wife of a craftsman, she had won such respect in Salem that the people addressed her by the gentlewoman's title of "Mrs." She and her husband, middle-aged and childless, had been in the town for a year. The shoes he made were superior in quality, and she had the habit of spending her free time reading the Bible. Little more had been found out about them. Now, when the people talked only of the astounding scene they had witnessed in the meetinghouse, it was learned that Mrs. Oliver, weak in body but strong in spirit, had suffered in England because of her Puritan convictions. At church in Norwich, her old home, she had persistently refused to bow at the naming of Jesus in the reading of the prayers and had been imprisoned for nonconformity.

She was brought before the General Court for examination on December 4, 1638. With ease she parried the questions, quoting at length from the Bible and refusing to admit the slightest degree of penitence. The Court was obliged to send her back to the house of correction. After a few days in the icy cell, with only enough food to maintain life, she obtained an audience with Governor Winthrop. In his presence she conceded that she had done wrong in disturbing others in their worship in Salem. The General Court again took up her case, and when her husband agreed to give bond for her good behavior she was released.

But within less than a year she was back in the Boston jail, charged with criticising church and government in the hearing of immigrants who had just arrived in Salem. This time the General Court sentenced her to be whipped. "She stood without tieing," wrote Winthrop, "and bore her punishment with a masculine spirit, glorying in her sufferings. But after, when she came to consider the reproach which would stick by her, she was dejected by it."

For six years she lived quietly in Salem. During this time, it appears, she tried more than once to convince the ministers and elders that she was worthy of church membership. Finally they let her know that a person with her questionable orthodoxy need never hope to be counted among the saints of God's State.

So she began to make trouble again. To Robert Cotty, an informer, she declared, "All the ministers in this country are blood-thirsty men."

"That's blasphemy!" interrupted Cotty.

She ignored the charge, and calmly said, in reference to her physical frailty, "My blood is too thin for them to draw it out."

Brought before Mr. Hathorne and the other Essex County magistrates on Cotty's complaint, she was sentenced to stand tied to the whipping post for two or three hours with a slit stick on her tongue.

She must have felt that Mr. Hathorne was mainly responsible for this particular punishment. For soon after undergoing the humiliation she was abusing him in the hearing of informers, "uttering divers mutinous speeches." She was saying to anyone who would listen, "You in New England are thieves and robbers!" One day she came to Robert Gutch's house and found several who were not members of the church. She said to them, "Lift up your heads! Your redemption draweth nigh!"

"Have you forgotten what you were punished for?" asked Gutch.

"I came out of that with a scarf and a ring," she answered, cynically referring to the tokens customarily given to ministers and magistrates at funerals.

As cryptic as she, Gutch answered, "There are some whose necks have iron sinews and whose brows are brass."

Assuming that Gutch was alluding not to herself but to Mr. Hathorne, she said, "I do hope to live and tear his flesh in pieces, and all such as he."

It was when she was brought into court on a charge of working on the Sabbath at the time of meeting that Gutch and other witnesses reported her abuse of Mr. Hathorne. For punishment she sat in the stocks for an hour, and she would have been sent to Boston for a term in jail if someone —not her husband, who had gone back to England—had not vouched for her decent conduct.

Once out of the stocks, she filed suit against John Robinson, the constable's helper, charging that he had handled her brutally while putting her into the machine of torture. The court ordered Robinson to pay her ten shillings.

In bringing this action Mrs. Oliver made a blunder, and Mr. Hathorne was quick to take advantage of it. He had long been determined to get the woman out of the colony, and she herself had at last shown him how he could render her exit ignominious. From this time on his informers were busy, probably swearing lies as often as they swore the truth. Mrs. Oliver was in and out of court, charged with living apart from her husband, defamation, and petty theft, and in turn charging others with like misdemeanors. She was clever, but in no position to outwit Mr. Hathorne. Instead of sympathizing with her, Salem came to regard her as a nuisance or worse, and to talk of her as possibly a witch. When, in the spring of 1651, she yielded to a command of the court and returned to England, there was about her nothing of the aura of martyrdom which had surrounded Mrs. Hutchinson. With her spirit at last broken, Mrs. Oliver died soon after reaching her old home. In 1652 her husband came back to Salem, and was soon married to a woman who was to make no attempt to challenge the Puritan theocracy.

Mr. Hathorne rarely committed a criminal to Essex County's one jail, the house of correction in Ipswich. The founders of Massachusetts Bay saw no reason in depriving the commonwealth of a wrongdoer's labor so long as there could be such a punishment as a fine, or a public humiliation, or a whipping, or a turn in the stocks. With all their visions of a Divine State, they were practical Englishmen, endowed with the traditional English regard for property.

Mr. Hathorne himself was too occupied with public affairs to build up a large private fortune, as several men in Salem were doing. Still he saw that his two farms yielded income, collected every farthing due him as an official of the colony, and reaped profit from shipments of goods—adventures he called them—to England and the West Indies. Moreover, about the time of Mrs. Oliver's expulsion, he erected a house on the town lot he had been granted on arriving in Salem, installed his family there, and in a room downstairs opened a shop. It was in 1651 that he first obtained from the General Court a license to sell strong waters. This lot, located on the main street a short distance east of the meetinghouse, extended down to the South River. Here Mr. Hathorne built a wharf and also a warehouse in which to store his adventures.

The trail which ran along the west side of the lot was called Burying Lane, because it led to the Burying Point, where, in graves unmarked, possibly rested Lady Arbella Johnson, the Reverend Francis Higginson, and many other victims of Salem's hard first years. The dwelling Mr. Hathorne erected was a "fair house"—probably a clapboard structure with an overhanging second story, a huge chimney in the center, a steep shingled roof, small leaded glass windows, a narrow vestibule, a spacious parlor on one side, a kitchen of the same dimensions on the other, a lean-to at the back to be used for the shop, and a turning difficult stairway leading from the vestibule to three or four chambers above. One looking out the front door saw on the opposite side of the street the fairest of Salem's "fair houses," the turreted wooden mansion built by Emanuel Downing, Governor Winthrop's brother-in-law.

Early in 1655 Governor Endecott moved to Boston. On the first Lord's day following his departure, at nine o'clock in the morning, his successor as Salem's most important lay personage, Mr. Hathorne, stepped from the front door of his town residence and started west on the main street for the short walk to meeting. He was a splendid figure, as he made his way between banks of snow, steadying himself on his magistrate's staff. He was wearing his great black magistrate's cloak, which had a square white linen collar and sleeves short enough to reveal from the elbows down the crimson and gold of his rich under jacket. His gauntlets were of white kid, and the silver buckles on his black shoes and white steeple-crowned felt hat glistened in the sunlight. A man whose whole wealth amounted to less than £200 was forbidden by the laws of the colony to wear such adornments as buckles and to deck his wife in silk scarfs and hoods, but Mr. Hathorne was worth several times £200. With his farms and his town house he would have been respected as a gentleman even in Berkshire.

Very different from the beautiful old churches in Bray and Binfield was the meetinghouse which he was approaching. It had been greatly enlarged in 1639, but it was still small and crude—unpainted and weatherbeaten. There was no spire. The bell which the sexton rang to summon saints like Mr. Hathorne and all others, on pain of law, was hung on rough scaffolding in the yard at the front. Perhaps nailed to the main door was the bleeding head of a wolf some man had slain the night before, thus entitling himself to a reward of five shillings from the town treasury. Undoubtedly nailed to the door were notices of various sorts, including possibly an anonymous attack, maybe in doggerel verse, on Mr. Hathorne or some other high official. If such was found, Mr. Hathorne before entering the sanctuary summoned an informer and sent him out on a search.

The "catted chimney" which had formerly heated the meetinghouse had been condemned as too likely to start a destructive fire. Now the holy interior was icy. As Mr. Hathorne crossed the threshold he saw that every inch of space, except the "open middle alley," was filled and that everybody was muffled in the heaviest woolen. On the side reserved for women sat his wife and three daughters, and possibly also his youngest boy, William, who was only ten. In the men's section sat Eleazar, the oldest son, already near eighteen. On the gallery or pulpit stairs sat the other two boys, Nathaniel and John, sixteen and fourteen respectively. Mr. Hathorne, with all eyes upon him, strode down the "alley" to the "bench of honor," and for the first time took the seat which had hitherto been reserved for Mr. Endecott.

The people, whom in meeting Mr. Hathorne called his brothers and sisters, seemed charitable enough as they looked at him in admiration. But he was a *practical* visionary: he understood these people as their minister, the Reverend Edward Norris, would never be able to understand them. Mr. Hathorne was in a position to pry into their most intimate secrets. He could make their homes happy or condemn them to misery. The deference accorded him was, he knew, only outward. Very few of these people had been redeemed from original sin. Within the breasts of most of them still slumbered such resentment and hatred as Mrs. Oliver had had the courage to express in words. He and his kind, with Cromwell at the helm in England, were in firm control in God's State. But Mr. Hathorne knew that they could not for a moment afford to relax their vigilance.

By order of the General Court, the people of Massachusetts Bay fasted on June 11, 1656, and prayed God to preserve Cromwell from the machinations of persons of evil mind, to bless the naval and land forces of England at home and abroad, to go out with the Protestant armies against Antichrist and his adherents, to settle unity and peace upon the churches in the New World, and to check the spreading errors of such as the Ranters and Quakers in the Old, "that the ordinances of Christ might become more effectual to all, especially to children and servants, the rising generation." This order indicates clearly that the leaders of Massachusetts Bay were alarmed over the rise in England of those who called themselves Friends, but who were known by their traducers as Quakers. Their founder, George Fox, had been preaching his doctrine of direct revelation and inner light for only eight years. But already his followers were many.

They were extreme rebels, critical of all sects besides their own, and of all governments. Interpreting the commandment, "Thou shalt not kill," in its strictest sense, they justified no war, not even the civil conflict which had raised the Puritans to power in England. In contending with their enemies their main weapons were faith and passive resistance.

They were given to strange practices. When they were receiving what they called a communication from God, their ecstasy was manifested in the trembling of their bodies. Hence they had been nicknamed Quakers. They had no ordained ministry. At their meetings all was silence until, as they claimed, the Holy Spirit descended upon some man or woman and spoke through his or her mouth. They argued that all persons are equal before God, and refused to take off their hats in the presence of their betters. No force could induce them to swear an oath. They insisted that they acted only upon the command of God. From the point of view of Massachusetts Bay, it was not the Lord who told George Fox to do such a foolish thing as walk barefoot through the streets of Lichfield on a wintry morning.

The Massachusetts Bay leaders wanted none of such strangers, as they called all visitors who were not of their faith. Yet God, the Quakers said, was appointing them to go among peoples everywhere. The leaders knew that sooner or later the fanatics would be in New England. They were a menace not to be tolerated, for, with their gentleness and charitableness towards the lowly and unfortunate, they quickly won sympathizers and supporters. No persecution, it seemed, could crush them. They invited punishment, and apparently reveled in it. If one was struck on his right cheek, he turned his left. If one was put to death, another took his place. Mr. Hathorne, as he heard reports of these erratic new visionaries, realized that he and all the other high officials of Massachusetts Bay faced a problem which was going to be difficult to solve.

While the fast of June 11, 1656, was being observed, two Quaker women were on their way to Boston. As soon as they landed, three or four weeks later, they were arrested and put in jail; and the books they had brought were burned. Before they were released and banished, eight more Quakers had arrived, among whom were two young men, Christopher Holder and John Copeland. All were immediately imprisoned, and again there was a burning of books, including copies of the Bible belonging to the heretics. Three months later the eight were given their freedom on condition that they leave Massachusetts Bay immediately. They departed, probably for Rhode Island.

But at the end of the summer of 1657 Holder and Copeland turned up in Salem, and were received as guests in the home of Lawrence Southwick and his wife Cassandra. The General Court, in which Mr. Hathorne was that year the speaker, had a few months earlier passed laws providing special punishment for any Quakers found in the colony and a heavy fine for any ship captain who brought them in. Furthermore, the town of Salem, acting at the instigation of Mr. Hathorne, had decreed that whoever took strangers into his home without official approval must pay into the town treasury an assessment of twenty shillings a week while entertaining them. On the first Lord's day after their arrival in Salem, Holder and Copeland went to meeting. At the conclusion of the exercises Holder rose to speak, but had said little in criticism of the faith of the Puritans when he was assaulted by one of Mr. Hathorne's subordinates. The attack was so ferocious that Holder would have been choked to death there in God's sanctuary but for the interference of a bystander, Samuel Shattuck, who acted from no more than an impulse of humaneness. As soon as Holder was freed from the assailant's clutches he and Copeland were placed under arrest. Both then were taken to Boston by foot. Although they arrived in a state of exhaustion, they were flogged with a knotted whip before they were cast into prison and for three days were denied food and water. "Take no thought of me," Copeland wrote to his mother in England on the third day. "The Lord's power hath overshadowed me, and man I do not fear; for my trust is in the Lord, who is become our shield and buckler, and exceeding great reward." For giving aid to the strangers Samuel Shattuck and the Southwick husband and wife, all three of whom were respected in Salem, were likewise taken to Boston and imprisoned.

So was started in Massachusetts Bay the persecution of the Friends and their sympathizers. From the beginning to the end Mr. Hathorne was active. With the arrival of each new group of the strangers in the colony his determination to crush the whole lot grew all the firmer.

On June 27, 1658, a Sabbath day, he heard that a number of Friends were holding a meeting at a private home in Salem. He at once ordered constables to go and arrest all present. The next day he presided at the court before which those taken appeared for trial.

"For what have you come into these parts?" he asked the strangers.

One of them answered, "The Lord God said, 'Pass away to New England and seek a godly seed.' "

Then the spokesman, seeing that the prosecution had no witnesses to prove his identity as a Friend, took the initiative and asked, "How may you know a person is a Quaker?"

"You are one, for coming into court with your hat on," said Mr. Bradstreet, an assisting magistrate.

"It is a terrible thing," the spokesman said, "to make such cruel laws, to whip, and cut off ears, and burn through the tongue, for not putting off the hat."

"You speak blasphemy!" broke in Mr. Hathorne. "Do you admit that you speak thus at your meetings?"

"If you would attend our meetings you would know," replied the man. "Then you could give an account of what was done and spoken, and would not conclude a thing you know not."

"If you meet together and say anything," said General Denison, another magistrate, "we may conclude that you speak blasphemy."

"Do we have no recourse to English law and courts?" asked the spokesman.

"None," replied Mr. Hathorne.

The accused then admitted that they were Friends, and Mr. Hathorne ordered all the strangers and several of the Salem converts to the Boston prison. Among the strangers was young William Ledra, who was to write on the eve of his martyrdom on the gallows: "Alas, alas, what can the wrath and spirit of man, that lusteth to envy, aggravated by the heat and strength of the king of locusts, that came out of the pit, do unto one that is hid in the secret places of the Almighty? The sweet influences of the Morning Star, like a flood distilling into my innocent habitation, hath so filled me with the joy of the Lord in the beauty of holiness, that my spirit is as if it did not inhabit a tabernacle of clay, but is wholly swallowed up in the bosom of eternity, from which it had its being." Among the converts sent to Boston were

Lawrence and Cassandra Southwick, who were to hear on the day they were sentenced to banishment that Mr. Hathorne had authorized the sale into servitude of their twenty-two-year-old son Daniel and their eighteen-year-old daughter Provided. The accumulated fine charged against the parents for absence from meeting and entertaining strangers was so great that the son and daughter were unable to raise the money to pay it. Mr. Hathorne's order that they pay with their freedom, perhaps because of its extreme inhumanity, was never to be executed. Among the converts who were only admonished that day was Mrs. George Gardner, whose husband was the brother-in-law of one of Governor Winthrop's nieces. Despite the prominence of her family connections, Mrs. Gardner was to be persecuted until she and her husband found refuge in Connecticut.

Still the number of converts in Salem grew, and from time to time new strangers, in pairs or in groups, came to meet with them. Mr. Hathorne had been a close friend of several of the converts. But now—as an historian of the persecution was to claim—Mr. Hathorne pursued all "like a bloodhound, and had his will on them, in person and estate." In an order to a constable he wrote: "You are required, by virtue hereof, to search in all suspicious places for private meetings; and if they refuse to open the doors, you are to break open the door upon them, and return the names of those you find."

With all his vigilance Mr. Hathorne failed to capture two strangers, William Robinson and Marmaduke Stephenson, who came to Salem and attended several meetings of Friends. The two had been previously banished, and realized that they were back in Massachusetts Bay at the peril of their lives. After their departure from Salem they had gone to no more than one or two other towns when they were arrested and taken to Boston. There they were immediately

tried, and sentenced to be hanged. On the day of their execution the General Court, in which Mr. Hathorne was influential during the entire period of the persecution, called up the
militia to keep order in the capital. Public resentment at the
cruel course which the government was taking had to be
checked at all costs.

Condemned with Robinson and Stephenson was Mary
Dyer, a Boston convert. She had been banished, and had
spent some time in Rhode Island before returning to her
home in defiance of the law. The two men were hanged
before her eyes. Then, just as her turn came to mount the
scaffold, an officer rushed upon the scene and announced
that the General Court, through the intercession of her son,
had commuted her sentence to a second banishment. Again
she went to Rhode Island. But the next year, as she claimed,
God commanded her to return to Boston. This time she was
hanged. Hundreds in the years to come, including perhaps
descendants of Mr. Hathorne, were to vow that they had
seen the ghost of Mary Dyer, clad in the Quaker gray in
which she died, walking Boston Common late at night, showing by the very gentleness of her mien that the meek truly
inherit the earth.

To Mr. Hathorne the zeal of the Quakers was a form of
madness. Certainly one case which he had to judge justifies
such a conclusion. A shy young Salem wife, Deborah Wilson,
daughter of the converts Joshua and Thomasin Buffum, got
the notion that God was commanding her to walk entirely
nude through the streets of Salem in order to exemplify to
the people the nakedness of the established religion. She
forthwith obeyed the command. But only a few had seen
her abroad in her nudity when a constable stopped her and
took her back to her home. When court met, she was brought
before Mr. Hathorne. The decision of the magistrates was:
"For your barbarous and inhuman going naked through the

town, you are sentenced to be tied to a cart's tail with your body naked downward to the waist, and whipped from Mr. Gedney's gate till you come to your house, not exceeding thirty stripes; and your mother Buffum and your sister Smith, that were abetted to you, are to be tied on either side of you at the cart's tail naked to their shifts to the waist, and accompany you." To the letter, the sentence was executed. Several times during the months that followed Deborah Wilson was fined for absence from meeting. Finally the court agreed that she was "distempered in the head."

Following the death of Cromwell and the restoration, in 1660, of the monarchy in England, the great reaction against Puritans and Puritanism began. While the Massachusetts Bay leaders were pressing at full vigor the persecution of the Quakers, they suddenly found that the face of Jehovah was no longer shining upon them, that in all respects they were definitely on the defensive. The first act of Charles II directed against them was a command, dated September 9, 1661, stating that any case involving a Quaker held in Massachusetts Bay on a capital charge must be transferred to courts of law in England. Two Salem converts, Samuel Shattuck and Nicholas Phelps, had gone to London, had received permission to state their grievances before the king, and had persuaded him to interfere. The government in Massachusetts Bay was in no position to ignore the royal edict. The hangings, the cutting off of men's ears, the boring of holes through women's tongues with red hot irons, and the starving of the imprisoned in Boston were at once stopped.

Even whippings and fines were exacted only after careful deliberation on the part of the magistrates. It must have been agony to Mr. Hathorne to have to pass light sentences on certain Quaker blasphemers who appeared before him. One, according to witnesses, had said in speaking of the Salem minister, "No, I will not go to hear old Higginson, nor to any of their meetings, but when the Church of England shall be set up, with the organs, then I shall go." Another was accused of saying, "Mr. Higginson bawls like a bear." A Quaker servant was charged with saying, "Mr. Higginson is a cheat. He told my mistress, Mrs. Corwin, that he had no bread, and when I was sent to his house with two bags of wheat I found his storeroom so full that there was no place to put them." The worst of all the blasphemers was reported to have declared, "Higginson is one of Baal's priests, and Major Hathorne was drunk, and I had to lead him home."

Goody Small, a Quaker convert, had no money to pay a fine assessed against her for not attending meeting. One day while she was toiling in her corn field a constable came and took her oxen from the plow.

She at once made her way to John Gedney's tavern, where the court was in session. Granted permission to plead before the magistrates, she abruptly asked, "Why were my beasts taken?"

"They will be sold, and the money will go to the poor," answered Mr. Hathorne.

At that moment John Gedney, noted for the excellence of the food and the variety of the drink served in his house, walked into the room.

"Is he the poor to whom the money will go?" asked Goody Small, pointing to the innkeeper.

Mr. Hathorne—not to his godly credit—asked in reply, "Would you have us starve while we sit about your business?"

The Friends, fighting with their weapons of sincere faith, passive resistance, sobriety, and industry, won a great victory over the builders of God's State. Mr. Hathorne was to live to see Thomas Maule, a Quaker stranger, establish himself in Salem and, in spite of grievous discrimination, rise to a position of prominence. Mr. Hathorne was to live to hear that Maule was planning to erect a Quaker meetinghouse in the town. Mr. Hathorne was even in time to allow a Quaker witness to give testimony in his court on mere affirmation rather than on a sworn oath. And Mr. Hathorne was to live to see his son John married to a daughter of the Mrs. George Gardner whom he had hounded into fleeing with her husband and children to Hartford in Connecticut because of her Quaker faith.

WITH BIBLE AND SWORD

IN 1662, when he was in his fifty-sixth year, Mr. Hathorne was taken from the General Court and made an assistant, a member of the governor's advisory council. Known henceforth as "the worshipful Major," he entered the period when life for him and every other leader in the colony meant compromise after compromise and often complete surrender. Massachusetts Bay, built on the Puritan dream, was a success; and ambitious outsiders from all directions were looking covetously towards the promising new commonwealth. The founders, their backs already to the wall in 1662, grew more and more out of favor in the mother country. In moments of defeat and despair they no doubt felt that they were also out of favor in heaven.

Still, as the difficult years passed, they held on all the more stubbornly to the conviction that their creed alone embodied the truth of the Bible, and they maintained at all times the courage to use their swords. Before Major Hathorne's mind's eye the vision of God's State upon earth still loomed, and his will to do all in his power to bring about moral perfection among the people never weakened.

The Quakers met with growing leniency in his court because they settled down and proved themselves peaceable, honest, and willing to work. They were heretics, and therefore were despised. But so long as they paid their fines for absence from meeting, abstained from blasphemy and proselyting, and made their labor count, they were tolerated. This was not true of thieves, vagrants, loafers, tipplers, merrymakers, and philanderers. Nor was it true of men who aped dandies and wore long hair, nor of women who adorned themselves with "superstitious ribbons" and went abroad clad in "bodices revealing naked breasts and arms," nor of couples who "rode from town to town upon pretense of going to lecture but in truth to drink and revel in taverns and ordinaries." It was not even true of children, who now at divine worship were required to sit in a corner to themselves with a "grave and sober" tithingman watching over them. The prestige which came to Major Hathorne on his elevation to the governor's council served to make him all the more severe and all the more dreaded. Whippings of thirty-nine stripes, and fines running into pounds, were common sentences in the Essex County quarterly court after 1662.

In his struggle to tighten discipline and strengthen the country from within, the worshipful Major missed no opportunity to exhort the people. In the old days after uniting a couple in marriage he had mildly instructed them in their duties as husband and wife. Now he bluntly told them that they would burn in hell if they failed to train their children in the godly virtues of courage, diligence, and thrift. Endowed with "the quick apprehension, strong memory, and rhetoric" which a contemporary ascribed to him, he often supplied the pulpit in Salem and other towns when the ministers were sick or away. In the manner of the most effectual of the preachers, he used his booming voice to terrorize his hearers with pictures of the horrors of hell and with stories of the mysterious portents sent by Providence to warn the wicked. The refrain in each of his discourses was, "Where the idler lies at his ease the Devil lurks."

Within less than a year after he became an assistant, his oldest son, Eleazar, was married to Abigail Corwin, daughter of Captain George Corwin, seventeenth-century Salem's richest man. Major Hathorne, burdened by the duties which his assistantship added and awake as never before to the necessity of promoting godliness in the country, had no time for private business. Since Eleazar had proved his aptitude for trade, his father deeded to him his town property, including the residence, shop, warehouse, and wharf. When the groom and his bride moved in, the Major, with Mrs. Hathorne and the children still in the family fold, went back to the Mill Pond farm to live. This was the Major's last move. And except for sending to sea occasional adventures —entrusted to the management of Eleazar, who was soon to become a partner of his brother-in-law Jonathan Corwin —Major Hathorne was to have no more to do with trade.

As a magistrate of the Essex County court he had been judging minor offenders for a full quarter of a century. With these he still had to contend. Now as a member of the court of assistants he also had to pass judgment on the innocence or guilt of the colony's worst malefactors. The convictions he helped bring about were many, and the punishments decreed were extreme.

A killer found guilty of manslaughter was sentenced "to be burned in the hand and to forfeit his goods and chattels." The executioner did the burning in the presence of the worshipful assistants. An African slave, called Maria Negro, convicted of setting fire to her master's house in Roxbury, was burned at the stake in Boston. On the same occasion another black slave, a man, also convicted of arson, was hanged, and as soon as he was pronounced dead his body was cut down and thrown upon the flames which were consuming Maria. A man found guilty of treason was sentenced to run the gantlet through all the companies of soldiers stationed in Boston, forfeit his lands to the commonwealth, and go into exile for the rest of his life. For "contemptuous carriage before the court of assistants" Maurice Brett was sentenced to stand in the pillory with one ear nailed to it, then to suffer the amputation of the ear, pay a fine of twenty shillings and receive a whipping of ten stripes.

Persons charged with gross moral uncleanness came again and again before Major Hathorne and his worshipful colleagues. To a Boston woman taken in adultery they gave a choice of two punishments: she might leave the colony, or she might receive thirty stripes from a knotted whip and then exhibit herself on a stool in the market place for one hour with a paper on her bosom reading in capital letters, THUS I STAND FOR MY ADULTEROUS AND WHORISH CARRIAGE. A man and woman of Boston found "not guilty of adultery but of very suspicious acts leading to adultery" were sentenced to stand for an hour on the gallows with ropes about their necks, and then to be tied to a cart's tail and whipped not exceeding thirty-nine stripes through the streets of both Boston and Charlestown. Sentenced to die were a man of Haverhill for raping a neighbor's wife in the woods on a Christmas day, a servant for raping his master's three-year-old daughter, and an Indian for raping a squaw. Another Indian, found guilty of raping a nine-year-old Indian girl, was sentenced to be carried to the Caribbean Islands and sold into slavery. A Roxbury youth, convicted of "the unnatural and horrid act of bestiality on a mare," was sentenced to stand at the foot of the gallows and see the abused animal killed with "a knock on the head" and then to ascend the ladder and die by hanging. To a woman who complained that her husband had been bewitched into impotency the court denied divorce, recommended "a more loving and suitable cohabitation one with the other," and suggested that the pair "might use all due physical means." A Braintree man and his recently wedded wife, who had been his brother's widow, were found guilty of incest: cohabitation between them was forbidden, and the woman, judged to be the aggressor, was ordered to make confession of her guilt at meeting.

The measures Major Hathorne and the other leaders adopted were doubly hard. But hard even to a greater degree were the times. In England the fallen Puritan masters were being brought to the block if they were aristocrats, and hanged and drawn and quartered if commoners. Stuck on poles in market places throughout the kingdom were their stinking heads for the populace to spit at. What retribution would the revengeful Charles II and his government of sycophants work in Massachusetts Bay? This question outweighed all others in the mind of Major Hathorne. The Dutch of New Amsterdam, who had given little trouble to the Puritans, surrendered in 1664 to English forces loyal to Charles II. To the north and east of Massachusetts Bay were the king's friends and supporters, the French. Everywhere in the colony, even in the Salem town center, were the children of the Devil, the red men, only waiting to be incited. The times called for prayer, holy living, industry, thrift, courage, watchfulness, and tactful statesmanship.

In 1645 the General Court had appointed Mr. Hathorne and other negotiators to go to St. Croix, in Canada, and demand satisfaction from a French adventurer, Charles d'Aulnay, who had seized at sea a Salem vessel carrying merchandise to his chief rival in fur trading, Charles de la Tour. The negotiators, favored by Providence and led by Mr. Hathorne, succeeded in effecting a settlement without leaving Massachusetts Bay. After that time, according to a contemporary, "the godly Mr. Hathorne was consulted when the colony had to do with any foreign government." Mr. Hathorne had also learned lessons in diplomacy at meetings of the New England Confederation, in which he had been one of the Massachusetts Bay delegates for more than twenty years.

But until Charles II sent over commissioners to make an investigation the Major had never been called upon to treat with opponents who held most of the advantages. When these emissaries began to manifest an overbearing attitude, and especially when they started the rumor that Charles II was going to exact of Massachusetts Bay a levy of £5,000 a year for his private purse, Major Hathorne lost his head and showed that after all he was an unskilled diplomat. Addressing the Salem trainband on the drill field on an afternoon when the royal commissioners were still in the colony, he expressed his dissatisfaction with them and with what they were doing. In the course of his speech he even dared to declare that prerogative rests in the laws of a people rather than in the will of a king. Governor Endecott, leader of leaders in Massachusetts Bay since the death of Winthrop in 1649, held that his first duty was to guard the charter, and in dealing with the commissioners followed the policy of circumvention. Within his heart he no doubt approved of his old friend's bold speech, which was not unlike his own most celebrated deed, his cutting the St. George's cross from the royal standard in 1634. Still his position demanded that he rebuke Major Hathorne. So upon the governor's recommendation the General Court relieved the Major of his command of the Salem unit of the Essex County militia and ordered him to write a retraction of his insurrectionary words and an apology for his rashness. Copies of his statement were nailed on meetinghouse doors throughout the country.

But after the despised commissioners had gone on to New York a chance event vindicated Major Hathorne. The messenger who was carrying the report on Massachusetts Bay back to London was captured at sea by the Dutch, then at war with England. On being taken the man dropped the receptacle containing his papers into the ocean. When news of this "visitation of Providence" reached Massachusetts Bay the leaders, overlooking the fact that the Dutch were the enemies of their mother country, freely gave vent to their joy. From the pulpits of Boston and other towns ministers declared that Jehovah was again smiling upon His saints in the New World. Thus emboldened by the churchmen, magistrates on all sides repeated what Major Hathorne had said about a people's laws and royal prerogative. Instead of being a rebuked official publicly humiliated the Major found himself a hero. It was probably of his own will that he was not returned to the command of the Salem trainband.

John Endecott died soon after the commissioners left Massachusetts Bay. If he had lived to hear of the loss of their report he would surely have asked the General Court to proclaim a day of thanksgiving. His successor as governor, Richard Bellingham, was a less impulsive man. Though younger than Endecott, he was "an ancient gentleman near eighty years old, attended with many infirmities of age, as stone-colic, deafness, etc." Still he had the strength to suppress rebellious talk in Massachusetts Bay. He and all other leaders realized that the commissioners would eventually get back to England and report orally to the king. The colony was in a state of dread until the summer of 1666.

Then came a royal letter, written the previous April 10. It listed the commssioners' complaints, and threw Massachusetts Bay from dread to frustration. Among many odious items was the order: "His Majesty's express command and charge is that the Governor and Council of Massachusetts Bay do forthwith make choice of four or five persons to attend upon His Majesty, whereof Mr. Richard Bellingham and Major William Hathorne are to be two, both which His Majesty commands upon their allegiance to attend." Must the king be obeyed? Was it his intention to announce to Governor Bellingham at Whitehall that the Massachusetts Bay charter was forfeit? Was it the royal will to have Major Hathorne arrested immediately upon landing in England on the charge of making a treasonous speech? These questions and a hundred like them the members of the government pondered and discussed. Finally a course of action, determined by the policy of circumvention, was decided upon.

Within a few weeks a ship sailed from one of the Massachusetts Bay harbors bearing to His Majesty an obsequious yet evasive letter and two "brave masts," the loftiest and sturdiest that could be cut in the forests. His Majesty's liege subjects in the Massachusetts Bay plantation, said the letter, had long been considering how they might show their affection and loyalty, and so were sending as a gift the two superb masts, shaped for immediate raising on a vessel like the *Prince George,* the pride of the king's navy. Moreover, said the letter, a ship bearing twenty-eight similar masts would soon follow. Then the letter pointed out that of all His Majesty's dominions Massachusetts Bay had the tallest and strongest trees and the devoted subjects most willing to fell them and prepare them for use on the royal fighting ships. So wordy were the framers of the letter in pouring out their love for Charles II and in offering him gifts of masts that they failed to allude to his order regarding the appearance of Governor Bellingham and Major Hathorne at Whitehall. These two apprehensive gentlemen remained respectively in Boston and Salem.

In the autumn of 1666 another letter intended for the ear of Charles II was sent from Massachusetts Bay. It was dated October 26, and was addressed to one of the king's secretaries of state, Sir William Morice. The communication, about three thousand words long, was signed "Samuel

Nadorth." Any person capable of the strong style in which
the letter was written would have been known in the colony.
Yet nowhere in the Massachusetts Bay records does the
name "Nadorth" appear. It must therefore be considered
a pseudonym. Since it is almost a perfect anagram of the
name "Hathorne," several descendants of the Major were to
conclude that he was the writer and sender of the letter. If
Mr. Hathorne, an assistant, took the liberty of addressing
the king "without the authority or advice of any person
whatsoever," and if moreover he was foolish enough to sign
the message with an anagram of his own name, he was a
far worse diplomat than the proved facts show. The letter,
on the whole a repetition of the official dispatch, could have
served only to make a complex situation more complicated.
It remains a mystery.

Providence, the ministers claimed, was again favoring
God's State and chastising the mother country. Charles II at
the end of 1666 was too absorbed in adversities at home to
give attention to letters and gifts from his subjects, loyal or
disloyal, in New England. He was beset by his troubles
with the Dutch and by internal problems resulting from
the plague which was sweeping England and by the fire
which had destroyed a great part of London. Massachusetts
Bay, to the great satisfaction of the leaders, especially Governor Bellingham and Major Hathorne, was ignored. The
revered charter was safe in Boston and still in force, but
every high official knew that the king would again make
demands.

One of the early cases which came before Major Hathorne
as a member of the court of assistants was a suit for divorce
in which his oldest daughter, Sarah, was the plaintiff. She
had married Edward Helwyse, probably a native of her
father's Berkshire, and he had taken her to England. There

he served in the army of Charles II, first as a private soldier in the Tower, and then as sergeant of a foot company in Ireland. After Sarah bore him a son, christened Gervais, he deserted her and married "a woman of Westminster." Sarah, required by English law to leave her child in the custody of the father, had come back to Salem. Depositions proving her husband's desertion and bigamy were read before the court of assistants on September 9, 1664, and she was granted a divorce and given the right to be known again as Sarah Hathorne. The next April she was married to Joseph Coker of Newbury, her father probably officiating at the marriage ceremony.

A woman of violent temper, capable of great cruelty, Sarah Hathorne probably forced Edward Helwyse into leaving her. But her father, nurtured in the traditions of English family loyalty, could never have hesitated in holding out help when she found herself in trouble. Besides, she was the oldest of his children, born in Dorchester when he was still learning the New World ways, and she had given him his first grandson, a boy he was to remember. Providence had been singularly kind to him and Mrs. Hathorne. They had seen all of their children grow to maturity with strong bodies and good minds, while the majority of the babies born in Massachusetts Bay failed to survive infancy. But the blow of hearing that Sarah was in distress had scarcely fallen upon the Hathorne parents when Providence sent a second blow, the loss of their son Nathaniel, probably at sea. He was accomplished at keeping accounts, and often, it appears, went as supercargo on trading voyages to look after the sale of adventures. He reached at least the age of twenty-five.

On July 15, 1665, lightning struck a powder magazine belonging to The Castle, the fortress in Boston harbor which Major Hathorne's brother-in-law Richard Davenport had commanded since 1644. In the terrific explosion, which Massachusetts Bay looked upon as some sort of rebuff from Providence, several soldiers were killed, including Captain Davenport. At the time he took over The Castle he was pronounced by Winthrop "a man approved by his faithfulness, courage, and skill." He received a steady salary, and was rewarded from time to time with grants of land. But in rising in the world he had not kept pace with his wife's brother William. His career as a chief military defender fell in a period of peace, when he had no opportunity to show his worth as a leader of soldiers. He had held on to his house on the main street in Salem, and at his death it came into the possession of his oldest son, Nathaniel Davenport. Within a few years it was sold to Jonathan Corwin, Eleazar Hathorne's partner in business. Captain Davenport's widow and unmarried children had by this time established a home in Boston.

John Hathorne, still the keeper of an ordinary in Lynn and now the father of numerous children, was as usual bringing shame to his highly respected sister, Elizabeth Davenport, and his brother, the worshipful Major. The latter could scarcely have disapproved when he was asked to draw up the indenture which forced one of John's sons, no more than seven or eight, into servitude for ten years. How the father and uncle felt at the death of the boy, possibly from overwork, can only be imagined. As to the Major's humiliation and disgust over other deeds committed by his wayward brother there need be no doubts.

John was a defendant in quarterly court much too often. He was presented for failure to report cases of drunkenness in his house. "A tippler's money is as good as any man's," he was reported to have said. Once he was brought before his brother for not ejecting from his ordinary a crowd of intoxicated revelers, among whom was a married woman who sat wedged in between two men friends "singing merrily with them to her husband and the other profane laughers present." Twice John was brought before Major Hathorne for speaking contemptuous words to Lynn constables, one of whom he called "a lying, prating fool and knave." Once he was convicted of defamation and ordered to read a confession of repentance at meeting.

On another occasion he was the plaintiff in a defamation suit. The defendants were William Longley and his wife Joane, whom he accused of saying that he had "put more in a writing than should be." This meant forgery, of which he had once been convicted. But he was determined not to allow the name Hathorne to be slandered. So he had called in a constable to arrest the Longleys, and had attached their property. At the trial a witness, a man of Lynn, testified that he had said to Goody Longley, "I suppose John Hathorne esteems his name more than all your estate." The witness swore that she had asked in reply, "Is his name so good? What is it worth? Has he redeemed it?" Then the witness said to the court, "The whole drift of her discourse was a disesteeming of Hathorne's name and reputation." But the testimony of the defense witnesses was so strong that Major Hathorne and his associate magistrates dismissed the case.

However honored John Hathorne might have considered his family name, he found himself dragging it in the mud at a session of the court presided over by his brother in June, 1672. He was charged of keeping a disorderly house, selling strong waters to Indians and habitual drunkards, holding profane revels, brawling with his neighbors, and disturbing the peace. Two statements of grievances against him, one signed by fifteen men of Lynn and the other by six, were read to "the godly court."

The witnesses for the prosecution were many. One testified that "on last Christmas day at night," despite the law forbidding festivity at Christmas, a crowd had gathered at Hathorne's ordinary. "Joseph Collins," the witness swore, "drank *seventeen* quarts of rum. He and many more were disguised with drink. Goody Collins was so drunk that she had to be carried to bed. A daughter of a lady, Mrs. Laton, was there, and that's why nobody talked." Another witness testified, "An Indian working for me came to my house in the morning and said, 'My head no well. Me no work today.' I found a pint of liquor on him, and he said he got it of John Hathorne for a shilling." The wife of this witness swore, "Several Indians came from Hathorne's ordinary to my house so disguised with drink I was afraid. One fell down and slept in my yard." A neighbor whose family had engaged in a bloody brawl with Hathorne's family, clapboards and "knockers" for splitting clapboards having been freely used on both sides, testified, "When I went into the ordinary and asked Hathorne why he suffered the like of Daniel Sallman to be there drunk he said, 'What? Do you come to quarrel? You came to do that the other night. It repents me that I did not seat you headlong out of doors.' " The wife of the drunkard Sallman swore, "My husband spent his money at Hathorne's house, and when there were no more shillings for Hathorne to get he got our house and land."

The trial lasted for several days, the witnesses for the defense being also numerous. The verdict suggests that Major Hathorne was once more swayed by brotherly solicitude. For John was found guilty of only one charge, breach of the peace. The sentence was the temporary suspension of his license to sell strong waters and a considerable fine, one third of which was ordered paid to those who had testified against him.

The following September the General Court granted John a new license. He was not always in bad repute. For several

years he was a deputy constable for the town of Lynn, probably detailed to administer floggings. He served at various
times as a Lynn selectman, and was often called to Salem or
Ipswich to serve on a jury. He received the appointment of
quartermaster for the Essex County militia, an appointment
due undoubtedly to the Major's influence. He drew up wills
and made inventories for his neighbors.

On one occasion, in 1668, he addressed a plea to the quarterly court in behalf of an ill-treated Indian servant girl who
had appealed to him for help. In stating his reasons he said he
believed that all Negroes had surely been foredoomed to
damnation but that an Indian might possibly be destined to
spend the hereafter with God's elect. That observation
would scarcely have been made by him or anyone else in
Massachusetts Bay after the outbreak of King Philip's War
in 1675.

For thirty-eight years there had been peace in New England
between the red men and the white. Encouraged by the
success of such missionaries as John Eliot, many leaders had
come to conclude that the reds were going to be fitted into
the white civilization and made faithful subjects of the King
of God's State. But when news of the atrocities of the Indian
warriors began to pour in, that attitude was abandoned.
Major Hathorne never held it. His original distrust and
hatred of the Indians had grown with the years. In his view
they had developed more and more the traits of their sire,
the Devil.

An early victim of the war was one of Major Hathorne's
nephews, Captain Nathaniel Davenport, killed with a musket
ball in the campaign against the Narragansetts in December,
1675. Another victim in the same campaign was Captain
Joseph Gardner, commander of troops from Salem. He was
succeeded by his first lieutenant, Major Hathorne's young-

est son, thirty-year-old William, who was at once promoted to a captaincy.

Of all the young Salem officers who fought in the war Captain William Hathorne was the most dashing and ruthless. After the campaigns in Rhode Island and Connecticut he came back to Salem, and, while training recruits, got married. Then, in August, 1676, he was ordered to march with his company to the east and seek out and slay all hostile red men. At Dover in September, in violation of all the rules of warfare, he commanded his men to take captive a host of Indian warriors who had assembled at the invitation of the whites to discuss terms for a truce. When two hundred of the prisoners were sent to Boston to be disposed of as the government saw fit, many were shipped to the West Indies to be sold as slaves. From Dover, Captain Hathorne went into Maine, where in the vicinity of Wells, Winter Harbor, and Casco Bay he searched for more reds to crush either in fair fight or by treachery. Though the foray was in the main fruitless, he proved himself a daredevil leader. By the end of 1676 his troops, many of whom had been impressed, were demobilized, and he was back in Salem with his bride.

The Indian fighting power was already broken. Still it was almost a year before the war ended. The victory belonged to the whites, but it was only temporary. Almost a century was to pass before the red men of New England, with the French at the north to stir them up, were completely subdued.

The cost of the war to Massachusetts Bay, in both lives and wealth, was enormous. All agreed that God's State was under punishment. Major Hathorne and the other leaders, clerical and lay, were shouting to the people, "Jehovah in the wrath of His vengeance is scowling upon you, and not again will He show His smile until you return to the paths of godliness which your fathers trod." To steer Massachusetts

Bay back into the old ways the General Court passed more stringent laws, such as decreeing that any man who wore a periwig would be subject to a fine. At the same time the magistrates, desperately eager to run down criminals of all sorts, kept informers on the alert. But the people, unlike their fathers and grandfathers, appeared prone to treat lightly the harsh regulations. To one another they were whispering, "God is angry, and is chastising all of us for the blood the ministers and magistrates spilled in persecuting such as the Quakers."

Major Hathorne and his wife, both aged now, were living by themselves on the Mill Pond farm. It had been reduced to sixty acres, and the Major owned no other land except half of a mile-square tract in Groton. He had deeded the other half to his son William. The Salem Village farm had been divided into two equal parts and conveyed to the younger daughters as marriage portions. The sisters were wedded to brothers, Ann to Joseph Porter and Elizabeth to Israel Porter. Already born to the latter pair was the daughter who was to marry Joseph Putnam and become the mother of General Israel Putnam, of Revolutionary War fame. It was to Elizabeth that the half of the farm containing Hathorne Hill had fallen. The Major had given his son John a part of the Mill Pond property. This scion of the family, though married to the daughter of a Quaker woman, was showing an inclination to walk in the steps of his father. Just now John was planning to build a residence in the town center, near the plot on which had stood in early days the dwelling occupied by the Reverend Roger Williams.

Major Hathorne had long ago done what he could for the two oldest children. Eleazar, on the town property received as patrimony, was getting rich. He had lost three of his six children, but in other ways he had experienced little adversity. Sarah, who must have been given a money settlement at the time of her first marriage, was the unfortunate member of the family. She was living in Newbury, a woman of the people. Her second husband, to whom she had borne several children, was known to his neighbors as Goodman Coker. Unable perhaps to forget her unhappiness as the wife of Edward Helwyse and the son she had left in England, she had become monstrous in her cruelty. On one occasion she had been forced to appear before her father's court, sitting in Ipswich, on the charge of repeatedly beating in very brutal manner one of her white servant girls.

If Major Hathorne had directed his energies towards the accumulation of riches rather than towards the development of godliness in Massachusetts Bay, he might have left great wealth to his sons and daughters and their descendants. Of the many grants he had received, he had attempted to develop only one, the mile-square farm in Groton. The lands more distant voted to him by the General Court in recognition of his services to the country had been sold for little or abandoned as worthless domains. He had long ago given up plans to establish a trading post on a tract allotted to him in New Hampshire and to settle farmers on his share of a grant of a hundred square miles in the hills west of Springfield. Except for encouragement from the General Court and promise of title to a vast territory, nothing had come of a scheme which he, young Richard Saltonstall, and others had worked out for forestalling the Dutch and planting a colony on the Hudson in the vicinity of Albany. He had practically given away the quarter of Block Island which had been voted to him. A great parcel of land in Maine which he had been granted had been seen by few whites. Whatever titles the Major still held were so vague that he was to make no mention of these faraway properties in his final will.

Though the Mill Pond farm was diminished to only sixty

acres, it was one of the best equipped holdings in Essex County. There were cows, pigs, quite a herd of sheep, horses, and, running wild in the woods around, seven mares and a colt. The farming implements were plentiful, but there were no wheeled vehicles. The dwelling was so sturdy that it was to be habitable for three quarters of a century. The furnishings, similar to those in the house in which the Major had grown to manhood in Berkshire, consisted of cupboards, chests, tables, chairs, joined stools, bedsteads, cushions, and floor coverings, including a "Turkey carpet." The feather bed, bolster, pillows, curtains, and valances belonging to the bedstead on which the master and mistress of the house slept were valued at £8. There was another feather bed, valued at £4, and there was a "flockbed" worth £2. The Major's books, among which was a cherished copy of Sir Philip Sidney's *Arcadia*, were kept in a chest. There were pewter vessels, brass kettles, a warming pan, a pair of scales, and iron skillets and pots. There was also plate, valued at £8. The Major's firearms consisted of three guns and two pistols; and he also owned a rapier and a cutlass, probably brought from Berkshire. His wearing apparel—including his magistrate's robes—was valued at the high figure of £15. Mrs. Hathorne had at this time more than sixty yards of cotton and linen already woven, and six yards of wool, in addition to twenty-two pounds of linen and cotton yarn. Major Hathorne, it appears, distilled strong waters for home use, for he had a still in one of his outbuildings. There were two habitable cottages on the farm, probably occupied by servants.

Major Hathorne—making trips to Boston for meetings of the assistants, presiding at sessions of the Essex County court, performing marriage ceremonies, and drawing up wills and other important papers—might have had a contented old age. But Providence struck him with blows which

became steadily harder during the years following King
Philip's War. John Hathorne of Lynn, who despite his tend-
encies to commit crimes held his brother's affection, died
while in his late fifties, leaving an estate appraised at £263,
with a feather bed willed to each of his many children. The
Major lost his sister, Elizabeth Davenport, about the same
time. Towards the end of 1678 came a much stronger blow,
the death of the Major's youngest son, Captain William
Hathorne. The exposure and privations this daring soldier
suffered during his foray into Maine to hunt red men in
1676 had broken his bodily vigor. Yet during his limited
period in business he had prospered sufficiently to leave to
his childless widow an estate valued at £500, not inconsid-
erable in Massachusetts Bay at that time. Among the items
listed in the inventory of his possessions were £5 still due
from the country for military service and two hundred
gallons of rum molasses, received in exchange for an adventure he had sent to the West Indies.

In January, 1680, before the Major had grown resigned
to the loss of William, his son Eleazar, who as the eldest
was most counted upon to keep alive the Hathorne traditions
in the New World, sailed in one of his own vessels to Wells,
Maine, where he had a sawmill. His aim was to bring back a
cargo of pine lumber. He was in his forty-third year. Associated with Jonathan Corwin, he was enjoying the characteristic Corwin success in trade, and promised to become one
of the wealthiest men in Massachusetts Bay. He had little
inclination towards the social, political, and religious leadership manifested by his father and by his father-in-law, Captain George Corwin. Though a member of the church and
a freeman, Eleazar had actually been brought before Major
Hathorne in court and fined for absence from meeting. If
the father admonished the son too severely for committing
this crime, the son might have pointed out that the father

had also been required to pay a fine—for the crime of leaving a meeting of the court of assistants before official adjournment was declared. The father could only have taken the greatest pride in the son's one notable service to the commonwealth. That was supervising the erection of the fortification which secured the Salem peninsula against Indian attack during King Philip's War.

Eleazar was sure of life that January day when he bade his wife and three children farewell and set out for Maine. He had thought so little about death that he had never bothered to make a will. But two or three weeks after his departure a letter was brought by special messenger to Jonathan Corwin, a letter written by the overseer of the Wells sawmill. Dated January 31, it began: "Mr. Eleazar Hathorne died this afternoon at two o'clock. Please, sir, let us have some of his relations here at his funeral." Then the overseer explained that the vessel had been loaded with lumber as Mr. Hathorne directed, and had been accurately inventoried, but that Mr. Corwin must expect a slight shortage, for a few boards of the pine had been taken from the cargo to make for Mr. Hathorne a comely coffin.

Providence had the Major bowed down with personal sorrow, and then Providence visited upon him the physical ailments of age. There was no longer strength in his legs, and he got about with difficulty. When the hundreds who had suffered from his hard judgments saw him hobbling along the main street, they no doubt said in undertones, "Heaven is giving him the justice he denied us."

But what disturbed him most during his last days was not his grief over his dead sons, nor his bodily weakness, but his concern over the fact that Edward Randolph, in whom Charles II had found a commissioner far more shrewd than any previously sent over, was in and out of Massachusetts Bay. Major Hathorne and every other official of the colony knew that this highly efficient emissary, unscrupulous enough to stoop to any subterfuge to gain a desired end, had one aim—to revoke the old charter and thus bring Massachusetts Bay under direct royal control, with the Church of England the established church, and the Puritan order forever broken.

Randolph first came in 1676, while the colony was under the greatest pressure from King Philip's warriors. In one of the reports which he at that time addressed to Charles II he named those who "directed and managed affairs as they pleased." Specially condemned among them was Major Hathorne, referred to as "still a magistrate, though commanded by His Majesty upon his allegiance to come into England, yet refused, being encouraged in his disobedience by a vote of the court not to appear, upon some reason best known to themselves." That the Major, who had failed to obey a royal command in 1666, was still in the magistracy was pointed out in several reports which Randolph sent back to Whitehall during his second visit to Massachusetts Bay, in 1678. In one the Major was spoken of as belonging to the "small faction which keep the country in subjection and slavery, backed with the authority of a pretended charter." Major Hathorne could not have known what Randolph was saying of him. But the Major perceived clearly that the loathed commissioner was creating dissension in the colony and making headway towards attaining his goal.

In spite of the fact that he saw dark days ahead for God's State, and in spite of his illness and grief, the Major held on to much of his old stamina. He remained active in the court of assistants until a few months before Eleazar's death, and was still presiding over the Essex County court in March, 1680. One of his last official acts was to decree proper punishment for a man of the people who had spoken of him insultingly in the hearing of an informer. The fellow, perhaps under the influence of the calumnious gossip which Randolph's agents were stealthily encouraging, had referred to the Major as "a white-hat limping rogue."

By the beginning of March, 1681, Major Hathorne was not even strong enough to limp. The people would not again have an opportunity to gloat over his infirmities while watching him struggle to make his way over the trail leading to the Mill Pond farm. At last he was bedridden, with little to do except wonder what Edward Randolph's next move would be, admit to himself that it would take more than a single lifetime to bring about all-reaching godliness in Massachusetts Bay, and thank Heaven that at least one of his sons had been spared to fight on in his stead. Before the old man's inner eye still gleamed the vision of the Divine State upon earth, but often in his daydreams he saw this Promised Land attacked by an army of demons and imps led by the Devil.

While the Major with his fears and illusions lay dying, three inhabitants of Salem were accused of an ugly crime. In dealing with the affair, which was to have an important bearing upon the history of the Hathornes, the authorities, unaware of what they were doing, played into the hands of Randolph. The central figure in the sordid life drama was Captain Nicholas Manning, whom Major Hathorne knew well.

A native of Dartmouth, in Devonshire, Manning came to Salem in 1662. Though only eighteen, he was so expert at his trades of gunsmith and anchor maker, and so efficient in business, that before long he was the owner of two workshops and a dwelling house. He met the requirements demanded by the deacons and the minister, the Reverend John Higginson, and was received into the church, henceforth to be classed among God's elect. Made a freeman, he served as juryman, as constable, and on the board of selectmen with Major Hathorne a colleague. For a time he was one of the Major's informers, and testified at court against critics of church and government. Once he appeared before the court as an offender, charged with wearing a periwig, and was fined. Within less than a year after his arrival in the New World he married a Salem widow, Elizabeth Gray, who had a son only seven years his junior. Still she bore Nicholas Manning four children, all but one of whom, a boy, died in infancy. At the outbreak of King Philip's War, Manning at once marched to the front, and served with such distinction that he was soon a captain, in command of a corps of troops. His last assignment as a soldier was to lead the fighters on the ship *Supply*, which succeeded in running down the Indian marauders who had taken thirteen boats in Salem harbor and escaped in them to the open sea. This mission accomplished, Manning returned to civil life, to direct the craftsmen in his employ and also to engage in trade. In the spring of 1679 he chartered a ship, the *Hannah and Elizabeth*, and sent it to England loaded with adventures. On the following November 18, a little more than two months before the death of Eleazar Hathorne, the ship got back to Salem with forty-seven passengers, among whom were Captain Manning's widowed mother, Mrs. Anstiss Manning, two brothers, Jacob and Thomas, and three sisters, Anstiss, Margaret, and Sarah.

In the course of the year 1680 the wife of Nicholas Manning, so much older than he, developed a desperate jealousy for two of his sisters, Anstiss, a spinster of thirty, and Margaret, twenty-three, married to Walter Palfray. The frenzied wife—possibly with real reason, possibly from unbalanced mentality—summoned the courage to appear before a magistrate and swear to a complaint of incest between each of the two sisters and her husband. He, somehow forewarned, fled into the forest before he could be apprehended.

But the sisters were arrested, and their mother and brother Jacob gave bond for their appearance at the next session of the quarterly court, held in Ipswich. At their trial, conducted by four of Major Hathorne's former colleagues, five women in addition to the jealous wife testified against them. Each of the defendants was found guilty, and was sentenced to receive a severe whipping on the naked back or pay a fine of £5 and "at next lecture day in Salem to stand or sit upon a high stool in the open middle alley of the meetinghouse during the whole time of the exercises wearing on the head a paper with the crime written in capital letters."

Though it was difficult for Mrs. Anstiss Manning to raise £10, the fines were paid and her daughters were not whipped. The lecture day arrived—the third or fourth Thursday in March, 1681—when they were to fulfill the rest of the sentence. Early that afternoon the young women pinned to their caps papers marked INCEST, repaired to the meetinghouse, mounted the stools which had been set up for them in "the open middle alley," and began their ordeal of shame.

No one was to be fined for absence from lecture that day. The meetinghouse then in use, erected in 1672 to replace the building which had served since 1639, was sixty feet long by fifty wide and had two galleries. Against the side walls, both upstairs and down, the men of prominence had built their own private pews. The most conspicuous of all was Major Hathorne's, occupied on this occasion by John Hathorne and his family. In the pew belonging to the elder Mr. Porter sat the Major's younger daughters with their husbands and children. The pew built by the late Eleazar Hathorne was occupied by his widow, soon to marry James Russell of Charlestown and bear to him the son who was to become an ancestor of the American author and diplomat

James Russell Lowell. On the public benches which filled most of the space in the sanctuary the men and women sat apart, and on the pulpit and gallery steps were the children, watched over by tithingmen. Every bench was crowded. There was probably only one person among the people that day who had sufficient room for comfort—Bridget Oliver, clad as usual in clothes which even the women in the private pews envied. She had recently escaped hanging for witchcraft by an eleventh-hour executive reprieve; and the majority in Salem, still believing her a witch, dared not get close enough to her to brush against the gay garments. Major Hathorne, his son John, and others had urged the building of a larger meetinghouse. Certainly on this long-to-be-remembered lecture day more space was needed. Many, unable to get within the doors, were standing outside peering in through windows.

There was an extreme tenseness in the assemblage. Never before had a criminal convicted of such a disgusting crime been exhibited on a repentance stool in Salem or anywhere else in Massachusetts Bay. The psalm, with a deacon "lining and setting the tune," was sung without fervor. Mr. Higginson, at whose ordination as minister of the Salem church Major Hathorne had assisted in 1660, knew that his hearers were paying little attention to his words as he enumerated the ways in which the Devil entices even the wary into wickedness.

All were absorbed in gazing at the miserable creatures "sitting or standing" on the repentance stools. The younger of the two was obviously great with child, and the question in the mind of everybody was, "Is the father her husband or her brother?" Captain Manning, about whom the whole congregation was thinking, was wandering somewhere in the wilderness, a fugitive from Puritan justice. Here on one of the rough uncushioned public benches sat his outraged

wife, triumphant over her revenge. Within two years the
court of assistants was to grant her a divorce on the grounds
that "the said Nicholas Manning was guilty of incestuous
practices with his sisters of which they were convicted and
punished but himself escaped out of this jurisdiction thereby
avoiding the punishment and also that he hath not for several years past afforded the said Elizabeth any relief for
maintenance and hath lately declared in writing under his
hand and seal that he doth renounce the said Elizabeth and
that he will not own her for his wife or have anything to do
with her." Near the vindictive woman sat the Manning
mother, who was born a Calley of Devonshire. From the
beginning to the end she had insisted upon the innocence of
her accused offspring, swearing at the trial that she had at
no time since her arrival in New England been separated
from her daughter Anstiss. On the bench beside her sat her
youngest daughter, Sarah, not yet fourteen. In the men's
section sat her twin sons, Jacob and Thomas, both gun-
smiths, twenty years old. They were still single, but before
the end of the coming summer Thomas was to be married
to Mary Giddings, who belonged to a family of Ipswich.

Major Hathorne, lying on his bed at the Mill Pond farm a
mile away, did not need to be told what was going on at
the meetinghouse. He had seen so many women under punishment for crime that he knew precisely how the Manning
sisters, tears streaming from their eyes, were longing to get
away to a hiding place and remain forever shut off from all
humanity. He thought that he knew also just how the people
were reacting to the grim exhibition. There was scarcely a
man or woman among them with whom he was unac-
quainted. He had united scores of them in marriage—young
couples, their fathers and mothers, and their grandfathers
and grandmothers. For more than forty years he had strug-
gled to force these people into devout living. He had drawn

their secrets from them, and he was sure that he understood them perfectly. Today they were cowering because of the monstrosity of a crime committed by three of their kind. Tomorrow others would yield to the allurements of the Evil One. The significant truth about these people, as Major Hathorne saw it, was that they had been born totally depraved.

Such a vision as had led William Hathorne since his conversion to the Puritan faith always blinds. Likewise deadening to his sense of true perception was the power he had wielded for so many years. He was incapable of seeing that these people hung their heads not because of indignation at a crime which three of them had supposedly committed but because of pity for the two sisters on the repentance stools and resentment towards the rulers who had placed them there. It was impossible for him to realize that the hatred for the existing order which such punishments stirred up was of the greatest aid to Randolph in his endeavor to split the colony into factions. Though Major Hathorne had himself risen from yeomanry, he had forgotten that the urge welling strongest in the breasts of the unprivileged was not their predilection to listen to the voice of Satan and break the Ten Commandments but their will to rise up and exchange places with those in authority. If the old man sunk in Puritanism had been told that some day Providence might bring about a turning of the tables in the fortunes of the Hathornes, now so high, and the Mannings, now so low, he would have said with complete self-assurance, "Impossible."

What surprises would have had him quaking in wonder if he could have been lifted from out the bounds of time and endowed with the power to see the past, present, and future as one! He would have realized how limited was his own life when fitted into the life of generations of Hathornes. Mysterious beyond his wildest speculation would have appeared the ways of the Providence to which he had devoted so much of his Puritan thought.

Margaret Palfray, weeping on a repentance stool, was to leave the meetinghouse, tear the shameful paper from her cap, go home to her husband, and within less than two months bear him a son. After the change in social relationships which was to follow the witchcraft delusion in Salem, only eleven years away, she was to gain the respect of her fellow townsmen. Among her descendants were to be journalists able to sway the opinions of thousands in New England, including Hathornes.

The other sister exhibited on a repentance stool was to leave the meetinghouse, go to her mother's home, and, acting with her partner in disgrace, petition the Essex County court for the return of the fines the two had paid on the plea that they were "fatherless and strangers in a strange country." Within a few years she was to become the wife of a middle-aged widower, James Powling, whom Major Hathorne had once fined for "shooting a gun in the night."

Sarah, the thirteen-year-old daughter sitting on the bench with her mother, was to marry in 1686 James Williams, a cooper. Of all the seventeenth-century Salem women she was to have the largest number of distinguished descendants. Among her great- and great-great-grandsons were to be merchants with ships sailing to the earth's most distant ports, financiers, philanthropists, patriots, statesmen, diplomats, jurists, and lovers of learning and art. They were to bear in addition to the name Williams the names Crowninshield, Derby, Hodges, Lambert, Pickman, Ropes, and Stone. They were to live in Salem's mansions, while the Hathornes of their time were to dwell in humble houses on the town's mean streets. In several of the family lines descended from Sarah Manning the unusual Christian name of her mother and older sister, the name Anstiss, was to be kept alive, borne by women of great wealth, singular beauty, and marked cultivation.

Jacob Manning, who with his mother had given bond for the appearance of his sisters in court, was to marry into the Stone family, serve Salem as a selectman, and lead in organizing St. Peter's, the town's first Church of England parish. One of his grandsons, Captain Richard Manning, was to be counted among Essex County's most illustrious Revolutionary patriots. A rich eccentric bachelor, fond of old-fashioned customs, Captain Manning was to address, appropriately he thought, many of his Hathorne neighbors in Salem with the titles "Goodman" and "Goody."

But if the Major had been granted the power of foresight that lecture day, Providence would have given him a surprise still more startling. A great-granddaughter of Thomas Manning, never so prosperous as his twin brother Jacob, was to be Elizabeth Clarke Manning. In 1801 she was to marry Captain Nathaniel Hathorne, the Major's great-great-grandson, and on July 4, 1804, there was to be born to them the romancer, who was to restore the old spelling *Hawthorne* to the family name and lift it to the level of the names most honored in American annals.

Providence, in characteristic fashion, had made sport of Major William Hathorne. He had been used as an instrument in founding a state, but it was no more God's than thousands of others founded before and hundreds of others to be founded later.

Sometime during the month of April, 1681, the loyal old Puritan was gathered unto his Roman Catholic and Church of England fathers. Neither the exact day when he died nor the spot where he was buried is known. The cost of his funeral, estimated by the appraisers of his estate at £41, indicates that he was interred with the pomp befitting his station. The customary tokens of rings and scarfs went no doubt to a long procession of black-clad ministers and magistrates.

The total wealth of the Major at the time of his death, exclusive of the half interest in the Groton farm which he still held, was valued at a little more than £750. Mrs. Hathorne, named in the will as the executrix, received "all the movable estate, within door and out." John got "all land, orchards, and appurtenances, lying in Salem." Eleazar's three children —two sons and a daughter—received legacies amounting all together to £100. Since the two daughters married to the Porter brothers had been given the Salem Village farm, they were willed nothing. William's widow got the last two adventures the Major sent to sea, and her ownership of the half of the Groton farm which had been given to her husband was verified. The other half went to the Major's English grandson, Gervais Helwyse, on condition that he leave Europe—the Major spelled it "Urop" in the will—and come to New England to live. In the event the young man refused, the land was to go to the two oldest sons that his mother, Sarah Coker, had borne to her second husband.

LIKE FATHER, LIKE SON

BEFORE his hand had grown unsteady with age Major Hathorne wrote on the flyleaf of one of his books who his children were and when they were born. Opposite the name of the son marked by Providence to stand as his successor among the Hathornes of Salem he put down "4th day, 6th month, 1641." In the calendar prevailing in his century the sixth month was August.

Attended by a midwife who probably used as guide Eucharius Rhodion's old "borning book," Mrs. Hathorne had this son, her fourth child, under normal circumstances. But there is something unusual in the fact that the infant was baptized when only two days old. Perhaps Mr. Hathorne hastened the christening because he wished to have the rite administered by his highly valued friend, the Reverend Hugh Peter, who was just at this time on the point of embarking for England, to experience first fame and then martyrdom. The boy was given the name John, after his uncle, then only twenty and not yet notorious for his crimes of forgery, defamation, and breach of the peace.

The date of the child's birth seemed, indeed, auspicious. Mr. Hathorne must have felt that as a begetter he was blessed with divine favor. He now had a trinity of sons, born at intervals of almost exactly two years, Eleazar having come into the world on August 1, 1637, and Nathaniel on August 11, 1639. Each of the three had been conceived when the snows of winter were near, and each had been delivered from his mother's womb when summer was at the full. Such a falling of births in a family, from the Puritan way of looking at things, was due not to coincidence but to some sort of heavenly plan. Belief that he was a father marked by Providence for a special destiny doubtless had much to do in producing in Mr. Hathorne the abundant energy he manifested in the early 1640's.

Before John was old enough to store up impressions that would be remembered, the family was living on the Mill Pond farm. Even in Massachusetts Bay, with all the Puritan rigor, an infant was not expected to be completely sober. There were playthings to be bought in Salem during John's early years. One shopkeeper, William Bowditch, had in stock "a parcel of toys for children," valued all together at two shillings and six pence, and "thirty dozen whistles," valued at ten shillings. Some of these gewgaws must have got into the hands of little John Hathorne, and he probably inherited from Eleazar and Nathaniel such a homemade rocking horse as could be found in many a Puritan household. Besides, at the Mill Pond farm there were the wonders of the barnyard, stables, fields, and the upper reaches of an arm of the sea, the South River.

But like all boys and girls belonging to the first generation brought up in Massachusetts Bay, John learned at an early age that he was born in sin with little chance of ever being redeemed out of it. At meeting, to which he was taken from the time he was a few months old, he heard the Reverend Edward Norris, Mr. Peter's successor, shout again and again in a terrifying voice, "God has no mercy on the unregenerate child!" Often the boy's sister Sarah, or uncle John, or some other older person pointed a finger of scorn at him and said, "You were born totally depraved. If you'd die tomorrow you'd go to hell and burn forever." He was often prevented from playing as he wished to play by the remark, "The Devil told you to do that." He lived in constant dread of turning a corner and running into the clutches of the Black Man, who was as real to him as his mother and father. That he was a full inheritor of Adam's sin gradually took on meaning in the boy's mind.

The Puritans, guided by the Bible in all transactions, gave particular heed to the statement of the wise Solomon, "He that spareth his rod hateth his son." Mr. Hathorne, who loved his children, no doubt beat them for the slightest offense. John was probably required to receive the stripes and then thank his kind generous father for the punishment.

While a good deal was made in the Hathorne home of affection for one's family and charitable feeling towards all godly Puritans, much more was made of hatred. John was taught the he must despise the Indians, the Baptist heretics, and some among the Devil's offspring he had never seen, the Cavaliers warring against the Puritans in England and the Pope at Rome with his hordes of criminal followers.

When John was six, the General Court, his father the speaker, passed one of the most famous of Massachusetts Bay statutes, the "old Deluder law." The act provided for the establishment of a school to teach reading and writing in each town having as many as fifty householders and, in each town with twice that population, a grammar school for fitting boys for "the university." Salem belonged in the latter category. The aim of the law, as stated in the preamble, was to combat the determination of "that old Deluder, Satan, to keep men from the knowledge of the Scriptures, as in former times by keeping them in an unknown tongue." Salem had long had a school for the sons of the privileged, taught in recent years by Edward Norris, the minister's son and namesake. Under the new law this school was open to all boys. If a father could show that he was too poor to pay tuition, his sons were taught at the expense of the town. In this democratic environment, under the tutelage of Mr. Norris, John learned how to read, spell phonetically, write, and cipher.

He used a catechizer, a horn book, a primer, and, as he grew older, the Psalter and a treatise on arithmetic, Johnson's or Cocker's. The school term began in the early spring and lasted until the end of November, with classes in session every week day except Thursday, which was given over to lecture at the meetinghouse.

Nothing is known of the building to which John first went for "books," except that the selectmen voted funds to provide the place with a chimney. But it is certain that after the Hathornes moved into their new residence on the main street, John, then in his last years as a scholar, reported to Master Norris on the lower floor of Salem's first town house. This edifice, put up in the early 1650's, provided two names, School Lane and Town House Lane, for the wide important avenue which crossed the main street at the meetinghouse. The two-story building, thirty feet square, stood right in the center of the avenue, splitting it into two roads. The site was about halfway between the main street and the North River. If the schoolroom seat assigned to John was placed so that he could look out an east window, he was able to see what was going on in the front of the "fair house" which was to be occupied until 1655 by Mr. Endecott.

The boy had time for much else besides "books" during his seven or eight years at school. He went on swimming and fishing excursions with his older brothers. He became proficient in shooting, riding, and boating. His father, ever a believer in the disciplinary value of labor, required his sons to work in the fields on both the Mill Pond and Salem Village farms. In this way John learned that a husbandman's life was a life to avoid.

A grave problem at the Salem meetinghouse was how to keep adolescent boys full of animal spirit from growing restless and getting into mischief during the exercises. The tithingmen had their hands full. But Mr. Hathorne was never obliged to fine himself for the misbehavior of his own boys in the house of God, as he fined other fathers. His sons were too subdued by threats of his rod and by backbreaking toil in his fields to join the "young mockers" who played pranks while sitting on the pulpit or gallery steps during sermon.

While John was in his teens, on a day to which he had looked forward with trepidation, he appeared before the deacons of the church and the minister, his teacher's father, to announce that through the redeeming blood of Christ he had been lifted from depravity to sainthood. He told how he had been "wounded in his heart for his original sin" and how penitent he was for his transgressions, each of which he was asked to describe in detail. Convinced by his answers that he had been "showered with heavenly grace," had "submitted unconditionally to divine will,' and was filled with "a sense of peace and joy in God," the authorities on the next Lord's day gave notice of his application to become a member of the church and named the time when he could appear before the congregation. On that occasion John rose, and, in a solemn speech lasting for as long as a quarter of an hour, repeated in public what he had said in private to the Reverend Mr. Norris and the deacons. Then, in democratic fashion, he was voted into the church. Recognized as a saint, an approved member of God's elect, he proceeded to take his first Communion.

All his life he had been absorbing the faith which admitted him to this supreme ordinance. As far back as he could recall he had been in the meetinghouse at nine o'clock every Lord's day morning ready to join in the singing of the psalm, which usually lasted until half past nine. Then he had heard the "long prayer," which often occupied a full hour, and the sermon, which rarely ended before one o'clock. At home for dinner during the "nooning" he had been allowed to speak only of religious matters. Then at two o'clock he had rushed back to the meetinghouse for more psalm singing, another "long prayer," and another sermon. On lecture day for hundreds and hundreds of times he had answered questions about the sovereignty of God, predestination, original sin, total depravity, and the regenerating grace of the Christ who rose from the dead. At school the lessons of the church had somehow been introduced even into the drill of reciting the multiplication tables. The years of training had brought about the result the father wished: John Hathorne became and was to remain a conservative Puritan.

But his conversion was not what his father's had been. He was in no sense a rebel. To renounce the religious order under which he had grown up and sail to a wilderness three thousand miles away to assist in establishing a new order never once occurred to him. No vision of a Divine State upon earth gleamed before his inner consciousness. He had no comprehension of the power of his father's will. A chip off the paternal block, historians have called him. He aspired to be that. But to the spiritual forces mainly responsible for making the first Hathorne of Salem a man of distinction John Hathorne was wholly a stranger.

When he reached the age of twenty-one, in 1662, his father deeded to him a portion of the Mill Pond farm. But John apparently gave little attention to husbandry. He was already engaged in the sort of work which occupied his brother Nathaniel, keeping accounts for merchants. At times he was obliged to go to sea. On December 10, 1665, he was in Jamaica, making out bills of sale for a cargo, which included no doubt adventures belonging to his father.

On the return from this voyage the ship on which he was sailing as supercargo called at some settlement on the Maine coast. There, probably for a few baubles brought from

Jamaica, John Hathorne purchased from a sagamore known
as Robin Hood a tract of land computed to consist of about
nine thousand acres. It was situated between Lake Dama-
riscotta and the Sheepscott River, in the section of Maine
which was to become Lincoln County, and embraced
"islands and islets, meadows, harbors, marshes, creeks, and
coves." The deed John procured was recorded in Salem
on June 16, 1666, shortly before Major Hathorne received
the command to appear before Charles II at Whitehall.
The tract, usually referred to by the Hathornes as "the
eastern land," was of little concern to John, but to his
descendants it was to be a matter of hopes, dreams of great
riches, and then disappointments and regrets.

As to John's activities from 1666 to 1671 nothing seems
to be known. By March of the latter year he was back at
home, living no doubt with his father, who had turned the
main street property over to Eleazar and was again on the
Mill Pond farm. For the next four years John was engaged
in drawing up wills, making inventories of estates, surveying
highways, and getting launched into an independent merchant's career. In 1674 he was appointed to his first public
office, that of deputy marshal.

Late in March the following year, when he was near
the age of thirty-four, he was married to Ruth Gardner,
granddaughter of Thomas Gardner, a man of prominence
among the pioneer settlers. The bride, only fourteen, had
been born when the Quaker persecution was at the most
violent stage. Her mother was an open convert to the faith
of the Friends, and her father was a sympathizer. Still, when
Ruth was four or five she was taken to the Reverend John
Higginson, then the Salem minister, for the rite of baptism.
Fined persistently, however, for absence from meeting and
molested in other petty ways, her parents, Lieutenant and
Mrs. George Gardner, finally, in 1673, moved to Hartford,

Connecticut. If, as appears most likely, Ruth was left in Salem in the household of her childless uncle, Captain Joseph Gardner, and his wife, the daughter of Emanuel Downing, John received from them permission to pay court to the girl and made his prenuptial calls at the splendid Downing mansion, where Captain and Mrs. Gardner had lived for many years. Ruth had been married for only a few months when her uncle, looked upon as a gentleman in his own right and all the more exalted because of his union with John Winthrop's wealthy niece, marched with his troops to meet death at the hands of the Narragansetts in King Philip's War.

Major Hathorne must have objected sternly when he found out that John was contemplating marriage with the daughter of a Quaker woman. Nor could he have approved of his newly wedded son's behavior during the first year and a half of the Indian war. While Eleazar was giving time to the erection of defense fortifications, which cut through a portion of the Mill Pond farm, and William was at the front fighting, John was entrenching himself in business, purchasing a wharf, securing a license to sell strong waters, and building for himself and his bride a mansion on the west side of School Lane, near the South River.

But during the four years beginning with 1677 John proved that he too was a Hathorne willing to serve the country. He accepted the commission of a captaincy, and took over the training of a foot company. He contributed liberally towards financing the expedition sent out under the command of Captain Nicholas Manning to clear the Salem waters of Indian marauders. He took the oath as a freeman, became a selectman, was a constable, and, for reasons unknown, declined an appointment to serve the church as a deacon. In 1679 he was made the town clerk, and began penning records with the peculiar spelling which

hints that even at this early period in his life he was suffering
from defective hearing.

When Major Hathorne, during his last days, dwelt upon
the loss of first Nathaniel, then William, and then Eleazar,
he must have consoled himself by the thought that Providence had spared the son who, though a late starter, was
showing the will to fight as he had fought for God's State.
The Major had not been long in his grave when the freemen
of Salem showed that they too respected the promise of
his sole male heir. At the election in May, 1683, John
Hathorne was chosen to represent Salem as a deputy in the
General Court.

In this position he satisfied the Salem electorate, and the
next year was voted into the high office of assistant. So it
was that John Hathorne, at the age of forty-three, found
himself the full inheritor of his father's privileges—and
responsibilities.

The Major had infrequently been called upon to face
problems more trying. Edward Randolph, ever resource-
ful and persevering, was winning victories in his struggle
to overthrow the old order. The position of John Hathorne
as assistant, as well as the whole framework of the government in Massachusetts Bay, was in 1684 illegal. Acting
upon Randolph's reports, a high English court, with the
sanction of Charles II, had in June the previous year an-
nulled the charter. Following the old policy of circumvention, the government in Boston had continued in power
as before. The decree of the king's bench was simply
ignored.

Randolph had succeeded well in dividing the leaders
into parties. A numerous group, led by wealthy traders
who placed commercial advantage above all else, favored
compromise with him and his abettors. Another group,

encouraged by the most influential of the ministers, argued that the old institutions, including religious intolerance and theocratic rule, must at all costs be upheld. John Hathorne, true to the principles of his father, was a member of the latter party. He defended the exclusion of the Book of Common Prayer from use in any Massachusetts Bay church, the restriction of the franchise to freemen, and the exaction of the dealth penalty for religious heresy. He was prepared to answer Randolph's charges that the colonial authorities had protected at least two of the judges who had voted for the death of Charles I, had coined money without approval from the mother country, had blocked appeal to the English courts, and had required an oath of fidelity to their own government while neglecting to demand an oath of allegiance to the king.

Still John Hathorne did not come directly under Randolph's condemnation until 1686, a year after the death of Charles II and the succession of his Roman Catholic brother, James II. Then, in a letter to the king, Randolph definitely cited Hathorne for disloyalty. As his father had done when accused by the hated commissioner of maintaining the same treasonous attitude, John Hathorne kept to his usual course.

Instead of bothering about a place of refuge if flight should become advisable, he joined his Salem neighbors in a move to safeguard their property. The titles to the lands they held were based on provisions in a charter which from the point of view of the mother country no longer existed. Could such titles in any way be replaced? Some ingenious person—possibly John Hathorne's brother-in-law Israel Porter—thought of securing an over-all deed from the descendants of the sagamores who had held sway over the lands before the coming of the whites. Fantastic as the proposal was, it was put into operation; and, at a cost of only £20, it worked. On October 11, 1686, the selectmen of Salem, as trustees, received by court order from several Indians with unpronounceable names titles to all the land making up the town. The deed was written so as to appear as pretentious as possible. Whether the Puritan conscience of John Hathorne was ever disturbed by his formally admitting that the Salem earth and the fullness thereof had once belonged to the children of the Devil was not recorded.

Mr. Hathorne had been present at the meeting of the General Court the preceding May 20, on which day the government passed into the hands of an interim committee, headed by Joseph Dudley with the title of president. This grandson of Governor Thomas Dudley and nephew of the first wife of Governor Bradstreet, had gone to England to serve the interests of the colony and had returned an appeaser. Though his attitude was directly opposed to Mr. Hathorne's, the two were still close personal friends. So Mr. Hathorne had been named a justice of the peace for Essex County and made a member of the board to regulate trade.

The first royal governor, Sir Edmund Andros, arrived in Boston the following December 19, and at once took over the rule from Dudley. Randolph was made an assistant, now known as councilor, and his influence from the start was great. Still Justice Hathorne was permitted to go his way unmolested, and to exercise his duties as a local magistrate as his father had done. The ministers at Salem, Mr. Higginson, in service for almost thirty years, and the Reverend Nicholas Noyes, a younger man, set the example of political detachment which Mr. Hathorne followed. He was politic enough to remain silent when he saw taxes mount to unbelievable heights, and offices which he and his father had held with small compensation yielding huge fees to sycophants. Yet frequent and fervent must have been his prayers for the delivery of New England from the "tyranny of Andros," especially when the governor attempted to restrict local powers hitherto exercised by the freemen of a town gathered together in free assembly.

During the years of the "tyranny of Andros" Mr. Hathorne lived his life in comparative ease, entertaining distinguished visitors in his mansion on School Lane, or enjoying treats in Meers's tavern at the expense of his friend Samuel Sewall while on business in Boston, or receiving a scarf or ring for serving as pallbearer at the funeral of some Essex County notable. Despite the growing worldliness of the people under the rule of Andros, Mr. Hathorne encountered every day something to remind him of the Puritan ideals according to which he had been reared.

The death in Salem on October 17, 1688, of young Nathaniel Mather, son of the Reverend Increase Mather, proved that the old spirit was by no means dead. This remarkable youth upon his graduation from Harvard at the age of sixteen had delivered an oration in Hebrew. Having dedicated himself in mystic fashion to "abstemious holiness and a complete mastery of divine revelation," he had burdened his mind with study and forgotten his body. A victim of melancholia, he appeared at the end like a worn old man. He was interred at the Burying Point, and the epitaph on his tombstone was probably written by his brother Cotton. It reads: "An aged person that had seen but nineteen winters in the world."

At the end of 1688 came the "glorious revolution" in England, the abdication and flight of James II, and the succession of William and Mary, staunch Protestants, as joint sovereigns. When news of these great events reached Massachusetts Bay, about the middle of January, 1689, Mr. Hathorne and everybody else knew that the days of the "tyranny of Andros" were numbered. Yet three months passed before the people in and around Boston rose up and carried out a revolution of their own. The result was that on the morning of April 20, 1689, Andros and more than twenty of his chief satellites found themselves imprisoned or under guard.

Whether Justice Hathorne had a part in the uprising of the day before is unknown. But it is certain that he was immediately summoned by the eighty-seven-year-old Simon Bradstreet to become a member of the committee of safety which took over the government. Despite party strife the old order within a few weeks was carrying on as if there had never been a nullification of the original charter. Mr. Bradstreet was again governor and Mr. Hathorne again an assistant.

Whatever the appearances might have been, all directly responsible for the conduct of affairs faced heavy uncertainty. As the months passed the anxiety mounted. Agents, headed by the Reverend Increase Mather, were in England trying to obtain a new charter as much like the old as possible. Reports on what they were accomplishing were not encouraging. While they had found the Roman Catholic James II ready to grant concessions to dissenters in order to strengthen the general opposition to Church of England supremacy, they met in King William an uncompromising Church of England defender.

The war with France which his and Mary's accession to the throne had precipitated soon spread to the New World. To win his favor Massachusetts Bay ventured too much. The cost of the 1690 expedition against Quebec, which ended in disaster, was greater than the colony could afford. The war moreover almost extinguished commerce at sea. The waters were infested not only with privateersmen but with pirates, most of them English born. In the course of

1690 sixteen buccaneers were captured off the New England coast and brought to Boston for trial. Mr. Hathorne and his fellow assistants with quick dispatch sentenced them all to death on the gallows.

For Mr. Hathorne himself the time was not altogether barren of business. For £250 he purchased a prize towed into Salem harbor by the ship *Pelican.* One of his own vessels, the brig *Dove,* safely made the voyage to and from Newfoundland, bringing back wine, brandy, and articles of English manufacture. Mr. Hathorne spent some of the money he was making to procure from Henry Curtis, of Beverly, a quitclaim to "the eastern land," the nine thousand acres in Maine, which the sagamore Robin Hood had evidently disposed of more than once.

While Mr. Hathorne was enlarging his private fortune, thousands of others in Massachusetts Bay were near impoverishment. Dread of another sort was also felt in the country. The French were reorganizing the red men to the east and north. What could prevent a repetition of the Indian atrocities of 1675 and 1676? To add to the public fear an epidemic of smallpox in violent form broke out in Boston at the beginning of 1691 and rapidly spread to other towns.

"Satan is marshaling his forces for a final decision," shouted the ministers, led by the Reverend Cotton Mather, sole preacher of Boston's Old North Church since his father's departure for England. In sermon and pamphlet the people were told that the Prince of Darkness was beyond a doubt determined to exterminate the fearers of God in New England and return the country to his own children, the red men.

Nothing reflects more clearly the press of problems upon the authorities in Massachusetts Bay during these years than the loose manner in which they dealt with certain criminals.

Andros had not been long in power when the notorious Captain Nicholas Manning, who had turned up in Maine as one of his supporters, was given a judgeship. After the fall of the Andros government Manning was arrested, brought to Boston, and put in prison on the sole charge of complicity in the "tyranny." That he had never stood court trial on the complaint for which two of his sisters had suffered exhibition on repentance stools in the Salem meetinghouse eight years before seems to have occurred to neither John Hathorne nor Jonathan Corwin, the two Salem men then serving as assistants. In a time less beset with anxiety the old charge of incest against Captain Manning would surely have been revived.

As it was, Nicholas Manning, citing his services to Massachusetts Bay in the Indian wars and picturing his record as stainless, addressed to the General Court two or three petitions for deliverance from prison. Finally his plea was granted. Again a free man, he settled in Boston and pursued successfully his trade of gunsmith. He was to remain in New England until 1696, when he moved to New York— to remarry, sire a new line of Mannings, and end his days in obscurity somewhere on Long Island.

In dealing with another monstrous love crime the authorities apparently made no effort to prosecute the man known to have been involved. The woman belonged to a respected family of Haverhill. At her trial before the court of assistants witnesses testified that on March 7, 1691, she gave birth to twin bastards. To cover up what she had done she killed the infants, sewed them in a bag, and hid them in the cold room of her father's house. Then on May 10, with the coming of warm weather, she took them from the place of concealment and buried them in the yard. It was on the following September 26 that she stood trial. Mr. Hathorne was in attendance, and concurred with the other assistants in sentencing the young woman to die.

Once more a Hathorne would have been astounded at the paradoxes with which Providence strews a family's history if the worshipful John while looking upon this miserable creature could have seen beyond her into the future. From a line of her family was to spring one of the greatest of Americans. But to John Hathorne she was only a criminal who had yielded to the temptations of Satan and was now found out and marked for the hangman's rope. In passing judgment upon her the court of assistants had not taken into account the fact that her brutal father had warped her character with beatings and other cruelties. The Essex County court, of which Mr. Hathorne was the head magistrate, did not even hold for trial on a charge of fornication her notorious sex-mad seducer.

At Whitehall on October 7, 1691, less than two weeks after the condemnation of the unfortunate woman of Haverhill, the new charter for the commonwealth was declared in force. Massachusetts Bay as reconstituted was a province rather than a colony and included Plymouth. It was not until the end of the year that the thousands of persons affected understood the sort of government under which they were to live in the future. Mr. Hathorne must have felt that the Reverend Increase Mather and his colleagues in London had let Massachusetts Bay down in agreeing that the governor and lieutenant governor were to be appointed by the crown. Nor could Mr. Hathorne have approved of the provision in the charter which gave the right of suffrage to any man with land yielding an income of forty shillings a year or with personal estate amounting to forty pounds. That membership in the church was no longer a qualification for voting meant that the theocracy which Mr. Hathorne and his father before him had fought to preserve was at an end. The clause in the charter allowing religious freedom to all Christians except Roman Catholics might be circumvented, as a like ruling by Charles II had been. The provision which left the right of taxation to the exclusive control of the General Court, chosen by popular suffrage, no doubt won Mr. Hathorne's full favor. With the people holding the purse strings any royal governor would have to be wary.

King William, observing to the letter Mr. Mather's recommendations in appointing officers for the new province, had named as governor Sir William Phipps. This native of Maine, born into a family which numbered twenty-four children, had, through the luck of recovering a vast treasure from a Spanish ship sunk in the waters of the West Indies, attained wealth and a title. His staunch ruggedness and steadfast Puritanism appealed to most in Massachusetts Bay, even to those dissatisfied with the charter. It was true that he had led the unfortunate expedition against Quebec. But he had succeeded elsewhere in the war against the French and Indians—so much so that all Nova Scotia was now nominally included in the province of Massachusetts Bay. Mr. Hathorne received no doubt with great satisfaction the notice that he had been chosen to serve as one of Sir William's advisers—not with the old title of assistant, but with the new title of councilor.

Sir William was now in England. Until his return in the spring with the new charter the government under the aged Mr. Bradstreet was to carry on. The beginning of 1692 found Mr. Hathorne more hopeful than he had been at any time during the eleven years since his father's death.

His optimism was not shared by the majority in Massachusetts Bay. Owners of real property remembered too keenly the threat of Andros to nullify their land titles to put trust in any government directly responsible to the crown. The winter was unusually severe that year. All felt the sting of hard times, and some among the people went hungry. The epidemic of smallpox had not been fully checked. Rumors of woes sped rapidly from town to town, from house to house. Night and day a desperate watch was kept to spy out the movements of the Indians who had ravaged certain settlements in Maine. And every Sabbath day and lecture day the Reverend Cotton Mather in Boston, the Reverend Nicholas Noyes in Salem, the Reverend Samuel Parris in Salem Village, and ministers in chilly meetinghouses throughout Massachusetts Bay were repeating to the people that the Devil, bent upon reclaiming the country, was using all his wiles to win disciples from among them.

WITCHCRAFT, ALAS!

WHEN the assistants assembled in Boston on March 1, 1692, for what turned out to be their last meeting under the old charter, the members from Salem, John Hathorne and Jonathan Corwin, were not present. A dread duty demanded that they remain in their own county. The preceding day they had received calls from several landholders of Salem Village, which was to become in 1753 the independent town of Danvers. Responding to a petition presented by these men, Mr. Hathorne and Mr. Corwin had issued warrants for the arrest of three persons suspected of witchcraft. The three were now in custody at Nathaniel Ingersoll's tavern in Salem Village, and preliminary hearings were scheduled for this very day.

Early in the morning the two magistrates, attended by marshals and constables, set out on horseback for Salem Village, five miles from the Salem town center. Mr. Hathorne and Mr. Corwin were in magisterial garb. It is possible that they had on periwigs and broad-brimmed feathered hats, now worn by the handsome Reverend Cotton Mather and therefore not too much condemned as adornments of vanity. The constables and marshals, bearing long staffs, were in the bright red surtouts which since the founding of the colony had been the official dress of men charged with the enforcement of the laws. The ride over the muddy roadway, as reported by a contemporary, had all the appearances of a progress in state.

But Mr. Hathorne, as he observed the awe with which the people watched the cavalcade, was not thinking of his superior rank. He was on a mission of the gravest seriousness. In his heart were prayers to God for guidance.

Like every other faithful Christian of his time, Catholic or Protestant, he believed that human beings often signed agreements with the Evil One, pledging their immortal souls in exchange for temporary supernatural powers. In so believing he was supported by the Bible, by the statutes of every Christian state, and by explicit admissions from some of the most enlightened men of his century. Among these were the father of empiricism Francis Bacon, the learned writer Robert Burton, the mellifluous churchman Jeremy Taylor, the scientist and essayist Sir Thomas Browne, the jurist Sir Matthew Hale, the mathematician Isaac Barrow, the wisest of English Puritan divines Richard Baxter, the diarist John Evelyn, and the philospher Joseph Glanvill. If any one of these men had been a magistrate in Salem on March 1, 1692, he would have gone to Salem Village feeling about the task awaiting him as Mr. Hathorne felt.

To him witchcraft was the most weighty of capital crimes, more horrible than murder, rape, bestiality, arson— or even blasphemy, to which it was akin. He was nearing seven when Margaret Jones, of Charlestown, was hanged as a witch. He could recall the excitement over the case of Mrs. Ann Hibbins. Though a gentlewoman, the widow of a wealthy Boston merchant who had served as an assistant and had been sent to England as an agent for the colony, she was convicted of consorting with the Devil and on May 27, 1656, was sent to her death on the gallows. Mr. Hathorne's father had not been made a member of the court of assistants when these two women were tried; and he had already retired from public service when, in 1680, the next important case came up, that of Bridget Oliver. The jury had found her guilty of witchcraft, and the court had sentenced her to be hanged. But Governor Bradstreet, on the basis of new evidence, had issued a reprieve, saving her life and restoring her freedom. Then, during the administration of Sir Edmund Andros, Mary Glover, a native of Ireland reared in the Roman Catholic faith, had been hanged on the charge of bewitching the four children of John Goodwin, of Boston.

Though Mr. Hathorne had not sat in judgment of this victim, he was well acquainted with the details of the case. For Mr. Cotton Mather had published an elaborate and most readable account of it in a book called *Memorable Providences*. This work, issued in 1688, had superseded in popularity a similar work, Mr. Increase Mather's *Illustrious Providences*, published in 1684. In writing on witchcraft the father and son had endeavored alike to strengthen the propaganda they were sponsoring. The people, they felt, must be convinced that New England was at a time of awful crisis, that Satan had made up his mind to regain the country, and that the Fiend's plots had to be combated with the greatest resourcefulness. Nor had the two leaders and their fellow ministers neglected to arouse interest in the well-known English treatises on demonology, such as the treatises by King James I, William Perkins, Sir Matthew Hale, and Joseph Glanvill. Even if the people of Massachusetts Bay had forgotten the traditions of witchcraft which their fathers brought from England, they would have been familiar with the pattern of the cult as it existed in the seventeenth century.

Mr. Hathorne felt that Massachusetts Bay had been specially blessed. For while the cases rising there had been only occasional, scores of persons in recent decades had been convicted of the crime in England, hundreds in Scotland, and thousands on the Continent. The European victims had been burned at the stake, in compliance with the tradition that fire alone is completely obliterating. But the Bible in stating that a witch must not be allowed to live says nothing about how she should be put to death. In Massachusetts Bay the legalized punishment for witchcraft was hanging, as for most of the other capital crimes. Mr. Hathorne and his colleagues in the government looked upon their country as far ahead in enlightenment. They dismissed as popish superstition the contention that a woman guilty of witchcraft would float if cast into water, an element to which all who had sold themselves to the Devil were supposed to be alien.

Gossip over the case now in the open at Salem Village had been going on for weeks. But Mr. Hathorne had gained his knowledge from intimate talks with the persons involved. The chief of these was the Reverend Samuel Parris, a graduate of Harvard College, a merchant in Barbados for several years, and since 1688 minister of the Salem Village church. Mr. Hathorne must have seen that Mr. Parris, man of business rather than spiritual leader, was unfitted to maintain harmony in his parish, which had been split by dissension since its organization in 1680. From Barbados Mr. Parris had brought two slaves, John and his wife Tituba, each part Indian and part Negro. They had inherited the primitive wisdom and childlike craftiness of both races, and their names must have turned up often as the minister talked with Mr. Hathorne. In another who had been consulted, Sergeant Thomas Putnam, a prominent Salem Village landholder, Mr. Hathorne should have seen a stubborn yeoman without initiative, yet a man capable of effectual action when spurred on by his high-strung vindictive wife.

It was Tituba who had precipitated the trouble. She began, in complete innocence it appears, by showing off her skill in magic for the amusement of two little girls in her master's household, a daughter, Elizabeth, aged nine, and a niece, Abigail Williams, aged eleven. Tituba could have learned her art from her own people in her native Barbados, or she might have invented it. The children, greatly delighted at her exhibitions, were soon inviting the young girls in the neighborhood to come in and see Tituba work wonders. Among the visitors was Sergeant Putnam's precocious daughter Ann, aged twelve.

With her to lead, the girls themselves acquired the art, and before long were surpassing Tituba in proficiency. To the consternation of their elders they would dart unexpectedly from dark corners, from under tables, and from behind chairs. They would walk about rolling their eyes with only the whites visible. They would fall to the floor as if in a state of trance, and describe the marvels they saw while lying there. They would go about speaking in a gibberish, claiming that it was an unknown tongue.

Evening after evening, in rooms lighted only by dying fires, they heard their fathers and mothers talk in hushed voices about the tortures inflicted upon human beings and animals by warlocks and witches. Again and again they listened to readings from books on demoniacal providences written by Mr. Increase Mather and his son, both of whom the children in Salem Village as in all Massachusetts Bay had been taught to revere as next to God in goodness and wisdom. At meeting and lecture they heard little from Mr. Parris except warnings to be forever mindful of the power of Satan, who was represented as the arch instigator of New England's troubles and on the alert day and night to bring about more suffering.

The children naturally drifted into a world where their fearsome fancies assumed all the qualities of reality. About the middle of January Abigail Williams began to contend that in performing Tituba's tricks she was not herself but what she pretended to be. Not long afterwards she succumbed to an illness much like that which Mr. Cotton Mather in *Memorable Providences* ascribed to one of the Goodwin children. Soon Elizabeth Parris, Ann Putnam, and other suggestible girls who had learned Tituba's art fell sick in a similar manner. The chirurgeon called in, unable to detect organic disturbance, had one pronouncement for what those belonging to his profession were in the future to call hysteria. That pronouncement was "Witchcraft!"

Mr. Parris, surely not surprised at the diagnosis, then appealed to neighboring ministers—Mr. Noyes and old Mr. Higginson of Salem, Mr. Hale of Beverly, and others. These men of God came to Salem Village, and, as Mr. Cotton Mather claimed he had done with effect in the Goodwin case, joined Mr. Parris in fasting and praying.

But Mr. Parris was not a man to remain without food on his knees when action was called for. He consulted books on witchcraft, one of which was sent up from Boston through the kindness of Mr. Cotton Mather. The authorities, Mr. Parris found, agreed that Satan worked only through human agents and that his victims could not be relieved until the identity of those who had them under control was revealed.

Again and again one sick girl after another was asked, "Who is hurting you?" Each upon hearing this question invariably fell into a fit and became dumb.

One of Mr. Parris's neighbors, Goody Mary Sibley, versed in demonology as it had been handed down in her family from generation to generation, recalled a rite which would empower an afflicted girl to speak the name of the wizard or witch who was torturing her. Without consulting Mr. Parris, Goody Sibley saw that the rite was performed. "Make a cake of rye meal mixed with the children's water," she said to John Indian, Tituba's husband, "and put it in hot ashes on the kitchen hearth. When it is baked, give it to the dog. If he eats, the children will name the torturer."

John made the cake as directed, and the dog swallowed it. No sooner was it in his stomach, Mr. Parris declared at meeting, than the children answered the question, "Who is hurting you?" At first they accused only Tituba. Then they added the names of two women who were looked upon in Salem Village as social outcasts. One was Sarah Good, married to a man so thriftless that she had to go from neighbor to neighbor and beg food for her children. The other was Sarah Osburn, a sickly shrew whose husband had deserted her.

These were the three who were to appear this day before Mr. Hathorne and Mr. Corwin. If they failed to show beyond a doubt that the charges brought against them were groundless, the law demanded that the magistrates send them to prison to await the action of a grand jury.

The Salem Village through which Mr. Hathorne and Mr. Corwin rode was made up of scattered farms, with little to mark the center besides Deacon Ingersoll's tavern, the crude meetinghouse—and the manse, to which Mr. Parris was scheming to gain title of personal ownership. To the northwest, beyond a stretch of field and copse, stood Hathorne Hill, looking down upon the house in which Mr. Hathorne had been born.

On arriving at the tavern, where the accused women were held in a private chamber, the magistrates found such a crowd as all Deacon Ingersoll's public rooms joined together could not begin to accommodate. It was announced that the hearings would be held in the meetinghouse.

Thither the throng scrambled, and within a few minutes all was in readiness for the hearings to begin. Back of a long table at the foot of the pulpit sat Mr. Hathorne, Mr.

Corwin, Mr. Parris, probably other ministers, and the clerk who had been appointed to keep a record of the examination. Before the table was an open space where an accused was to stand while being questioned. In the front row of seats sat the afflicted with their mothers and other attendants. Then came the spectators fortunate enough to gain entrance. Most of them, in order to see and hear the better, were on their feet. Everybody in the meetinghouse, and probably no one more than Mr. Hathorne, was tense with expectancy.

The proceedings were opened with prayer. Then Sarah Good was brought to the front by constables, who had to force their way through the thronged "main alley." The examination, conducted by Mr. Hathorne without a single interruption from Mr. Corwin, was brief. Repeatedly Mr. Hathorne tried to trap the woman into a confession of guilt by asking leading questions, as his father and every other magistrate in Massachusetts Bay had always done at preliminary hearings. Goody Good at first warded him off with ease. Then he asked her to confront the afflicted children. As soon as they saw her eyes fixed upon them, they fell into fits, uttering weird shrieks and making wild gestures. It was the presence of Goody Osburn which was tormenting the girls, she said, forgetting that the Osburn woman had not been fetched from the tavern. "Many lies Sarah Good was taken in," wrote the clerk. A spectator cried out, "Her own husband says she's a witch or will soon be one!" Goodman Good was in the audience, and was at once brought to the front. He denied having seen the Devil's mark anywhere on his wife's body. "But her carriage to me is bad," he declared. "Indeed I may say with tears that she's an enemy to all virtue."

She was sent back to the tavern, and Sarah Osburn was brought in. At Mr. Hathorne's command the children stood up and looked at her, and again they were all "hurt, afflicted, and tortured very much." When they finally came out of their fits, they declared that Goody Osburn, though sick in bed at her house several miles away, had more than once appeared to them precisely as she was now. Mr. Hathorne followed with leading questions, and in the end the accused admitted that "she was frighted one time in her sleep and either saw or dreamed that she saw a thing like an Indian, all black, which did prick her in her neck, and pull her by the back part of her head to the door of the house." Mr. Hathorne also led the frail trembling woman, scarcely strong enough to stand, into admitting that the Devil might have visited the children when disguised in her own likeness.

Her examination was even briefer than that of Goody Good. It was Tituba whom the magistrates wished most to question, and it was Tituba whom the spectators were eager to see and hear. She had no more than stepped across the threshold, with marshals at her right and left, when the children began to scream. To the people, whose shouts of hate raised the noise to a horrifying din, she, with her dark skin and mysterious black eyes, was the perfect witch. This time there was no trouble in getting the "main alley" cleared, for everyone was in deadly fear of her touch.

The girls, their voices spent, were still writhing as if in great pain when Mr. Hathorne, frowning upon the slave woman, asked, "Why do you hurt these poor children? What have they done unto you?"

Tituba, submissive yet composed, answered, "They do no harm to me. I no hurt them."

"Why have you done it?" broke in Mr. Corwin, ignoring the woman's statement.

"I no do nothing," she said. "I no can tell when the Devil works."

"What?" exclaimed Mr. Hathorne. "Doth the Devil tell you when he hurts them?"

"No. He no tell me nothing."

"Do you never see something in some shape?" asked Mr. Hathorne, waving Mr. Corwin to silence.

"I no see nothing."

"What familiar does the Devil employ when he approaches you? What is it that you converse with withal? Tell the truth. What sort of creature is it that hurts the children now?"

"The Devil, for aught I know."

"How does he appear when he hurts them? What is he like?"

"Like a man, I think. One night in the lean-to chamber at my master's house I see a thing like a man. He tell me to serve him, and I tell him I do no such thing. It's Goody Osburn and Goody Good that hurt the children. They come to me one night while I wash the room, and the man he with them, and two other women. They tell me to hurt the children too. They say if I no do, they hurt me. Then I obey, but after I do I tell them I do so no more. They try to make me go to Boston."

By now Tituba was more than composed. Forced by slavery to be adept in acting, she instinctively knew that she had this crowd at her feet. Everybody was alert to catch her every word, and at the merest hints from Mr. Hathorne she talked. She regretted hurting the children, she said. Then she told of the man's first visit, at the time the girls first fell sick. "He say they never be well," she declared. "He say he kill them, and he say if I no serve him he kill me too." He had not appeared always as a man, she said. Once he was a hog, and four times he was a great black dog.

"What other creatures have you seen?" asked Mr. Hathorne.

"A bird."

"What sort of bird?"

"A little yellow bird."

"Where did it keep?"

"With the man. He had pretty things more besides. He tell me he show them me some time, and if I serve him he give me the bird."

"What other creatures did you see?"

"I see two cats, one red, one black, as big as dog."

"Did the cats speak?"

"They say, 'Serve us.'"

"When did you see them?"

"One night."

"Did they do any hurt to you or threaten you?"

"They did scratch me, because I no serve them. They before the fire."

"Do they suck you?"

"No, no, sir. Never yet. I no let them."

"Did you never go anywhere with the women you mentioned?"

"They very strong. They haul me and make me go with them."

"Where did you go?"

"Up to Mr. Putnam's house to hurt his daughter Ann."

"Just how did you go? What did you ride upon?"

"I ride upon a stick, with Good and Osburn behind me. We ride taking hold of one another. I see no trees, I see no path. We right away there, when we are up."

"Why did they want you to go to Putnam's?"

"To kill the child."

Here Ann Putnam broke in and stated that at the time of which Tituba was speaking Good and Osburn appeared and said, "You must cut off your own head. If you refuse, Tituba will cut it off." The girl claimed that she had felt the knife piercing the skin of her neck. But apparently all signs of the wound had vanished.

"Tell me again," said Mr. Hathorne, "just when it was that you were told to do this awful thing."

"One night, when Mr. Parris was at prayer," said Tituba, "Goody Good stop my ears, so I no hear my master's words. The man he give her the yellow bird. It was in her right hand, and it suck between the forefinger and the long finger."

"What hath Osburn to go with her?"

"She hath two things. One hath wings, and two legs, and a head like a woman. The children see it one day, and before their eyes it turn into a woman. Osburn hath also a thing all hairy, with two legs. It goeth upright like a man, and one night it stand before the fire in my master's hall."

Tituba then denied that she had ever practiced witch-craft in her own country, and proceeded to describe the Devil as he had appeared in the likeness of a man. He was tall, she said, and had white hair. Usually his clothes were black, but sometimes he wore a serge coat of another color.

"What apparel do the unknown women wear?" asked Mr. Hathorne.

"One hath a black silk hood," Tituba answered, "with a white silk hood under it. She hath topknots. I no know her name, but I see her in Boston when I live there. The other woman, the small one, she wear serge coat and white cap."

All the afflicted at this point fell into violent fits.

"Who hurts them now?" shouted Mr. Hathorne above the clamor.

"It's Goody Good," Tituba shouted back.

The children, having recovered consciousness, agreed

with her. But suddenly one of the girls fell into a second fit, still more extreme. When she came out of it she claimed that her torturers were several, and that they had blinded her so that she was unable to see their faces. Then, all at once, she became dumb.

The afternoon was growing late, and there had been no recess for dinner. One of the ministers present prayed a closing prayer, and the hearing was adjourned for the day.

By the next morning news of the slave woman's dire revelations had spread to every corner of the town of Salem. A score were in the grip of the hysteria where there had been one the day before. Many, too stricken with terror to venture forth for their daily work, stayed at home to fast and pray. Still the number seeking to be present at the hearing was much greater than on the preceding day. By eight o'clock the roads were thronged with the disappointed who had failed to gain admission to the Salem Village meetinghouse.

Again the proceedings were opened with prayer. Then the feeble Goody Osburn was brought in for further questioning, and proved to be still uncommunicative, answering all charges with denials and accusing no one.

The rest of the day was given over to Tituba. For hours she skillfully hedged as Mr. Hathorne tried to lead her into admitting that she had entered into a formal pact with the Devil. But late in the afternoon she came out with what seemed to be a straightforward confession.

"The man he come," she said, "the Wednesday before Abigail get sick, six weeks ago, a little more. He tell me my master go pray, and then he read in book, and he say if I promise to serve him six years he let me see inside book. Then he leave, but the next Friday he come back, when it's light, betimes in the morning, and he show me the book again."

"Did he not make you write your name?"

"Yes, sir. I make mark. I make it with red, like blood."

"Did you see any other names in the book?"

"Yes, sir. I see several. Some marks red, some yellow."

"Did he tell you the names of them?"

"Yes, sir. Two, no more. Good and Osburn. He say they make marks for themselves and he point them out."

"How many marks do you think there were all together?"

"Nine," she said, and a gasp of horror rose from the spectators.

"And what did he say when you made your mark?" Mr. Hathorne asked.

Her eyes glittering unashamedly, Tituba answered, "He say, 'Serve me! And serve me always!' "

At the close of this second day of the hearings no one doubted that the three women would be committed. Yet Tituba had spoken of two strangers, and had seen seven signatures in the Devil's book besides Good's and Osburn's. Determined to establish the identity of as many of these as possible, Mr. Hathorne and Mr. Corwin continued the hearings March 3 and March 5. No new suspects were named, and on March 7 the magistrates jointly issued mittimuses for the imprisonment in Boston of Sarah Good, Sarah Osburn, and Tituba Indian.

On March 19 Mr. Hathorne and Mr. Corwin—the country's men of the hour, acknowledged victors in a bout with three who had sold their souls to the Devil—were accorded the commendation of the church. Justification of their course of action came in the form of a sermon delivered in their presence in the sanctuary where a few days earlier they had listened to Tituba's awful story. The preacher was the Reverend Deodate Lawson, intimate friend of Mr. Cotton Mather and predecessor of Mr. Parris as minister in Salem

Village. The discourse, bearing special dedicatory acknowl-
edgments to Mr. Hathorne and Mr. Corwin, was at once
printed and placed in circulation.

Then on April 11, when five or six more whom the sick
children had cried out against were under examination,
Mr. Hathorne and Mr. Corwin won the full approbation
of their superiors among the civil officers. The hearings
for this day were transferred to the much more spacious
meetinghouse in Salem; and Deputy Governor Thomas
Danforth, Mr. Samuel Sewall, and other noted jurists who
had come from Boston took charge. That night Mr. Sewall
wrote in his diary: "Went to Salem, where, in the meetinghouse, the persons accused of witchcraft were examined;
was a very great assembly; 't was awful to see how the
afflicted persons were agitated. Mr. Noyes prayed at the
beginning, and Mr. Higginson concluded." In the margin
Mr. Sewall added: "Witchcraft! Voe, voe, voe!" He might
also have added that Mr. Danforth's method of conducting
the hearings was on the whole that which Mr. Hathorne
had followed from the beginning.

The only innovation introduced by Mr. Danforth was the
Lord's Prayer test. An accused woman whom he was questioning was called upon to repeat Christ's words. When she
made a trivial slip, the judges agreed that it was the Devil
who had led her into the error.

In time Mr. Hathorne would certainly have used this
test on his own initiative. As he had shown in the examination of Tituba, he was well acquainted with the conventions of seventeenth-century English witch lore. From
time to time he drew from those he questioned elaborate
descriptions of black sacraments—baptism by immersion
in putrid pools which had been cursed by the Devil, and
mock communions in Mr. Parris's orchard with the Fiend
himself the celebrant and such witches as Good and Osburn

the deacons, serving bread that was red like blood and wine that really was blood. Mr. Hathorne listened credulously while the afflicted told of ghostly visits from those whom the accused were supposed to have murdered. At a hearing he frequently ordered an accused to touch an afflicted who was being hurt—stuck with pins, pinched, struck, kicked, bitten, scratched, strangled, or suffocated; for he believed that through such contact the accused if guilty would reabsorb the diabolic energy causing the torture. He found to his satisfaction that immediately when the accused were manacled and locked in prison those whom they were charged of hurting were relieved. He ordered the premises of a number of the accused searched for witches' poppets, and such objects as rags and loose hair supposedly rolled to resemble human bodies were found and placed in evidence. He held the theory that neither the Devil nor a witch or wizard could appear in the likeness of a person or animal who was not a diabolic minion. He believed that at least one accused woman whom he examined had followed a ship to sea and but for the prayers of the sailors would have destroyed it in the storm she raised as she flitted about the rigging. He accepted as sound evidence of demoniacal power reports of preternatural strength, such as a man's "putting his fingers into the bung of a barrel filled with molasses, and lifting it up, and carrying it around, and setting it down again."

He paid the strictest attention to the reports of the women and chirurgeons he appointed to search the naked bodies of the accused for witch marks and teats for suckling familiars. But he seems to have asked no question which led to other revelations suggestive of the erotic. Demons did not cohabit with mortals in Massachusetts Bay. Witchcraft there was not so unclean as in Connecticut, where a confessed witch admitted that the Devil was her lover and came every night to her bed. Mr. Hathorne wished to hear no further particulars when an accused woman with a shapely body declared that Satan took her to the top of a mountain, showed her New England spread out before her, and told her that the entire country would be hers to reign over as queen if she would only sign his book and fall to the ground and worship him.

On at least one occasion Mr. Hathorne himself, in order to bring about an identification, resorted to magic. Certain afflicted girls and women were having difficulty in pointing out a man they were charging of wizardry. Mr. Hathorne ordered all to move into the yard in front of the meeting-house. A great circle was drawn on the ground, and it was no sooner completed than one of the girls, in a trance, cried, "There's John Alden, a bold fellow, with his hat on before the judges! He sells powder and shot to the Indians and French, and lies with the Indian squaws, and has papooses!" Mr. Hathorne and Mr. Corwin a few days later committed as a wizard the man thus identified. He was an aging well-to-do Boston merchant, son of the John Alden and Priscilla Mullins who had brought romance into early Plymouth. Through breaking jail and fleeing he was to evade trial.

By May 14, when the frigate *Nonesuch*, bearing Sir William Phipps, the Reverend Increase Mather, and the new charter, arrived in Boston harbor, Mr. Hathorne and Mr. Corwin had the prisons of Essex and Suffolk Counties crowded with supposed witches and wizards. With the apprehension of each new suspect the country had become more alarmed. Nearly everybody was afraid of nearly everybody else. When two neighbors met, each was likely to be thinking, "Have you also signed the Fiend's book?" The new governor found Massachusetts Bay in unprecedented terror. He saw that something would have to be done immediately, and he knew that months would pass before the judicial machinery provided for in the new charter could be set up. Sir William therefore took advantage of an old English law and appointed a court of oyer and terminer to meet in the Salem town house at once and begin the trials of Their Majesties' subjects who were charged with witchcrafts.

The court consisted of nine magistrates, headed by Lieutenant Governor William Stoughton. He was a close friend of Increase and Cotton Mather, and held to the full their beliefs regarding witchcraft. Among the eight named to assist him were Samuel Sewall, Mr. Corwin, and Mr. Hathorne. Five, according to the governor's decree, constituted a quorum.

Certain historians were to make Mr. Hathorne a central figure in this court of oyer and terminer, the magistrate most assiduous in seeking death sentences for those on trial. The truth is that Mr. Hathorne rarely, if ever, took advantage of his right and sat as a member of the court. Not one of his contemporaries who wrote of the trials listed him among the judges. During the summer and early autumn he continued holding preliminary hearings, as he had done since March 1. With the trials at the town house attracting the curious, he questioned suspects at his own home, or at Deacon Ingersoll's tavern in Salem Village, or, more frequently, at Mr. Corwin's residence, which for this reason was one day to be known as the "witch house." Between the first of June and the middle of October as many as a hundred appeared before Mr. Hathorne and were committed. He could have had little time for other duties—except witnessing the executions of those whom Mr. Stoughton, Mr. Sewall, and others active in the court of oyer and terminer had condemned.

The first hanging, which came June 10, was that of Bridget Bishop, who twelve years before, when she was Bridget Oliver, had been sentenced to die for witchcraft and then, at the eleventh hour, had been pardoned by Governor Bradstreet. She had prospered as keeper of a tavern, where on occasion the merriment was loud. She had moreover worn clothes such as most of her women neighbors could not afford. After her commitment by Mr. Hathorne a grand jury —sitting probably at Mr. Corwin's residence—returned a bill against her. Brought before the court of oyer and terminer, she was obliged to take care of her own defense. For there were still no lawyers, except counselors for the crown, in Massachusetts Bay. The woman's trial, on the upper floor of the town house, was a bedlam. Time and again the reading of the depositions stating her alleged acts of witchcraft were interrupted by the shrieks of the stricken girls and women. But at last Bridget Bishop heard the clerk—Stephen Sewall, brother of Samuel Sewall—read the jury's verdict of guilty. Then she listened as Mr. Stoughton pronounced the sentence of death.

Mr. Hathorne, on horseback, was a prominent figure in the procession which followed her to the place of execution. She rode in a cart—standing, so that the hundreds of spectators could see her all the better. From the jail the procession moved south on Prison Lane, and then west on the main street. When the woman drew near the meetinghouse, she happened to cast her eyes in the direction of the sacred edifice. As she did so, said Mr. Cotton Mather, a board on the inside of the building broke from the heavy nails which held it and flew with the speed of a bullet to the opposite wall, hitting with a crash that could be heard throughout Salem. What more was needed to prove that Bridget Bishop had signed the Devil's book? At the corner of the Mill Pond farm—which for Mr. Hathorne and his family was a second home—the driver of the death cart turned from the main street into a narrow roadway which led northwest a short distance and then up a rocky mound, to be known in time as Gallows Hill. Mr. Hathorne, fulfilling his duty as a magistrate, looked on while Bridget Bishop was hanged, possibly from a gibbet, but more likely from the limb of a tree. When the hangman was sure that she was dead, the body was cut down and tossed into a shallow grave which had been dug at the foot of a rock.

On July 19 Mr. Hathorne witnessed the first mass execution. This time five women were hanged.

Among them was Sarah Good. When she came to Salem to be tried, she left in the Boston jail her little four-year-old daughter, Dorcas, also committed by Mr. Hathorne on a charge of witchcraft. He saw with his own eyes, he believed, the prints of her little teeth on the arms of two of the afflicted girls, bitten when the child's physical body was asleep in her own bed a mile or two away. The Boston jailer had to have special manacles made to fit the tiny wrists and ankles, and required the mother to pay for them. When Goody Good, sure of herself despite her fear and rancor, was about to be hanged, the Reverend Nicholas Noyes cried out, "You're a witch, and you know you are!" Turning upon him a look which in itself sent forth curses, she shouted, "You're a liar! I'm no more a witch than you're a wizard! And if you take my life God will give you blood to drink!"

Future commentators were to claim erroneously that this curse was addressed not to Mr. Noyes but to Mr. Hathorne and was spoken not by Sarah Good but by another woman hanged that day, Rebecca Nurse. This Christlike victim of the hysteria met death pitying her murderers rather than wishing evil upon them. Her husband was Francis Nurse, a large landholder and leader of influence in Salem Village. She was seventy-one, and all her life had been noted for her goodness and godliness. But because of disagreement over certain land boundaries she had won the enmity of Thomas Putnam's wife. Besides, Mrs. Nurse and her husband had never transferred their church membership from Salem to Salem Village, and were known to be in opposition to the scheme of Mr. Parris to obtain possession of the manse in which he was living. So Ann Putnam and two other girls cried out against Mrs. Nurse, and Mr. Hathorne committed her. She was so deaf that she missed most that was said at her trial. Mr. Stoughton, taking advantage of an equivocal answer she made to a question she failed to hear, finally succeeded in forcing from the trial jury a verdict of guilty. Then the Reverend Mr. Noyes, in a dread ceremony in the meetinghouse with Mrs. Nurse present in chains, pronounced upon her the doom of excommunication, and in doing so induced the politics-minded Governor Phipps to recall a reprieve he had issued. The passageway to hell freed of all churchly obstacles, Rebecca Nurse was crowded into the death cart with the four others and taken to the execution mound. Before she died she said, in complete resignation, "God will clear my innocency!"

On August 19, exactly one month later, Mr. Hathorne saw hanged four men, including the Reverend George Burroughs, and one woman, Martha Carrier, of Andover.

Mr. Burroughs was the short dark man, of great physical strength, whom the afflicted spoke often of seeing in their visions. The young woman who first identified him by name had been a servant in his house when he was the minister in Salem Village. Unable to bring about harmony in the quarrelsome parish, he had resigned, to return to his old home in Wells, Maine. He was in charge of the church in that settlement when Mr. Hathorne and Mr. Corwin issued the warrant for his arrest. Since he was a minister, his trial was specially sensational. Both the celebrated Mr. Mathers were in attendance. Even the ghosts of his two former wives, seen by the afflicted in their trances, came from their graves to testify against him, claiming that he had been their murderer! Mr. Stoughton had no trouble in getting the jury to agree at once on a conviction.

But at the execution mound, just before he was hanged, Mr. Burroughs proved that a man convicted of wizardry could, with great eloquence, repeat the Lord's Prayer. Then, in words so touching that many of his hearers were brought to tears, he addressed the crowd, avowing his innocence but dwelling more upon his fearlessness of death. Mr. Cotton Mather, present on horseback, in periwig and feathered hat, was quick to sense the effect of the speech, and as soon as he was sure that the body of Mr. Burroughs was lifeless, he too addressed the crowd. Unwilling in his piety to speak the name of a wizard, he called the hanged man G.B. Defending the action of Lieutenant Governor Stoughton and the rest of the court of oyer and terminer, he shot one thunderbolt of theological reasoning after another, each stronger than the preceding. The incontrovertible final discharge was, "This foul fiend G.B. preached from Christian pulpits—but never was he ORDAINED!"

When Mr. Mather saw the body of Martha Carrier dangling in the air, he shouted, "This is the hag whom the Devil promised to make the Queen of Hell!" She belonged to Andover, where the hysteria raged with a violence almost as great as in Salem Village. It was in Andover that a dog, supposed to have the power of bewitching, was by process of law executed. At Goody Carrier's preliminary examination Mr. Hathorne heard three of her children, among whom was a girl of eight, admit that they had yielded to their mother when she appeared in the likeness of a cat and threatened to tear them into pieces if they refused to sign Satan's book.

Mr. Hathorne let jailers and constables witness the next execution. The one victim this time was eighty-year-old Giles Corey. Because he stood dumb when he was asked to plead guilty or not guilty, he was sentenced by the court of oyer and terminer to suffer the ordeal of peine forte et dure until he admitted or denied being a wizard, or died. All he would say as he lay naked in jail while stone after stone was stacked on his chest was to be echoed in a song sung in eighteenth-century Massachusetts Bay, a ballad of the people bearing the refrain,

> "More weight! More weight!"
> Giles Corey he cried.

The ordeal, requiring three days, ended with the death of the old man on September 19.

The strength of character he showed in choosing to die an agonizing death rather than submit to trial by a court for which he had no respect was in time to make of him a popular hero. But the records credit him with little which his own age considered admirable. He and his middle-aged wife Martha, his third, inevitably became suspects as soon as the accusers began to look for victims. Though the Coreys in recent years had followed godly paths as church members, Salem could not forget that Giles had more than once been whipped for petty crimes and that Martha, who was of pure English origin, had some time previous to her marriage to Giles borne a mulatto son. Whether she had been wedded to the unidentified slave or freedman who was the child's father was not recorded.

She too, vowing to God her innocence as she prayed, was courageous when on September 22 she was taken with seven other women to the execution mound. As Mr. Hathorne sat on his horse looking at the swung bodies, he heard the Reverend Mr. Noyes cry out, "What a *sad* thing it is to see eight firebrands of hell hanging there!'" Mr. Hathorne might have wondered whether the minister, who had pronounced excommunication on both the Coreys, was being ironic in his use of the adjective *sad*.

Seven more women were under sentence to die, and Mr. Hathorne expected to see them hanged in October. But after that September 22, 1692, no one was ever again to witness an execution for the crime of witchcraft in New England.

Not all the people in Massachusetts Bay had by any means fallen victim to the hysteria. It had seemed so at the start, so stunned were the clear-eyed at the quick penetration of the madness into the minds of men and women of every social level. But as the weeks passed and the frenzy grew in intensity, those who were still capable of rational thinking showed their stand by word and act. They granted that the Devil was busy in the land. But they refused to believe the silly tales told of him at the trials. They maintained rather that the Evil One was at work in the hearts of the promoters of the delusion, such as Mr. Cotton Mather, Mr. Parris, and Thomas Putnam's wife. First the Fiend had deadened their sensibilities to reality. Then, without their awareness perhaps, he had stirred up their personal hates, their neighborhood enmities, their passion to step up in the world, and their primitive instincts of cruelty for the sake of cruelty.

Mr. Parris, leader of the accusing gang to the end, showed meanness throughout. When persons of prominence began to express alarm over the prosecutions, they themselves or those dear to them were cried out against. Among the high in rank directly accused were the Reverend Samuel Willard, minister of Boston's Old South Church, and Lady Mary Phipps, wife of the governor. Those indirectly attacked included the venerable Governor Bradstreet, two of whose sons were arrested on charges of wizardry, the Reverend John Higginson, one of whose daughters was arrested, and the Reverend John Hale, whose wife was named a suspect. Even Mr. Corwin, whose reticence at the preliminary hearings came to be frowned upon, found out one day that his mother-in-law in Boston had been accused. Strongly outspoken was the protest of the rational when Mrs. Hale, a gentlewoman widely beloved, was cried out against. Still Mr. Parris and his crew were so bloated with success, after sending twenty to their deaths, that they continued to name suspects until several of Andover who had been charged of familiarity with the Devil instigated suits for damages against their accusers. With purses threatened, Mr. Parris, still eager to own outright the Salem Village manse, was ready to call a halt.

Among the fearless protesters against all engaged in the witchcraft prosecutions were close relations of Mr. Hathorne. His youngest sister and her husband, Elizabeth and Israel Porter, were directly responsible for two petitions addressed to the court of oyer and terminer in behalf of Rebecca Nurse. When the women charged with examining Mrs. Nurse for witch marks reported that they had found spots on her body dead to all sensation, she asked that she be examined again by those who would tell the truth and in listing them gave first the name of Mrs. Porter.

The eldest of the Porter daughters—also named Elizabeth —was married to the man who in time was to be the most admired of all involved in the delusion. He was twenty-two-year-old Joseph Putnam, brother, paradoxically enough, of Thomas Putnam. Young Joseph kept his head clear and his ammunition ready. He sent word, says tradition, to the constables and marshals that he would resist to the death any attempt they might make to arrest him or anyone belonging to his household on a charge of familiarity with the Devil. To his friends he confided that if the officers of the law should come in numbers too great for him to fight he had horses in his stables day and night to speed to places of safety any in his keeping who might be accused. He was never in any way molested, and it is highly possible that he enabled certain suspects to flee. A fit father he was for the son his wife Elizabeth was to bear to him in January, 1718, the eleventh of their twelve children. This son, Mr. Hathorne's great-nephew, was to become one of the most daring and colorful of Revolutionary War heroes, General Israel Putnam.

With men of the courage of Joseph Putnam to stand up against them, the accusers by the end of 1692 were definitely silenced. Common sense was at last in the ascendancy in Massachusetts Bay. Though the Reverend Cotton Mather tried to revive the hysteria in Boston early in the new year, his vociferous appeals were ineffectual. With no suspects to examine and commit and no executions to witness, Mr. Hathorne was free of the witchcraft prosecutions. He had failed to be made a member of the permanent superior court which had been chosen to replace the court of oyer and terminer.

This new court had jurisdiction over pending cases, and the jails were filled with suspects slated for trial. But in the spring of 1693, Sir William Phipps, acting under pressure of public opinion, issued reprieves for those under sentence of death, and at the same time ordered all the accused held in custody to be set free.

Two or three of the committed had died in the Boston prison, probably from lack of food and brutal treatment. Among them was the sick old woman who had been so indifferent at her examination, Sarah Osburn.

The two slaves who had played such important parts

in starting the hysteria came out alive. John Indian was clever enough to save his neck by joining the group of the afflicted. He had even outdone Ann Putnam in wriggling on the floor, moaning under imagined torture, and shouting in gibberish. Tituba, because she was an openly confessed witch and might on any day name more suspects, had never been indicted. She had bided her time in silence.

The opportunity to speak out as she wished came when she left the Boston prison. Since she was a slave, her master was supposed to pay her prison fees—for lodging, board, and such incidental necessaries as manacles. When Mr. Parris refused to do this, Tituba was put up for sale, and was purchased by an unidentified man for the amount charged against her by the jailer. But before she departed for a destination unknown, she talked. On several occasions, in the presence of persons of integrity, she claimed that Mr. Parris had forced her with beatings and threats of more beatings to tell the story she told to Mr. Hathorne.

The spring and summer of 1693 saw the return home of the Salem suspects who had been freed from prison at the governor's order or had fled to places of refuge. Belonging to the latter group were the merchant Philip English and his wife Mary. They were well-to-do, and lived in an attractive dwelling which stood near the bay at the east end of the main street. Mr. English, part French, had come from the island of Jersey. He and his wife had been slow in adjusting themselves to Puritan ways, and had frankly admitted their preference for the Church of England. So they had been charged of witchcraft, and Mr. Hathorne had committed them. But through the aid of the Reverend Samuel Willard, who remained rational throughout the delusion, they had broken jail in Boston, and then had fled to New York.

After their return to Salem the day inevitably came when

they met Mr. Hathorne and his wife face to face, possibly in the street, possibly at meeting. Mr. Hathorne as a magistrate had abetted the legalized confiscation of much of their property, and if he had had his way their hanged bodies would long have been in shallow graves on the execution mound. Surely during the few moments of the chance encounter eyes shot hatred. But if the Providence which brought about the meeting could have whisked the four from out the bounds of their age and they could have seen themselves living on in their progeny, they would all have felt forbearance.

Standing in the summer of 1693, on a lane near the Philip English mansion, was the modest newly built house in which the author of *The Scarlet Letter* was to be born. Already a year old in 1693 was the romancer's great-grandfather, Mr. Hathorne's son Joseph. Two of the sons of this Joseph Hathorne were to marry granddaughters of Philip and Mary English. The romancer, descended from a third son of this Joseph, was to envy in his boyhood the social position of his cousins who had the blood of the Englishes in their veins. It was one of these cousins who was to give to the world the authentic story of the incarceration, sufferings, and escape of Philip and Mary English during the witchcrafts, telling of the arrest of the latter by Constable Jacob Manning, another relative of the romancer.

As Mr. Hathorne, his wife clinging to him, turned away from the pair whom he would have stamped out, thus altering greatly his family history, he possibly thought, "Only the Devil could provide the fires which darted from the eyes of that man and woman!"

THE TABLES TURNED

JOSEPH, the fourth of Mr. Hathorne's sons destined to reach maturity, was born in May, 1692, when the excitement over the witchcrafts was greatest. One of his earliest vivid recollections must have been the funeral of old Governor Bradstreet, who gave up the ghost on the last Lord's day in March, 1697, about ten o'clock in the evening. This longest-lived of all the Massachusetts Bay founders was in his ninety-fourth year. Since his marriage, in 1676, to the widow of Captain Joseph Gardner his home had been the turreted mansion built by her father, Emanuel Downing, on Salem's main thoroughfare. It was here that Mr. Bradstreet, in public service from the day of his arrival on the *Arbella* in 1630 until the period of the witchcraft madness, breathed his final breath. When news of his end reached Boston, the General Court, which happened to be in session, at once appropriated £100 for a state funeral. Excavators digging under pressure of time at the Burying Point and masons building the first family tomb seen in Salem made a deep impression on boys even as young as Joseph Hathorne. On the morning of the day set for the obsequies, Saturday, April 2, rain fell heavily. The boys were not to forget the picture the workmen made as they bailed out water from the flooded underground chamber.

That morning notables from Boston and every town in Massachusetts Bay kept arriving in Salem. Most of them were on horseback, and came drenched to the skin. Mr. Samuel Sewall, accompanied by Madam Sewall and the wives of Elisha Cooke and John Leverett, was among the lucky who arrived in calashes. The throng of guests for the funeral included both supporters and opponents of Mr. Bradstreet's political views. All alike wished to pay homage to the man who had served the country so long and so faithfully.

Providence interceded in behalf of Massachusetts Bay that afternoon. At two o'clock the rain stopped, the clouds dispersed, and the sun shone, filling Salem with warmth and the smell of growing April. No one could have prayed for more fitting weather for the rites about to be performed.

In the hall of the Downing mansion, in a simple pine coffin covered with a black pall, lay the body of the aged governor. No candles burned at the head and feet, and there were no flowers. But pinned to the pall were scraps of paper, on which admirers who had the talent for making verses had written eulogies. Assisting Madam Bradstreet in receiving the scores of gentlemen and gentlewomen who crowded the downstairs rooms were the children and grandchildren of the governor and his first wife, born Anne Dudley. For a quarter of a century she had been in her grave in Ipswich. A few of the older guests remembered that she had published poetry and had been dubbed "the tenth Muse, lately sprung up in America." Among her offspring present were the two sons who had fled the country in order to evade trial for wizardry.

There was no service for the dead. Many ministers were present, but there were no spoken prayers, no tributes— nothing which might hint of popery. Sermons in honor of Governor Bradstreet were to be preached later in many meetinghouses. But the present occasion—as a funeral had always been in Massachusetts Bay—was a time for social intercourse. Servants offered the guests cakes and tankards of wine and cider. For the pallbearers and persons of distinction there were the usual tokens of rings and scarfs.

Pleasantries were exchanged, and as more wine and cider were drunk mild laughter might have been heard.

It was time for gossip, and the talkers no doubt became critical when they saw Mr. Hathorne join the group of pallbearers. The preceding autumn he had brought upon the country a military reversal. Mr. Stoughton, the acting governor since Sir William Phipps's enforced retirement and death, had raised Mr. Hathorne to the rank of colonel and had sent him to Maine to replace a proved soldier, Colonel Benjamin Church. Mr. Hathorne took over the command as ordered, and set out to attack a fort held by Indians and the French in the Penobscot region. But after two or three days of skirmishing he withdrew, embarked his troops, and sailed with them back to Boston. He would be unable to fight, he reported, until he was given more men. "Colonel Church was able to fight!" said the Hathorne enemies, who were numerous. A few weeks later the General Court gave Mr. Hathorne an opportunity to redeem himself, at least partially. He was made a member of a commission to discuss terms for a treaty with the Indians whom he had previously been ordered to fight. This time he had met with success. But his failure as a soldier was still a live topic for conversation among those who hated him.

There had been a bit of compensation in his unhappy experience as a military man. He had gained a higher title than any other Hathorne had ever borne. For the rest of his days, and on his tombstone, he was to be called Colonel Hathorne.

Also among the pallbearers were Mr. Sewall, James Russell, and General Wait Winthrop, the founder Winthrop's grandson. They too had been judges in the witchcraft examinations and trials. But even if none of the men who had promoted the prosecutions had been on hand to stir memories, the talkers would have spoken of the witchcrafts.

The rationalism which checked the madness had within four years grown deeper and stronger. The concern of Mr. Cotton Mather and his kind over the Devil's endeavor to regain the country had been proved to be a nightmarish dread, born of superstition and misguided faith. The influence formerly exerted by Mr. Mather and his father was little felt now. Public opinion had forced Mr. Parris to leave Salem Village. Thomas Putnam's wife and his daughter Ann, the latter already a young woman, were the objects of general scorn. The preceding January 14 the people of the province, in obedience to governmental decree, had gathered in the meetinghouses to pray God to forgive any wrongs committed by the country in 1692 in condemning men and women on charges of familiarity with the Devil. In Boston's Old South Church Mr. Sewall had stood with bowed head while the plea of repentance he had penned was read from the pulpit by the minister, the Reverend Mr. Willard. Mr. Hathorne had not gone that far. But as one of the governor's councilors, as a judge in the court which had superseded the old Essex County quarterly court, and as a member of the church, he was acting with those who were trying to undo what had been done in violation of justice in 1692.

All talk was hushed when, at three o'clock, the meetinghouse bell began to toll. Marshals, in their customary red and with their staffs of office, cleared a passageway. General Winthrop, Mr. Sewall, and Mr. Cook on one side and Mr. Russell, Colonel Hathorne, and Mr. Samuel Phillips on the other took up the pall. Led by the constabulary, they started for the Burying Point. Directly behind them came four undertakers with the coffin on their shoulders. Then came Madam Bradstreet, escorted by Colonel Bartholomew Gedney and Major William Brown. In succession came the deceased's children, grandchildren, and other close relatives. Next came the ministers and high public officials, all, like the pallbearers, wearing the honorary rings and scarfs. Then came the wives and young children of ministers and notables, followed by such a throng as had not assembled in Salem since the witchcraft executions. So short was the walk to the Burying Point and so numerous were the mourners that the coffin was at the tomb before those in the rear of the procession had begun to move. There was no ceremony of committal—only the tolling of the bell and after the body was placed in the tomb the firing of three volleys, "but no great guns by reason of the scarcity of powder."

Colonel Hathorne could remember his father's return home from Governor Winthrop's funeral, in 1649. One after another the founders had been called to their final rewards. Now the last of them had been summoned, and men of Colonel Hathorne's age and generation were the patriarchs in the country. Did they have the strength to maintain what their fathers had built? Did they have the will? The Colonel was perhaps pondering such questions as he left the Burying Point and led homeward his wife and children, including five-year-old Joseph.

The boy was six when another memorable event took place in Salem, a dire visitation of Providence, a great fire. To the new Puritans it was what the presence of heretics had been to the old. For it involved property, the acquisition of which in Massachusetts Bay was more and more attracting the energy formerly devoted to the worship of Jehovah. The blaze started in the east end of the town, and, fanned by a gale from the sea, rapidly destroyed house after house as it sped westward. Powder was scarce. Yet a sufficient quantity from the town's store was used to blow up the dwelling Major Hathorne had built fifty years before on the main street at Burying Lane. With the razing of this structure—which belonged to the Hathornes of Charlestown, the heirs of Eleazar—the conflagration was checked.

By the summer of 1699 Joseph was in school, learning the lessons in the *New England Primer* under the mastership of one of Salem's most celebrated teachers, the Reverend John Emerson. On June 22, the most prominent families in the town gathered for an event which no doubt greatly aroused the boy's curiosity. Even his brother Benjamin, three years his junior, was old enough to remember the festivity of this day.

The scene was the home of Colonel John Higginson, merchant and magistrate. He was the son and namesake of Salem's aged minister and grandson of the pioneer Reverend Francis Higginson. The occasion was the marriage of Colonel Higginson's seventeen-year-old daughter Sarah to Colonel Hathorne's second son, Nathaniel, twenty-two. All the details leading to the engagement of the pair, including the matter of the bride's portion, had been arranged by the fathers. Sarah was possibly at no time consulted. If custom was followed strictly, her parents addressed to Nathaniel a formal letter of thanks after Colonel Hathorne had tendered the proposal. The ceremony might have been performed by either father, or by the bride's grandfather. For since the new charter had been in operation ministers had had the legal right to unite couples in marriage. Even if the old custom of having a magistrate officiate was observed, it is likely that after the nuptial vows were exchanged the Reverend Mr. Higginson, in a voice cracked by years, prayed for God's blessings to rest upon the union and made a few exhortatory remarks.

Colonel Higginson was noted for his hospitality—and for worldly ways scarcely to be expected of a minister's son. Surely great quantities of food and wine were served, and there might have been two or three fiddlers present to make music. It is highly possible that the bridal pair and other young couples, to the delight of the little Hathorne boys, danced several measures. The times were changing: as far back as 1686 a dancing master had made progress in teaching his art in Massachusetts Bay. But if Colonel Higginson did allow such merriment in his house it is certain that his father, in service as a minister in Salem for nearly forty years, kept his back turned upon the wanton frolic.

Among the guests no doubt was the bride's paternal aunt, Madam Anna Dolliver, of Gloucester, who had been accused of witchcraft in 1692. Present of course was Madam Hathorne, looking very tired and worn, though she was only thirty-nine. She had recently given birth to the last of her thirteen children. Providence had made of her a sorrowful mother. She had seen six of her babies buried, and this last, a son christened Freestone, was soon to be taken.

The oldest of the living children, John, twenty-three in 1699, was never to marry. Then came Nathaniel, and then Ebenezer, fourteen, also to remain single. Joseph and Benjamin, so much younger than their brothers, were doubtless made to feel in their growing up years that they were inferior in such pursuits as swimming, gunning, boating, riding, and working on the Mill Pond farm. Between the two younger boys came the one girl to survive, Ruth, born in 1694.

What Colonel Hathorne did for John when the latter reached manhood was not recorded. All that is known is that this oldest son was then at sea. It is certain that early in 1700 the Colonel deeded to Nathaniel several lots back of his mansion. No dwelling appears to have been built. Nathaniel and his wife had already established a home in another section of Salem. He too was a mariner, captain of a vessel which made regular trips to ports in England.

In 1702 Colonel Hathorne was raised to membership in the superior court of the province, a position to which he had aspired since the reorganization of the government. The elevation meant that he would serve no longer on the bench of the Essex County court of common pleas, that he would again sit at the trials of major offenders, and that he would have once more the opportunity of matching his judicial wits with the best in Massachusetts Bay. It also meant a fixed salary, which neither he nor his father with all their experience in the courtroom had ever enjoyed. The sum was small, only £50 a year; but it came in addition to the fees which had previously provided the only remuneration.

In assuming the duties of the new judgeship Colonel Hathorne practically ceased to be a merchant. As a man of business he had known little but adversity since the witchcrafts. While his wealth was shrinking some whom he had sent to prison in 1692 were in the heyday of prosperity. Among them was Philip English.

Once Mr. English fell ill. His family, thinking he was going to die, sent for a minister—probably old Mr. Higginson—to give spiritual consolation.

"Have you forgiven all your enemies?" asked the minister, sitting beside the sick man's bed.

"All but Colonel Hathorne," said Mr. English.

"Before departing this life you must forgive him too," the minister said.

"If I must, alas, I will," said Mr. English. Then, after a moment of hesitation, he added, "That is, if I'm going to die. If I get well I'll be damned if I forgive him!"

Mr. English did get well, and was typical of the competitors who had all but ruined Colonel Hathorne as a mer-

chant. The Colonel had the favor of the government authorities in Boston. But in free trade in Salem his position was
altogether different. It was probably his unpopularity which
induced his two oldest sons to change their place of residence to England. John, on settling in the old country,
appears to have given up the sea. Irresponsible and thriftless, he wandered from place to place, and was often penniless. Nathaniel, who remained a mariner, established a home
in Gosport, in Hampshire. In 1711 he died, leaving his
estate to his widow, who was soon to bear to him a posthumous child, the Colonel's first grandson and namesake.

Many months before 1711, Ebenezer, the Colonel's third
son, had become a sea captain, commanding vessels engaged
in trade with the West Indies. For the time being he showed
no intention of renouncing Salem as his home port. The
two youngest sons, Joseph and Benjamin—whether at
school under the threat of the Reverend Mr. Emerson's
ferule or at work on the Mill Pond farm or at the meetinghouse for religious exercises—had dreamed, not of following in the steps of their father and grandfather, but of going
to sea as their brothers had done. By 1711 both were before
the mast.

During his years on the superior court, his last decade
of health and strength, Colonel Hathorne worked with
great steadiness—and monotony. Many days out of each
month he spent in the saddle or in a calash or boat. He had
to take regular trips to Boston for the meetings of the
governor's council. Court sessions were held in towns as
distant as Braintree, Bridgewater, Scituate, Taunton, Wren-
tham, and Bristol. Often the Colonel was called upon for
a special judicial duty—perhaps to sit on a court of oyer and
terminer for the trial of an Indian charged with murder or
for the trial of a sea captain charged with flogging a sailor
to death. He was chosen several times during this busy

decade to represent the Salem church at synods, meeting as far away as Plymouth. More than once he was suddenly summoned to Boston—perhaps to help Mr. Sewall, always his friend, "steer between Scylla and Charybdis" in some matter involving public welfare, or to give advice both as judge and councilor over some problem demanding a quick decision from Governor Dudley.

The Colonel was too occupied to consider seriously the changes taking place around him. Without thinking of the possibilities of journalism, he read Massachusetts Bay's first newspaper, the Boston *News Letter*, circulated in Salem from the year it was founded, 1704. He probably disapproved of Salem's first house not made of wood, a brick structure put up in 1708. He, like many others, neglected to use the official name Queen's Highway, finally adopted for Salem's main street. At the same time he gracefully followed the new fashion of addressing women of quality with the title "Madam." Long accustomed to a Quaker meetinghouse in Salem, he apparently had no comment to make when he heard talk about plans for the erection of a Church of England chapel in the town. He could not have known that certain Salem families whom he had always looked down upon as belonging to the people were laying the foundations for fortunes which to him would have seemed fabulous.

Age did not strike the Colonel with force until 1712, when he was near the end of his seventy-first year. Then, "by reason of his great hardness of hearing," he was obliged to give up his judgeship and also his place on the governor's council. "Colonel Hathorne seems not to expect to go out of Salem any more," wrote Mr. Sewall in his diary.

The year the Colonel retired from public life Providence visited upon him a most unexpected trouble. His son Ebenezer on returning from Barbados brought back in his ship several sailors stricken with smallpox. A number in Salem caught the disease and died. The Colonel knew that many of the people were saying, "More suffering brought on by another Hathorne! Didn't the father do enough harm during the witchcrafts?"

A tradition, unsupported by any known record, claims that Ebenezer's mother was one of the victims of the epidemic in 1712. All that can be positively said of the time of Madam Hathorne's death is that it took place after 1699 and several years before 1717.

On an undesignated day in 1713 the Colonel witnessed the marriage of his one surviving daughter, Ruth, then nineteen. The groom was James Putnam, son of a first cousin of Joseph Putnam, the Colonel's nephew by marriage. No great Revolutionary soldier was to be numbered among the many descendants of James and Ruth Putnam. Yet theirs was to be one of the most evenly distinguished of the Putnam family lines, with the sons, generation after generation, graduating from Harvard College and serving the commonwealth worthily.

Then on May 30, 1715, the Colonel saw his son Joseph, already a sea captain, married to Sarah Bowditch. The Bowditches in the early days of the colony had been scorned as Baptist heretics, but with the years they had become acceptably orthodox. Sarah's father, Captain William Bowditch, was a mariner and merchant, and for several years represented Salem in the General Court. Counted among the town's richer men, he was able to give with Sarah a dowry of £200. Her mother, born Sarah Gardner, was Madam Hathorne's niece. So the bride and groom were cousins once removed. The marriage also brought closer the relationship between the Hathornes and Porters. For among the brothers of the bride's maternal grandmother, born

Mary Porter, were the husbands of Colonel Hathorne's sisters Ann and Elizabeth.

Colonel Hathorne and Captain Bowditch, close friends for many years, were no doubt highly pleased over the marriage. To them Joseph was a good boy and Sarah a good girl, and as they prayed for the blessings of Heaven to rest upon the union they thought only of average welfare. But Providence was laying other plans for the Hathornes and Bowditches. A common great-great-grandson of the deaf old Colonel and the still vigorous Captain was to be Nathaniel Hawthorne. But before the romancer's rise to great distinction his Bowditch kindred were to be well acquainted with the meaning of fame in the family. For the renowned mathematician, Nathaniel Bowditch, the Captain's great-grandson, was to antedate the romancer Hawthorne by a quarter of a century. Captain Bowditch, like Colonel Higginson, believed in occasional conviviality. The wedding guests, mindful only of the present, no doubt made merry and gave to the father of the groom a last sight of gaiety.

It must have been about the time of Joseph's marriage that the Colonel heard of the death, in England, of his firstborn, his son John. This young man stands as a mystery in the story of the Hathornes. There are hints that he followed evil courses.

Ebenezer and Benjamin were possibly at sea on the day Joseph got married. The men making up the third generation of the Hathornes of Salem were spending little time on New England soil. The two oldest before their deaths had even ceased to be subjects of Massachusetts Bay.

The Colonel spent his last days alone in his mansion. The downstairs rooms included, in addition to a great hall and the kitchen, a parlor, furnished with the bed on which the decrepit man slept. His housekeeper, "a faithful servant of many years," was Anna Foster. She was perhaps a relation of another Anna Foster, an aged woman of Andover whom the Colonel had committed for witchcraft. The widow of a man who had lived to be more than a hundred, this other Anna Foster told an astonishing story at her trial. She and Martha Carrier, she said, were riding in the air high above the treetops on a stick. Suddenly it broke in two, and they dropped to the earth. But neither had felt the slightest hurt. This older Anna had died in the Boston prison in December, 1692, while under sentence to be hanged. "A senile creature, with her wits gone," Salem now said of her. But the Colonel's Anna Foster was a woman of a different stamp. She was efficient, and loyal to her employer, whose deafness had shut him off from all in the outside world except his daughter Ruth Putnam, his sons when they were in the home port, and such friends as Mr. Sewall.

For his comfort Anna wove with her own hands "a great rug." In his will, dated February 2, 1717, he asked that it be given to her. He also directed that she be paid a legacy. Another legacy was to go to Nathaniel Hathorne's posthumous son, John, who was being brought up in England by his mother and a stepfather. The Colonel made provision for the payment of a debt of £50 which his dead son John had contracted in 1714 or 1715 with a London merchant, a relation of Colonel Higginson. The mansion, valued at £300, a warehouse, valued at £20, the Mill Pond farm, valued at £700, and the oxen and cows and sheep, valued at £45, with all furnishings in the mansion and farmhouse, were to be divided equally among Ebenezer, Joseph, and Benjamin. The two older sons were named executors. "And if I die while they are at sea," the Colonel wrote, "I desire my friend, Captain William Bowditch, to act as my executor until my sons return." The testament contained no reference whatsoever to the nine thousand acres of land in Maine claimed as late as 1690.

When the Colonel made the will he was nearing the end of his last year of life. A quarter of a century earlier it would have been considered a year of terrible omens. The preceding October there had been "the black Lord's day." About ten o'clock a strange darkness settled upon the land, so intense that ministers, in the middle of their sermons, had to stop and send for candles. The Reverend Cotton Mather —scientific as well as superstitious, agitator for vaccination to prevent smallpox as well as witch hunter—wrote an account of the phenomenon for the Royal Society in London, of which body he had been a member since 1713. The black Sabbath was followed by a winter of such snowfalls as the oldest Indians in Massachusetts Bay could not recall. At the time Colonel Hathorne wrote his will the drifts stood in some places in Salem to a height of twenty-five feet. But the worst came at the end of February. All low houses were completely buried. Cows, sheep, and fowl were almost exterminated. Foxes and wolves came right up to doors to get food.

The Colonel lived long enough to see the devastating snow melt away. It was on May 10 that he died. Three days later there was another great funeral in Salem, but not so splendid as Governor Bradstreet's. This time the government did not pay the expenses. Mr. Sewall, who came up from Boston for the occasion, made no mention in his diary of gifts of rings and scarfs. But when the funeral guests gathered at the mansion on School Lane to pay respects to the Hathornes who happened to be in Salem and to follow the corpse to the Burying Point, there must have been cakes, wine, cider, and gossip.

Some of the talkers perhaps whispered, "The sorrow

the Colonel did so much to bring about in 1692 is still felt
by hundreds. Providence has been working retribution.
Nine of the thirteen children he begot are in their graves,
and the three sons still alive are certainly not men of promise. A change of heart in his old age? Bah! If some distracted
girl should dash into this room and cry out that she'd been
bewitched, he'd rise from his coffin and start an investigation." Others might have declared, "None of us see now
as we saw twenty-five years ago. Wasn't the Colonel in
favor of the repentance act in 1696? Didn't he vote at meeting to revoke the doom of excommunication pronounced
upon Rebecca Nurse and the Coreys? Hasn't he supported the proposal to make financial restitution to the
families of the witchcraft victims? He has expressed his
sense of guilt in deeds while Mr. Sewall has expressed his
in words. Both will go down in history as great servants
of the commonwealth." If among the talkers there was one
who truly understood the ways of human nature, he said,
"Whether the Colonel ever repented of his acts in 1692
will in no way alter his reputation in the future. He played
an important part in the sensational tragedy of the witchcrafts. That is all the world will choose to remember about
him."

As at Governor Bradstreet's funeral, the tolling of the
meetinghouse bell stopped the gossip. The pallbearers, all
Salem men, included Colonel Higginson and the aged Mr.
Corwin. The internment was in a simple grave, about three
rods east of Governor Bradstreet's tomb, over which the
province had placed a sarcophagus bearing a tribute in
Latin. Mr. Sewall, writing that night of the Colonel's committal, put down, "Ten minute guns were discharged at
the fort and battery."

The Colonel was the first of the Salem Hathornes to
have a marked grave. The tombstone is a small slate slab,

decorated with a death's head. The inscription reads: "Here lyes inter^d ye Body of Col^{lo} Joh^n Hathorne Esqr Aged 76 Years Who Died May ye 10th 1717."

By this date Joseph Hathorne, just twenty-five, was a seasoned master mariner. At times he sailed a twenty-ton ketch manned by a crew of only four and at times a forty- or fifty-ton brig manned by as many as ten or twelve. In Virginia, the Carolinas, and the West Indies he sold cargoes of lumber, staves, hides, whale oil, and dried codfish. In turn he purchased to bring back to Salem cotton, wool, sugar, molasses for making rum, and occasionally Negro slaves. The pirates who had preyed upon Salem ships a few years earlier had been driven from the American coastal waters. Since the Treaty of Utrecht, signed in 1713, England, France, and Spain had been at peace, and Captain Hathorne had no opportunity to privateer. No case of insubordination on the part of the sailors he commanded was ever recorded. He was never brought to court on a charge of cruelty to his men, nor on a charge of dishonesty in carrying on the business of the owners of the ships he sailed. Among these merchants were his father-in-law, Captain William Bowditch, and John Cabot, ancestor of the Cabots who were to stand for wealth and distinction in nineteenth- and twentieth-century Boston. The pay Captain Hathorne received was a small percentage of the value of the adventures he transported. He had no other income, except from his third of his father's estate.

The accounts he kept were figured accurately, in a clear manly handwriting. His master at school, the Reverend Mr. Emerson, had given him a better education than Colonel Hathorne had received. Captain Joseph had a little library at home, and no doubt carried along books to read at sea. He surely kept a Bible in his cabin, and every Lord's day, as custom demanded, conducted religious exercises aboard ship. His Puritan training had been a formality, the acceptance of which he had never questioned. He had been "converted" from a state of original sin to a state of sanctity, and considered himself a member of God's elect. But in his age a man made little ado over his religious faith. It was out of habit that Captain Joseph followed the rules ordained by the Church. When he was in Salem on a Lord's day it never occurred to him not to go to meeting and sit with his wife and children in the pew formerly held by the Colonel.

In the spring of 1724 he set out for the Azores in the brig *Friendship* to bring back wines. A second brig bound for the Azores, commanded by Captain Jacob Willard, sailed from Salem the same day. When about a week out, the two vessels ran into a severe storm. Captain Willard saw his brig go down, but not before he and his crew were rescued by Captain Hathorne. The *Friendship,* too disabled to continue on to Fayal, was brought back to Salem. Everybody wondered how a vessel so battered could have proved seaworthy during the voyage home, and everybody praised Captain Hathorne for his skill as a mariner and for his heroism in saving the lives of Captain Willard and his men.

On August 15, 1729, Captain Joseph's brother Benjamin, also long since a master mariner, sailed from Salem for Barbados in command of the sloop *Two Brothers*. Seven days later he was forced to turn back. On reaching Salem on August 29 Captain Benjamin reported: "The afternoon of August 20 we ran into a very hard gale of wind at south-southeast. The sea was so great that about eight o'clock in the evening we were obliged to land all sails, except the foresail. About nine we perceived that the vessel was leaky. About four in the morning the storm was so violent that we were forced to scud before the wind, and the sea broke upon us several times and washed both horses off the deck, broke loose the boat, and obliged us to clear and heave what was in the ship overboard, as apples, bow sticks, etc. It also washed away two water hogsheads. About eleven o'clock we were forced to lay to the hulk. The next day about eight of the clock we fixed our sails and stood back for Salem again." Two of Captain Benjamin's seamen swore to the truthfulness of his deposition.

In 1729 Benjamin Hathorne had been married for two years to Hannah Derby, first cousin of Richard Derby, a mariner of seventeen, destined to found the great Derby fortune. Hannah had already borne a son, the second Benjamin Hathorne, who was to be the father of an adventurous young privateersman of the Revolution. In 1730 she had another child, a daughter named after her. This Hannah Hathorne was to live into the nineteenth century, the earliest of numerous spinsters belonging to the Hathornes of Salem.

In the early spring of 1732 Captain Benjamin set out on one of his regular voyages. This time Providence was against him. His vessel was a ketch, too light for an Atlantic gale. "On April 5 in a great wind," says the official report, "he and his crew of four men were cast away and drowned."

He was more spectacular than his brother Joseph. Of all Colonel Hathorne's sons he seems to have been the most likable. He was undoubtedly a mariner of great daring; and, if one of his friends who kept a diary may be trusted, he was an excellent companion for an evening of pleasure at a Salem tavern. Following in his steps, Hathorne after Hathorne was to go to sea and never return.

Joseph made up his mind that he would meet no such end. He had been saving money to buy his brothers' interests in the paternal estate, and in 1726 had purchased Benjamin's third. Now he raised the amount necessary to buy the third which belonged to Ebenezer. This bachelor Hathorne, following the example set by the older brothers John and Nathaniel, had moved to London, and was commanding vessels owned by English merchants. On the July 10 following Benjamin's death, when Ebenezer was in Virginia, the papers providing for Joseph's sole ownership of the land and houses left by Colonel Hathorne were drawn up and signed. Henceforth Captain Joseph Hathorne was to live in his father's mansion on School Lane and cultivate the Mill Pond farm, where his grandfather had died.

But the mansion was a lowly cottage when compared with "fair houses" farmer Joseph saw erected in Salem. While his fields and pastures all together amounted to only ninety acres, there were merchants in the town who owned great country domains. In the destiny of the Hathornes of Salem, so proud and influential for a whole century, the tables were turned. Joseph was back in the position of his great-grandfather, the Berkshire yeoman. He was obliged to bow to some whose ancestors Major Hathorne had ordered whipped because they had no money to pay fines.

Until his oldest son, William, born in 1716, went to sea, Joseph had three strong boys to assist in plowing and hoeing the corn, weeding the pumpkins and squashes, pruning the apples and pears, cutting the hay, shearing the sheep, milking the cows, piling the dung, slaughtering the pigs, and making the cider. The second son, also named Joseph, and the third, another John Hathorne, were unadventurous; they probably labored in the fields submissively. Two of the older boys, one of whom was christened Nathaniel, had died in infancy.

The sixth son, Daniel, the romancer's grandfather, was not born until 1731. When he grew big enough to hoe and plow and mow hay with a scythe, he probably had to be prodded. For he was very young when he came under the spell of the sea. No childhood experience could have pleased him more than hearing his father tell the story of the rescue of Captain Willard and his men in the storm. The boy's first hero was perhaps his drowned uncle, Captain Benjamin Hathorne.

Farmer Joseph's two older daughters also died in infancy. The two younger, Ruth and Sarah, the last of the ten children, were to survive their father and mother by almost half a century. Ruth indeed was to see the year when the marriage of the romancer's parents took place.

Though farmer Joseph lived by the sweat of his brow, he never forgot that he was a Hathorne, and always used the title "Captain." He was not the only scion of a great Salem family who had reverted to yeomanry. Certain descendants of John Endecott and Simon Bradstreet were in his company. He took comfort in the fact that his children shared the blood of a number of the mighty in Massachusetts Bay. His wife's brother, Captain Joseph Bowditch, who had followed Stephen Sewall as a clerk of the courts, was an important figure in Essex County. The Gardners, related closely to both Joseph and his wife, were among the families who were gaining power through wealth. There were Porter and Putnam cousins to stir pride. The Hathorne children were taught that they had every reason to hold their heads high and to be ambitious to marry into good families.

Yet they and their parents as well were reminded every day of the barrier which separated them from Salem's highest circles. No Hathorne was ever present at the gay gatherings in the luxurious homes on Queen's Highway. Farmer Joseph, smelling of cows and horses and hay, would have been altogether out of place in the drawing room of Brown Hall, erected by Colonel William Brown on his vast farm in emulation of the great houses which such families as the Byrds and the Lees were enjoying in Virginia. Farmer Joseph belonged to the people who nicknamed Brown Hall "Brown's Folly." When in June, 1746, Sir William Pepperell, a native of Maine who had risen from the ranks of the people, was given a dinner at the Salem town house in honor of his great victory at Louisburg, no Hathorne was included among the many guests.

Still, at town meeting Joseph Hathorne was sometimes appointed to serve on an important committee. Salem looked upon him as steady and reliable. But if the younger inhabitants had been asked how Hathorne Hill got its name, they would have answered, "From hawthorn bushes." The Major was forgotten, and the Colonel was remembered only as a judge of the witchcrafts, now a half century in the past.

Through the years farmer Joseph held his pew in the meetinghouse, erected in 1718 to replace the building in which Major Hathorne had worshiped during his last decade. It was Joseph's destiny to see the original congregation broken up. In this year 1718, forty or fifty members withdrew and organized the East Church in the quarter directly across the bay from Beverly. At least two among their leaders had every reason to hate what the old church represented. They were Jacob Manning, who had seen two of his sisters sit on repentance stools in the meetinghouse in punishment for the crime of incest, and Philip English, who had been jailed for wizardry and robbed of property with the full connivance of the church authorities. With a second congregation in Salem, the original congregation came to be called the First Church. In the 1730's another group withdrew and formed a third congregation, to be known as the Tabernacle Church. About the same time, again under the leadership of Jacob Manning and Philip English, those dissatisfied with the established Massachusetts Bay faith organized St. Peter's, a Church of England parish, and erected a simple chapel.

In passing this edifice after 1743, Joseph Hathorne might have heard organ music inside, a great novelty in Salem. He disapproved of it, as he disapproved of the preaching of the Reverend George Whitefield, whom he probably first heard on a December night in 1736 on the Salem Common. Mr. Whitefield wrote of the occasion: "I preached to about two thousand. Here the Lord manifested His glory. In every part of the great gathering persons might be seen under concern. Mr. Clark, a good minister, seemed to be almost in heaven." Four years later Mr. Whitefield preached again on the Common, and this time his hearers numbered six thousand. Yet the celebrated evangelist changed slightly, if at all, religious practice in Salem. The conservative formalists, like Joseph Hathorne, were greatly in the majority, and still held control in each of the town's churches.

Farmer Joseph could not have been happy when he saw two of his sons leave the First Church. In 1741 William, a sea captain, married a Church of England adherent, Mary Touzell, and went over to her faith. Her father was John Touzell, a Huguenot refugee, and her mother was the daughter of Philip English. Among her maternal aunts was the wife of Colonel William Brown, of Brown Hall. Mary and William, working hand in hand with the sons and daughters of Jacob Manning, were leaders in building up St. Peter's. William was to sire ten children and live until 1794. Five years after his marriage, his sister-in-law, Susannah Touzell, became the wife of his brother John, who also joined the Episcopalians. After the birth of a son and daughter—whose respective offspring were to cross paths with the romancer—John died, in his twenty-ninth year. His widow, never to remarry, was to live until 1802.

His brother Joseph, two years his senior, died when only twenty-seven. This Joseph was married to a daughter of Retire Becket, one of Salem's most celebrated shipbuilders, and left a son, Retire Hathorne. This scion of the family, old Puritan on his mother's side as much as on his father's, was to begin the line of Hathornes belonging to Bradford, near Haverhill.

Farmer Joseph was feeling his age by the time his youngest son, Daniel, took a wife. The day was October 21, 1756. The bride was Rachel Phelps, whose family was of a lower social standing than any into which a Hathorne of Salem had married. Her father was Jonathan Phelps, a blacksmith, originally of Beverly. In 1752 he had purchased a dwelling on a lane extending from Queen's Highway to the South River in the eastern part of Salem. Built about 1686 by Benjamin Pickman, ancestor of one of Salem's great merchant families, the house had two stories, an attic with a gambrel roof, and a massive center chimney. The structure was solid, but mean when compared with the residences the Pickmans were erecting in the eighteenth century. The parlor downstairs was the scene of the wedding of Daniel and Rachel, and in the northwest chamber upstairs the romancer, their one grandson to bear the Hathorne name, was to be born within a little less than half a century. Jonathan Phelps had a smithy somewhere in the neighborhood, probably on Queen's Highway adjacent to his house lot.

At the time of Daniel's marriage Massachusetts Bay was involved in the French and Indian War. Armed brigantines and schooners were sailing from Salem and returning with prizes. But most of the vessels engaged in the commerce which had to be carried on went to sea running the risk of capture by enemy privateers. Both of Joseph's surviving sons, William and Daniel, were serving as masters of such trading vessels. Good luck followed them.

But Providence appeared to be hounding with misfortune one of their cousins, another John Hathorne. He was in all probability the posthumous son, come home from England, of farmer Joseph's older brother Nathaniel. There is also the possibilty that he sprang from the Hathornes of Lynn, or from the Hathornes of Charlestown, the latter being the descendants of the Major's son Eleazar. Whatever might have been his origin, this Captain John proved himself a hardy and dauntless mariner.

He was in Salem as early as 1743, deep in a love affair with Sarah Russiew, whose name suggests that she belonged to a Huguenot family. The result of the liaison was a daughter, duly baptized in the Tabernacle Church and listed in the records as a bastard. Later Captain John married another woman, unidentified except by her Christian name Mary. Among his legitimate children was one who was to be for a time a close neighbor of the romancer.

During the early years of the war this Captain John Hathorne made successful voyages to and from Maryland, Virginia, and the West Indies. But on a trip to the Azores, which he knew as "the wine islands," his vessel, the sloop *Dolphin*, was taken by the French and then retaken by an English privateersman. He was not long in Salem when he went to sea again, in command of the eighty-ton sloop *Adventure*, bound for St. Eustacia in the West Indies with a cargo of fish and lumber. One afternoon, when he was near his destination, he found that he was being chased by three French privateers, two sloops and a schooner. His first thought was to try to outrun his pursuers. So he ordered the lumber thrown overboard. He then made such speed that he lost sight of the schooner and one of the sloops. But the other sloop kept up the chase, and when he ran into a calm about ten o'clock that night he was captured. With the *Adventure* held as a prize, he was taken to Martinique and cast into prison. After six days in irons he was released and allowed to go to St. Kitts under a flag of truce. He finally got back to Salem, but was soon at sea again, commanding another unlucky sloop, the *Charming Polly*. He evaded French privateers on this voyage, but on his return from the West Indies he ran into a storm. When he reached Salem in his crippled craft he had to report that the cargo, sugar packed in hogsheads, was "terribly damnified." Providence was to visit more trouble upon him after the end of the war.

Farmer Joseph did not live to hear of the treaty, signed in 1763, which brought all of Canada except the isles of St. Pierre and Miquelon under English control. But he did live to hear the bells of Salem ring for the victory of Wolfe over Montcalm at Quebec. He lived to become acquainted with French outcasts from Acadia, a number of whom were brought to Salem after the cruel expulsion. He lived to hear of the brave exploits in the fighting in the West of a young Virginia colonel, George Washington. Farmer Joseph lived to hear of the honors paid in England to an agent sent over by the colony of Pennsylvania, Benjamin Franklin, a native of Massachusetts Bay. Farmer Joseph also lived to hear of the brilliant arguments of James Otis before the Massachusetts Bay superior court against granting to collectors of revenue at ports of entry the right to issue over-all warrants for the search for smuggled goods. Farmer Joseph might have met in Salem the young circuit judge John Adams, who was to say of these arguments of Otis, "They breathed into the American nation the breath of life."

Joseph Hathorne died early in the summer of 1762. His will, dated July 25, 1759, was probated July 15, 1762. His wife Sarah, the executrix, was given a third of his personal estate, the right to live in his dwelling house the rest of her days, his best bed with "all the furniture belonging to it," his silver tankard marked H, and one milch cow. A half of his pew in the First Church went to Daniel, and the other half to his two daughters, Ruth and Sarah, with their mother granted the right to sit with them as long as she lived. A legacy of £200 was left to the children of the deceased son John, but no mention was made of Retire Hathorne, the heir of the deceased son Joseph. All the rest of the estate went in equal parts to William, Daniel, Ruth, and Sarah.

Joseph Hathorne's wealth at the time of his death was valued at more than £1600. The Mill Pond farm, on which the dwelling had been burned or torn down, was estimated at £900. The house on School Lane was listed as worth £500. Incidental possessions divided among the heirs included eight silver spoons, a bell metal skillet, a sifter, a mortar and pestle, a pair of bellows, a toilet table, several feather beds, two guns and a sword, a damask tablecloth, a diaper, a dozen damask napkins, candlesticks and snuffers, a gridiron, a draught chain, a hay fork, and a dung fork.

FREE AND EQUAL

W HILE Captain Daniel Hathorne was in his late teens or early twenties, he lost his heart, says tradition, to a maiden of Boston, Mary Rondel. To him she was as exquisite as her name, far too precious to be addressed in the words making up a mariner's vocabulary. Convinced that he should communicate with the fair one only in the language of romance, he searched the family library, and in a folio which had belonged to his great-grandfather, Major William Hathorne, found what he wanted, the amatory poems of Sir Philip Sidney. The volume, containing the prose *Arcadia* and the sonnet cycle *Astrophel and Stella*, was a few days later dispatched to Boston. As Mary turned the pages of the section in verse, she ran upon one of Astrophel's avowals of affection for Stella and in the margin in Daniel's handwriting, "Lucke upon this as if I my on selfe spacke it!" A page or two farther on came another passionate outburst from Astrophel and in the margin, "Pray, mistris, read this!" Daniel, spelling as well as he knew how, had shown in note after note that the cry of his heart was echoed in Astrophel's eloquence. Mary, ready to return the young man's love, found lines expressing Stella's satisfaction over Astrophel's suit, underscored them, and sent the book back to Salem. But the rejoicing of the shy young lover was brief. Providence entered upon the scene, and cut short the life of Mary Rondel.

If she ever existed and was actually the beloved of Daniel Hathorne, his grief over losing her left no marks upon his character. After his marriage, in his twenty-sixth year, to

Rachel, daughter of the blacksmith Jonathan Phelps, he showed all the conjugal consideration which could be expected from a sea captain. Except for brief interludes at home, he spent his life aboard ship. Many months would pass when Rachel would hear nothing of him, months when she could only hope that he had not gone down at sea or fallen fatally sick in a foreign port. He saw that she was well provided for during his long periods of absence, and he always came back. Regularly every two or three years for a stretch of two decades he got her with child.

On January 1, 1763, the year following his father's death, he sailed for Guadeloupe in the *Mermaid*, a sloop of sixty tons. He was scarcely back in Salem when, on March 13, he lost his first son, his namesake, aged four. Five days later his younger sister, Sarah, was married to Daniel Cheever, a collateral descendant of Cotton Mather's celebrated tutor, Ezekiel Cheever. The other sister, Ruth, had the preceding September married Daniel Ropes, who belonged to a Salem family which was soon to represent great wealth. Four weeks after the burial of his little boy Captain Daniel took over another sloop, the *Polly*, previously commanded by his unlucky kinsman, John Hathorne, and started on a voyage to Lisbon. Immediately upon his return to Salem, on August 26, he and his sisters and his one living brother, Captain William, agreed to a division of the property their father had left. To the sons went the Mill Pond farm, while their sisters got the house and lots on School Lane—now known by most as Town House Street.

All four had already joined relatives in an attempt to establish claim to the nine thousand acres of land their ancestor, Colonel John Hathorne, had purchased in Lincoln County, Maine. The heirs employed a Boston lawyer, James Noble, to represent them, and a merchant of Salem, James Ward, agreed to pay the costs of the litigation. According

to a contract signed March 12, 1765, the heirs if successful
in gaining title to the estate were to retain a third of it and
deed the rest, in equal parts, to Noble and Ward. These
men must have found it impossible to dig up supporting evidence, for the case was never brought to court. The heirs
were left to talk to their children and grandchildren about
how they all had been cheated out of a heritage which might
have meant vast riches. In time some of them were to say
that the land would have been theirs but for a curse pronounced upon Colonel Hathorne by one of the witchcraft
victims.

An agreement relating to this Hathorne claim was filed
in the office of the Essex County clerk a few weeks before
the Stamp Act of 1765 was declared in force in Massachusetts Bay. But if the indenture had been filed after the
Act became legal it would not have been stamped. The
organization known as the Sons of Liberty, having as motto
"Liberty, Property, and No Stamps," was strong in Salem.
How effectual the group was Captain John Hathorne discovered when he got back in January, 1766, from a six
months' voyage in the brig *Bradford*. In the Grenadines
he had been informed of the Act. Ignorant of how violently
it was being opposed, he paid to have his ship's papers
stamped when he deposited them in the Salem customhouse.
On learning what he had done, the Sons of Liberty forced
the custom officials to give up the papers, and then gathered
in a coffee house to discuss what disposal should be made of
them. The assembly unanimously agreed that such "marks
of tyranny were by no means to be lodged in a public
office." One proposed that "together with a jackboot, out
of which the Devil was peeping, they should be fixed to
a long pole and carried thus between heaven and earth, as
fit for neither, near to the Common whipping post." The
final decision was that the "marks of tyranny" should be

burned. So a bonfire was lighted on the Common, the papers were consumed, and "amidst the loud huzzas of the assembly the ashes were scattered in the air." Then, said the Boston *Evening Post*, the people dispersed without doing any harm or making any disturbance, and a number of gentlemen returned to the coffee house to spend the evening drinking "loyal toasts, such as long life and prosperity to His Majesty King George the Third and the destruction of the Stamp Act." Surely among these gentlemen was the forgiven Captain John Hathorne, with his eyes fully open to the true state of feeling in the country. Captain Daniel, who had just returned from a voyage to Newfoundland in the sixty-ton schooner *Salisbury*, was also probably in the company.

A few weeks later the luckless Captain John put out from Salem harbor for the last time. Somewhere in the Atlantic, before the first of April, 1766, Providence led him into a storm which was too much for his craft. He and all his crew went down. His widow and children, left with nothing, were the first to receive aid from the newly organized Marine Society of Salem.

In the meantime Captain Daniel, still sailing the *Salisbury*, was on his way to the island of Ivaca in the Mediterranean. It was the longest voyage he had ever undertaken, and July passed before he got back to Salem with a cargo of Spanish wines. Two or three trips to Monte Christi and other ports in the West Indies followed, and then, in June, 1767, he sailed to Fayal, where he took on another cargo of wines.

On returning to Salem he went far out of his way to call at Liverpool. He probably needed to recruit his crew. Anyway, when he departed from Liverpool he had on board the *Salisbury* a new apprentice seaman, Simon Forrester, a native of Ireland, nineteen years old. The young man was highly intelligent, ingenious, quick, and well bred. He soon showed that before long he himself would be in command of a vessel. Captain Hathorne thought he was being indulgent in his attitude towards the penniless youth. When the *Salisbury* reached Salem, Forrester was not allowed to go to a sailors' lodginghouse but was taken into the Hathorne home. Though he was treated with kindness and accorded a respect not shown the two Negro slaves, he was made to remember that he was practically an indentured servant.

Salemites had never taken to the name Queen's Highway for their long winding east-west avenue. By now most of them were reverting to the original name, but were writing it Main Street. On this thoroughfare, directly opposite the First Church meetinghouse, stood the residence occupied by Captain Daniel's brother, Captain William Hathorne. The older sister, Ruth Ropes, was living also on the north side of Main Street, directly opposite the entrance to Burying Lane, on the lot where the Downing mansion had once stood. The other sister, Sarah Cheever, had bought Ruth's interest in the old Colonel Hathorne mansion, and was to live in it until its destruction in the great fire which flattened much of Salem in 1774. Where Captain Daniel had dwelt since his marriage is unknown. But it is certain that on September 28, 1772, for a consideration of a little more than £466, he came into possession of the house his father-in-law had purchased in 1752. In this squat residence, with the gambrel roof and great center chimney, Captain Daniel was to maintain his family for the rest of his life. He and his brother had by this time sold the Mill Pond farm, upon which the expanding town center of Salem was encroaching.

A second son of Captain Daniel—a namesake of the father, like the first—was four years old when the family moved into their permanent home. A fourth daughter had been born in 1770. And Captain Daniel's wife Rachel had by no means reached her years of fruitlessness.

The Sons of Liberty, many of whom were now minutemen, were growing bolder in struggling towards the goal expressed in their new motto, "No Taxation without Representation." By the time of the Boston Tea Party, December 16, 1773, the wise in Salem knew that the differences between the mother country and the colonies were leading to war. Among the small minority of loyalists in the town were several of Captain Daniel's Gardner, Bowditch, and Putnam cousins, but no Hathornes. Among the leaders of the patriots were Captain Daniel's less affluent Gardner kinsmen, his brothers-in-law Daniel Ropes and Daniel Cheever, and his fatherless young nephew John Hathorne. One of the most outspoken of the younger leaders was an eccentric mariner with whom Captain Daniel was well acquainted. He was Captain Richard Manning, grandson of Jacob Manning, who had seen two of his sisters held up to shame in the Salem meetinghouse in 1681 and had later taken a prominent part in organizing St. Peter's Church. Descendants of another sister of Jacob Manning—bearing the names Hodges, Crowninshield, and Derby—were among the most aggressive of the patriots. Richard Derby, whose recently deceased wife was a great-niece of Jacob Manning, was owner of the ships Captain Daniel was now sailing.

By 1775 British troops were in Massachusetts Bay in numbers. Their immediate objective was to prevent the patriots from assembling arms. When agents reported that pieces of artillery were stored in Salem, Colonel Alexander Leslie, who was stationed in Marblehead with a regiment of regulars, was ordered to demand the cannon. He attempted the mission on a Sunday, February 26, 1775. His movement was observed by the patriot watch, the alarm was spread, men rushed from meeting, and when Colonel Leslie arrived with his troops at the North Bridge he found the Salem side of the river thronged with townspeople, many of whom were armed. Colonel Leslie estimated rightly their determination to bar his passage, and no more than hot words were exchanged before he marched his regiment back to Marblehead. If a single shot had been fired, this incident, to be celebrated as "Leslie's retreat," would be taken as the beginning of the Revolutionary War. Captain Daniel Hathorne was at home at the time, and it can scarcely be doubted that he was among the men gathered at the North Bridge ready to fight.

Two or three weeks later he left for the West Indies, in command of one of Mr. Derby's ships, the schooner *Patty*. He must have known that on his return, or earlier, he would hear of momentous events. Anchored in an undesignated port in June, probably Cap François, he received news—in the form of a letter from Mr. Derby, delivered by a Captain Cleaveland.

The communication, dated May 9, 1775, read: "I suppose you will be glad to hear from home, but things are in such a confused state I know not what to write you. Boston is now blocked up by at least 30,000 men. We have had no action since the 19 of April, which was very bloody. They, the regulars, came out in the night, silently up Cambridge River, and got almost to Concord before day, so that the country had a very short time to get out. Had we had one hour longer not a soul of those bloodthirsty creatures would have reached Boston. However, they got a dire drubbing, so that they have not played the Yankee tune since. We have lost a number of men, but we have killed, taken, and rendered justice, I believe, at least eight to one, and I believe such a spirit never was, everybody striving to excel. We have no Tories, save what is now shut up in Boston or gone off. There hath not been as yet any stopping of the trade, so I would have you get a load of molasses as good and cheap and as quick as you can and proceed home. If you have not sold, and the markets are bad where you are, you have liberty to proceed any other ways, either to the Mole, Jamaica, or to make a fresh bottom, or anything else you may think likely to help the voyage, but always to keep your money in your hands." The letter was subscribed, "Your friend and employer, Richard Derby."

To get into Salem harbor on his return Captain Daniel had to evade the British frigates lurking off the New England shore. His procedure was to keep to the open ocean until he was near the coast of Maine and then sail southwestward. He followed this course without mishap, and the hour finally came when he saw the *Patty*, loaded with barrels of molasses, tied up at the Derby wharf.

The Hathorne daughters—Rachel, already nineteen, Sarah, twelve, Eunice, nine, and Judith, five—had no doubt heard that the *Patty* was in and were at the wharf to greet their father and announce the coming of another brother. The child was born May 19, exactly one month after the fight described in Mr. Derby's letter, the Battle of Lexington and Concord. The christening rites had been administered—in the old First Church, of which Daniel alone among the Hathorne men of his generation was a member. The boy bore the name the Hathornes preferred above all others, the name Nathaniel. He was to be the father of the romancer.

During the year preceding the Declaration of Independence there was still, in Mr. Derby's words, "no stopping of the trade." On the contrary, with the ports of Boston and New York blockaded, commerce in Salem began to mount. The more sagacious among the merchants, remembering the profits reaped from privateering in the French and Indian War, were quick to see that Providence was dangling before them the opportunity to help the cause of the patriots and at the same time enrich themselves. They began to envision a great fleet of privateers manned by trained mariners.

More perhaps than any other Salem shipmaster, Captain Daniel Hathorne, forty-five years of age, set the pattern which the privateersmen were to follow. His glorious cruise during the latter half of 1776 on the *True American*, with ten guns and eighty men, was described in verse by his anonymous surgeon, a bad poet but an authentic reporter. The surgeon's ballad, known as "Bold Hathorne," was soon a favorite among sailors on Yankee ships. It follows, in the version which was to be printed in 1842 in Rufus Griswold's *Poets and Poetry of America*.

> The twenty-second of August,
>   Before the close of day,
> All hands aboard our privateer,
>   We got her under weigh;
> We kept the Eastern shore along
>   For fifty leagues or more,
> Then our departure took for sea,
>   From the isle Mohegan shore.
>
> Bold Hathorne was commander,
>   A man of real worth,
> Old England's cruel tyranny
>   Induced him to go forth;
> She, with relentless fury,
>   Was plundering all our coast,
> And thought, because her strength was great,
>   Our glorious cause was lost.

Yet boast not, haughty Briton,
　Of power and dignity,
Of all your conquering armies,
　Your matchless strength at sea,
Since, taught by numerous instances,
　Americans can fight,
With valor can equip their stand,
　Your armies put to flight.

Now farewell, fair America,
　Farewell our friends and wives;
We trust in Heaven's peculiar care
　For to protect their lives,
To prosper our intended cruise
　Upon the raging main,
And to preserve our dearest friends,
　Till we return again.

The wind it being leading,
　It bore us on our way,
As far unto the southward
　As the Gulf of Florida,
Where we observed a British ship
　Returning from the main;
We gave her two bow chasers,
And she return'd the same.

We hauled up our courses,
　And so prepared for fight;
The contest held four glasses,
　Until the dusk of night;
Then having sprung our mainmast,
　And had so large a sea,
We dropped astern and left our chase,
　Till the returning day.

Next morn we fished our mainmast,
  The ship still being nigh,
All hands made for engaging,
  Our luck once more to try;
But wind and sea being boisterous,
  Our cannon would not bear,
We thought it quite imprudent,
  And so we left her there.

We cruised to the eastward,
  Near the coast of Portugale;
In longitude of twenty-seven
  We saw a lofty sail;
We gave her chase, and soon we saw
  She was a British scow,
Standing for fair America
  With troops for General Howe.

Our captain did inspect her
  With glasses, and he said,
"My boys, she means to fight us,
  But be you not afraid;
All hands now beat to quarters,
  See everything is clear,
We'll give her a broadside, my boys,
  As soon as she comes near."

She was prepared with nettings,
  And had her men secured,
She bore directly for us,
  And put us close on board,
When cannon roared like thunder,
  And muskets fired amain,
But soon we were alongside,
  And grappled to her chain.

And now the scene it altered,
  The cannon ceased to roar,
We fought with swords and boarding-pikes,
  One glass or something more;
The British pride and glory
  No longer dared to stay,
But cut our Yankee grapplings,
  And quickly bore away.

Our case was not so desperate,
  As plainly might appear;
Yet sudden death did enter
  On board our privateer.
Mahoney, Crew, and Clemmons,
  The valiant and the brave,
Fell glorious in the contest,
  And met a watery grave.

Ten other men were wounded
  Among our warlike crew,
With them our noble captain,
  To whom all praise is due;
To him and all our officers,
  Let's give a hearty cheer:
"Success to fair America,
  And our good privateer!"

If the balladist had continued his account of the cruise, he would have said that the noble captain who deserved all praise quickly recovered from his wound, made by a musket ball which grazed his head, and that by the time he got back to Salem, on November 10, he had taken four or five prizes. He had shown the young privateersmen what persistence and bravery could accomplish.

Among the many eager to follow in his steps was his protégé, Simon Forrester. The ambitious Irishman, still in his twenties, had learned so thoroughly Captain Daniel's lessons that he himself for several years had been a shipmaster. He hated Britain in true Irish fashion, and he felt no fear at the prospect of grappling and boarding an English vessel at sea. But always foremost in his mind was the value of the prizes he might take and how great in pounds and shillings would be his reward. In buying cargoes and selling them at great profit he was a genius. Captain Daniel should have known that young Forrester got what he wanted on his own terms.

That he desired the oldest of the Hathorne daughters, Rachel, must have been long evident. Still, when he carried her to Danvers and made her his wife there was great resentment in the Hathorne household. The marriage took place on December 7, four weeks after Captain Daniel returned from his celebrated 1776 cruise. His satisfaction over his remarkable achievement was forgotten in his humiliation over the marriage. Young Forrester, though himself a Protestant, had sprung from the despised Roman Catholic Irish. The Hathornes had looked upon him as only a little better than a servant. Deep was the wound to the Hathorne pride. But it was to be healed, to a great degree, when Simon Forrester's riches began to mount.

Captain Daniel was not the kind to stay at home and nurse his indignation. Soon after Rachel's marriage he was again at sea on the *True American,* taking more prizes. Then he was commissioned to command the *Sturdy Beggar,* which carried eight guns and sixty men. While engaged on this ship he was entrusted with the sale in foreign ports of at least two vessels which his employer wished to replace, the *Cromwell* and the *Polly.*

On each of his returns he saw a different Salem. As a result of privateering, a town was being transformed into a city. Plants for manufacturing muskets and cannon were bedlams of activity. Blacksmiths and anchor makers were pounding red hot iron from dawn to dark. The shipbuilding yards, where hundreds were employed, were noisy with the sawing of wood, the joining, the hammering of nails, and the caulking with oakum. Trim ships were leaving the harbor, and battered ships were coming in. The wharves and streets were thronged with drunken sailors, shouting and singing, perhaps making sport of landlubbers who had come from the interior with cartloads of lumber only to find themselves impressed for service on privateers. In the countingrooms were the busy merchants, making money too rapidly to bother about the distinction between privateering and piracy. Great fortunes were being founded, among them the fortune of Captain Daniel's son-in-law, Simon Forrester. More than a hundred and fifty ships, equipped with more than two thousand guns and manned by several times that many sailors, were sent out from Salem during the war.

Essex County knew great prosperity, especially after the scene of the fighting was shifted from New England. But the people were by no means free of the trials and suffering which accompany warfare. With much money in circulation, prices rose to such heights that simple, rigidly honest privateersmen like Captain Daniel found it very hard to make ends meet. The toll of the dead, wounded, and captured on the privateering cruises was high. Captain Daniel's brother-in-law Daniel Ropes, after heroic achievement in an encounter at sea, died a prisoner in Halifax. A grandson of the first Benjamin Hathorne, in service on the privateer *Chase*, was captured and held on a prison ship in the harbor of Charleston, South Carolina, until he escaped, at great risk, by swimming a prodigious distance. Among the young men of Salem who endured for at least five years the hardships of fighting on land was a son of Captain Daniel's brother William, another Nathaniel. According to the service papers of this soldier, he was possessed of the dark complexion, dark hair, and blue eyes which marked the Hathornes.

It was sometime during the period of the Revolution, or shortly afterwards, that Captain Daniel had himself painted. The portrait, done by an unknown artist, is a miniature, showing only the head. The eyes are the Hathorne blue, but there is little else in the picture suggestive of the physical appearance of the Captain's descendants. The round fat smooth ruddy face, with a double chin, is set directly upon sloping shoulders. The nose is big. The painter was evidently most impressed by his subject's stoutness and genial mien. Yet the portrait reveals that Captain Daniel might have been handsome when, at the time he was supposedly in love with Mary Rondel, he could take a landsman's exercise and had not exposed his skin too much to the tropical sun. The face also shows determination and courage. One looking at it can easily believe the seaman who said of the Captain, "He's the sternest man that ever walked a deck!"

The Captain was beginning his fifty-third year when, on September 3, 1783, the signing of the Treaty of Paris formally ended the Revolution. He believed in the ideals for which the war had been fought as staunchly as his great-grandfather, Major William Hathorne, had believed in the creed of the Puritans. At home between privateering cruises he had drilled into the minds of his two little sons a hatred for British Toryism and a reverence for the principles enunciated in the Declaration of Independence.

For six years following the Revolution, Daniel Hathorne remained a shipmaster, sailing such vessels as he had commanded when a privateersman. But there were no guns to keep in trim, and the scores of fighting seamen had been re-

duced to normal crews. The merchants, finding themselves
in possession of a great fleet of ships heavy enough to venture into the most distant seas, were thinking of new markets
—in Zanzibar, India, Ceylon, China, Sumatra, Java, and the
Philippines. Captain Daniel, getting old, let younger mariners experience the excitement of rounding the Cape of
Good Hope. He stuck to trade routes with which he was
familiar. In command of the *Mary Ann* between 1785 and
1789, he made voyages to Guadeloupe, Turks Island, Cap
François, and other ports in the West Indies. Off the shore
of Martinique, on March 5, 1789, he saw the *Mary Ann* go
down in a gale. Always a lucky mariner, he had been rescued
just in time. His return to Salem on a ship commanded by
another captain was, it appears, his final voyage.

As a retired man, he at last had the opportunity to get
well acquainted with his children. The oldest, Rachel, Mrs.
Simon Forrester, with five or six children of her own, lived
in a mansion which faced the South River and looked directly upon the Forrester and Derby wharves. She was learning to adjust herself to the riches which her husband was
fast accumulating, but she was still a loyal Hathorne. The
second daughter, Sarah, had been since 1786 a discontented
childless widow, forced to return to her father's roof after a
marriage which lasted only a year or two. The husband had
been a mariner, John Crowninshield, a great-grandson of
the youngest sister of Jacob Manning, a nephew of the
founder of the mighty Crowninshield fortune, and a first
cousin of the two Crowninshield brothers who were to be
appointed to serve in turn under Jefferson and Madison as
Secretary of the Navy. John Crowninshield died at the age
of twenty-five, from a fever probably contracted in a foreign port. His debts had far exceeded his assets. Captain
Daniel's third daughter, Eunice, who apparently was never
taught to write her own name, was to remain single. The

fourth daughter, Judith, was married in 1792 to George Archer, a sea captain, who belonged to a family of merchants. Ruth, born in 1778, the fifth daughter and the youngest of the seven children, was, like Eunice, to be an old maid. The older of the two boys, Daniel, was already at sea and Nathaniel—seven years his junior—was soon to begin his apprenticeship before the mast.

For Captain Daniel there was little joy in retirement. Life during the seven years allotted to him after his final voyage was an ordeal to endure. His ways were the rough ways of the sea, and he had no patience with landsmen's habits. Whatever manners he had learned in his boyhood he had long ago forgotten. When the fat dyspeptic man ventured abroad, usually on the water front, no one remembered that he was a hero of the Revolution, sung about in the ballad "Bold Hathorne." In his tattered hat, soiled linen, and shapeless coat he was the living image—says Salem tradition—of "a back country gran'f'er." It is no wonder that the wealthy queer old bachelor, Captain Richard Manning, who lived on Main Street a little to the east of the Hathornes' lane, invariably greeted the Captain with, "Good day, Goodman Hathorne."

Sometimes, wobbling at a slow pace, knocking at the pathway with his heavy cane, the Captain went into the heart of the town and beyond. On such an excursion he could hardly avoid seeing kinsfolk and others in some way connected with the Hathornes. On Main Street, facing the entrance to his lane, lived the Crowninshield family into which his daughter Sarah, with great unhappiness to herself, had married. Her sister-in-law, Hannah Crowninshield, kept a boardinghouse for seamen. As Captain Daniel followed Main Street westward, walking on the north side, he crossed the lane leading to the Common and then came to the house where his widowed sister, Ruth Ropes, had brought up two worthy sons. One of them, Joseph Ropes, was to be the most noted of all American privateersmen in the War of 1812 and wreak vengeance on the British for taking the life of his father. Continuing on Main Street, Captain Daniel at some turn might have run into the town drunkard, his first cousin Habakkuk Bowditch. The Captain could never have dreamed that this ignoble kinsman's son Nathaniel, just two years older than his own Nathaniel, would one day rank among the great American mathematicians.

A few paces beyond the lane which extended northward to St. Peter's Church and the Essex County prison, Captain Daniel came to his brother's house. Captain William was a feeble man in his late seventies, and within very few years was to rest beside his grandfather, Colonel John Hathorne, at the Burying Point. His most prosperous son, Joseph, a goldsmith and silversmith, had only recently died, leaving three small children, one of whom, also named Joseph, was to grow up and be a saddler, unrecognized as a kinsman by the romancer. William's youngest sons, John Touzell and Nathaniel, the latter of whom had fought under Washington, were mariners, and his daughter Sarah was married to Joseph Endecott, a Danvers farmer, great-grandson of Governor John Endecott.

To reach the house where lived the most interesting of his brother William's children, the oldest daughter, Captain Daniel had to walk quite a distance westward, well past the busy junction with Town House Street and the stretch of Main Street which had been paved. The real name of this daughter was Mary, but Salem knew her as Molly Hathorne. She was a huckster, a very shrewd one, and was looked upon as more man than woman. It was said that she hoarded every penny she made, but not even discerning Captain Daniel could have believed that at her death, in 1802, her savings would be appraised at $40,000. She was of course an old maid: her interest in men had always been limited to their power to buy or sell. She shared a house with her married but childless brother William, who was her partner in business. The house stood on the south side of Main Street, and back of it was the land which had made up the Mill Pond farm.

Keeping to the south side of Main Street on his return home, Captain Hathorne came within ten or twelve minutes to the entrance of the large cloth shop owned by his nephew John, by far the most prominent Hathorne of the time. This scion of the family, fatherless since infancy, had been for a good many years Colonel Hathorne, commander of the Salem unit of the militia of the state of Massachusetts. Though an enthusiastic worker for the patriot cause during the Revolution, he had seen no fighting; and he was to be too old for active service during the War of 1812. His destiny was to train other men to fight. But most of his time was given to his business. While his wealth was far from approaching that of his cousin Rachel's husband Simon Forrester, he was by no means poor. Even the powerful Crowninshields and Derbys recognized him as a fellow merchant, and within a few years he was to be able to retire as a gentleman farmer. He was an active politician, a disciple of Thomas Jefferson, and often voiced his democratic views in public speeches. Included in his library of several hundred volumes were Boccacio, Milton, Pope, *Pamela, Cecilia,* the Earl of Chesterfield's letters, Thompson's *Seasons,* Hutchinson's historical volumes, Whitefield's sermons, the poems of the Negro slave girl Phillis Wheatley, Young's *Night Thoughts,* and the writings of Thomas Paine. His wife, born Susannah Herbert, had borne him ten children, and she was to keep on until there were fourteen. Colonel John's sister was married to Captain Samuel Ingersoll and lived on the water front in the eastern quarter of Salem in the old Turner home, one day to be known as the House of the Seven Gables. With her lived her mother, born a Touzell. This aged sister-in-law of Captain Daniel, widowed for forty years, had a remarkable memory and was frequently consulted on data relating to the past by Salem's ubiquitous antiquarian and gossip, the Reverend William Bentley. Colonel John and his sister, brought up by the Touzells, must have found their blunt dowdy uncle Daniel an oddity. Certainly to their genteel ways the stern old sea captain was a stranger.

After leaving Colonel John's shop he was soon at Salem's heart, the crossing of Main Street and Town House Street. Perhaps he turned south on the latter, and walked to the lot on which the house in which he was reared had stood. It had projected out into the street, but the residence erected to replace it was set back, in line with the houses on the right and left. In one of them, or in the near vicinity, lived Captain Daniel's sister Sarah Cheever, none of whose children was to rise above the ranks of the ordinary.

If the Captain retraced his steps back to Main Street and turned homeward, still walking on the south side, he was able to reach out and touch with his cane the town pump and then the north wall of the First Church meetinghouse, where every Lord's day he worshiped in the pew he had inherited from his father. If the stout old stroller was not already fagged out, he probably made detours on his way home and paid his respects to other Hathorne kindred in Salem. Some of these cousins were the descendants of his uncle, Captain Benjamin, and numbered also among their relatives the rich Derbys. Several descendants of the luckless Captain John Hathorne were still in Salem. Captain Daniel, in spite of his belief in the principle that all men are free and equal, could not have taken pride in a good many of the Hathornes he knew. Some were pretty low in the social scale. The clergyman of St. Peter's who baptized one, a girl, wrote opposite her name in the parish register, "Illegitimate, I suppose."

Sleeping, eating too much, ordering his wife and daughters about as if they were apprentice seamen, reading the Salem *Gazette,* voting against the Federalists, taking his walks, and going down to the wharves to smoke his pipe and gaze seaward—such, said a contemporary, were the activities which filled Captain Daniel's last days. For two centuries his paternal forebears in Berkshire and in Salem had been careful to make wills. Though he broke the tradition, he thought seriously about the place where he wished his bones to lie. No doubt more than one unfilled tomb belonging to an extinct family had been appropriated in Salem and nothing had been said. But when Captain Daniel openly turned covetous eyes towards Governor Bradstreet's tomb at the Burying Point, he set his hopes too high and brought upon himself an avalanche of hard criticism. Months before his death, which came April 18, 1796, he knew that since he was a poor man he would have to be content with an ordinary grave. His body was interred in the Hathorne plot at the Burying Point, where paralleling his final resting place came in succession the graves of his brother John, his grandfather Colonel John, and his brother Captain William.

FROM FORECASTLE TO CABIN

CAPTAIN Jacob Crowninshield—who was to represent eastern Massachusetts in the national Congress and to decline, on account of ill health, an invitation to serve in Jefferson's cabinet as Secretary of the Navy—spent several weeks of the summer of 1795 at Port Louis in the Isle of France. While there he disposed of the vessel in which he had left Salem the preceding December and bought a newer and heavier craft, the *America*. Within five months he had her at Calcutta, loaded with rice, coffee, bales of India textiles, and an elephant, the first ever purchased to be transported to the New World. His chief mate, to whom he entrusted the keeping of the ship's log, was Nathaniel Hathorne, Captain Daniel's younger son.

While Captain Crowninshield was twenty-four, Mate Hathorne was only twenty. Those who knew him best were to say that he was slender, athletic, silent but severe, and somewhat melancholy. A miniature, done by an unidentified artist, hints that the severity he manifested was a mask for a character innately visionary. Though the portrait shows that he resembled his father, there is nothing in the face which suggests either Captain Daniel's sternness or grossness.

The youth's maternal ancestors had been content to be numbered among the people. His mother's father, the blacksmith Jonathan Phelps, was in all likelihood the grandson of one of the three Phelpses, probably brothers, who were settled in Essex County by the middle of the seventeenth century. The most respected of the three was Christopher

Phelps, a Salem constable for the year 1683. He was married to an Elizabeth Sharp and had sons who reached maturity. The second of the supposed brothers was Nicholas Phelps, described by a contemporary as "a weak man and one whose back is crooked." Still the Quakers, whose faith he adopted, chose him to accompany another convert, Samuel Shattuck, to London to implore Charles II to stop the persecutions they were suffering. It is certain that this Nicholas and the most unworthy of the pioneer Phelpses, named Henry, migrated to New England on the same ship. Sailing with them was the woman, named Hannah, who married Nicholas and bore his heirs. But before, and after, becoming his wife, she showed that Henry was the man she desired. As much as Major Hathorne despised her husband because of his Quaker faith, he went to great trouble to prevent her and Henry from being attentive to one another. She retaliated by openly criticizing church and state, and was sentenced to suffer thirty stripes or pay a fine. Someone with sufficient money, perhaps her husband, saved her from the whipping post. Each time Henry was brought to court on a charge of "uncleanness" with her he was acquitted. But he failed to win the clemency of the magistrates when he was accused of beating brutally one of his young sons. That the boy was committed to the custody of his "uncle Batter" indicates that Henry Phelps's wife might have been a sister of Edmond Batter, a figure of importance in seventeenth-century Salem. Though there seems to be no positive evidence of kinship between these Essex County Phelpses and the illustrious Phelpses who settled in the Connecticut valley, both groups probably sprang from a common ancestor. Mate Hathorne could well be proud of at least one known kinsman on his mother's side, her brother Captain Henry Phelps, a Salem shipmaster who figured prominently in opening up trade with the East Indies.

Mate Hathorne could recall the excitement in Salem—the ringing of bells, the firing of salutes, the animated talk, and the running to and fro in the streets—on that day in 1783 when Captain John Derby sailed in on the *Astraea* bringing news of the signing in Paris of the treaty which made the United States of America a recognized sovereign nation. Nathaniel was then eight.

He was ten when an important visitor, the Reverend William Hazlitt, spent part of a summer in Salem. Because Mr. Hazlitt came from England and preached a shocking doctrine, Unitarianism, Salem called him a "stranger." He had his wife and children with him, and as soon as they were settled his son John, already a professional painter though only eighteen, advertised in the *Gazette* for sitters for portraits. It is possible that he was the artist who executed the miniature of Captain Daniel Hathorne. The youngest of Mr. Hazlitt's children was William—to be ranked among the great English essayists. Nathaniel must have remembered the two boys and the excitement with which his elders argued over Mr. Hazlitt's attacks on the doctrine of the Trinity. One Salem congregation, Dr. William Bentley's East Church, was by 1795 definitely turning towards Unitarianism, but the First Church, in which Nathaniel had been baptized, was to remain rigidly conservative for another thirty years.

The boy was fourteen when, in 1789, President Washington while on a tour of New England spent an afternoon and night in Salem. If Nathaniel was not already before the mast at this time, he was surely in the shouting crowd which greeted the celebrated visitor as he rode into Town House Square on his white charger. Mate Hathorne perhaps remembered how the moderator of the town's selectmen, a Quaker, stood on the receiving platform and, without removing his hat, shook the President's hand and said, "Friend Washington, we are glad to see thee, and in behalf of the inhabitants I bid thee a hearty welcome to Salem." In the multitude which pressed towards the platform to gaze at the President and listen to the speeches and the singing of an ode which had been written for the occasion were many Hathornes. But few of them were high enough in the social scale to be admitted to the Assembly Rooms that night for the grand ball given in honor of the esteemed guest, who appeared for the function attired in black velvet, with his hair powdered. Nathaniel's only kinswomen who might have danced with the President were Madam Rachel Forrester and Madam Susannah Hathorne, wife of Colonel John.

At a Salem school, possibly Master Belcher Noyes's, Mate Hathorne had learned to figure accounts with absolute accuracy and to record them in a bold clear hand. He had been taught how to spell and how to express his ideas without too many slips in grammar. But he had evidently had few lessons in the use of capital letters. At school or elsewhere he had been introduced to books. Occasionally in entering in a log a ship's position and the state of the weather he would add reflections echoing his reading. Sometimes he attempted to cast his comment into verse.

He was tired of India and homesick for Salem when the *America* set sail from Calcutta on December 3, 1795. That evening he wrote in the log, "Let this auspicious day be ever sacred!"

He was happy at the speed the new ship made after she got out of the Indian Ocean. On Wednesday, February 17, 1796, she was at St. Helena, taking on casks of fresh water, fish, pumpkins, cabbages, greens for the elephant, and a container of red paint. That night Nathaniel inserted in the log, "We have been informed since we arrived here that the ship *John* of Salem sailed from this place 4 Days ago. I think we have made our Passage 23 days Shorter than theirs was and at that rate we shall get in Salem before they Do." Two days later, at sea, he recorded the finding of a stowaway who had boarded the ship at St. Helena, and then wrote, "I wish there was a little more wind, for I want to get Home as soon as the ship *John* of Salem. Saw great Plenty of Flying Fish." On February 24 the *America* was in the Bay of Ascension, and the crew went ashore to catch turtles. Mate Hathorne wrote in the log, "The Island of Ascension has every Appearance of its being formerly a Volcano, the rocks appearing to be burnt and are so rocky that they may be broken to pieces by the hand of any Person." In mid-ocean on March 10 he wrote, "This Night we saw the North Star, which I think is a great pleasure to a homeward Bound Mariner after a Long Voyage to India."

Mate Hathorne's dream of reaching Salem in advance of the *John* was shattered when Captain Crowninshield decided to call at New York, where he felt that he would have a better chance of selling the elephant than at any New England port. The *America* passed Sandy Hook April 10, just eight days before the death of Captain Daniel Hathorne. Nathaniel, it appears, did not get home until autumn was beginning.

The delay was probably due to the difficulty Captain Crowninshield had in finding a buyer for the elephant. Finally the animal was disposed of, for $10,000. Before Mate Hathorne set out on another voyage to the East Indies he had the opportunity of seeing on exhibition in his home town the beast which had been his companion on the *America* for more than five months. An ostrich had already been shown in Salem, and in the immediate years to come the curious of the town were to pay to see in turn a moose, a walrus, a camel, a lion, a leopard, and "a wonder of natural history, a pygarg from Russia, having the likeness of a camel, bear, mule, goat, and common bullock, and spoken of in the Bible, Deuteronomy, Chapter XIV." On July 4, 1806, Salem was to witness a combat between a zebu brought from China and a Spanish bull. In transporting the elephant Captain Crowninshield and Mate Hathorne advanced an amusement which was rapidly becoming popular.

Anxiety over the state of his father's health might have been a reason for Nathaniel's impatience to get home from the first of his voyages to the East Indies. But there was a stronger reason. Directly back of the Hathorne house, in a clapboard residence recently built, lived Richard Manning, a blacksmith, who had come from Ipswich. Historians were almost invariably to confuse him with Captain Richard Manning, Salem's wealthy aristocratic queer old bachelor. The two men were second cousins and had the same name. But in all other respects they were far apart. Among the older of the blacksmith's nine children was Elizabeth Clarke, a girl of remarkable beauty, now in her sixteenth year. She and Mate Hathorne were in love.

One hundred and fifteen years had passed since that lecture day in 1681 when two Manning sisters sat on repentance stools in the Salem meetinghouse wearing on their caps papers marked INCEST. Descendants of the brother charged of being their partner in crime, Captain Nicholas Manning, were now respected citizens of New York, Boston, and other places. Warwick and Edward Palfray, descendants of one of the accused women, were soon to begin careers as editors, respectively, of the *Essex Register* and the Salem *Advertiser*. Among the descendants of Sarah

Manning, the young sister of the notorious trio, were the richest and most powerful of the Hodgeses, Lamberts, Derbys, and Crowninshields, including Captain Jacob. One of the younger brothers of the disgraced family was Jacob Manning, five of whose grandchildren—related to the Lamberts through their mother—were living together in east Salem, aged bachelor and spinster hoarders of wealth, including Captain Richard Manning. Jacob's twin brother, Thomas Manning, had married Mary Giddings of Ipswich. Among her father's descendants were to be Joshua Reed Giddings, the celebrated antislavery orator, and the two great lawyers Joseph Hodges Choate and Rufus Choate. Thomas Manning had prospered as an Ipswich gunsmith and blacksmith. In 1692 he forged manacles for those whom the first Colonel John Hathorne committed to the Ipswich prison on charges of witchcraft. Thomas Manning was Elizabeth Clarke's great-grandfather.

His two sons who had issue were, though twins, pronounced opposites in character. One, Dr. Joseph Manning, who married into the prominent Boardman family, was a graduate of Harvard College, class of 1725, and for many years a practicing physician in Ipswich. The other, John Manning, Elizabeth Clarke's grandfather, was a yeoman of little property who signed documents with his mark. He was married first to Jane Bradstreet, then to Elizabeth Wallis, and finally to Ruth Potter, mother of six of his twelve children.

The youngest was the blacksmith Richard Manning, born in 1755. At the age of twenty-one he married Miriam Lord, seven years his senior. Her father's family had been in Essex County since the founding years, and among her maternal ancestors were Waites, Days, and Clarkes. It was early in the 1790's, after the birth of his youngest child, that blacksmith Richard moved with his family to Salem. By 1796 he was buying land in Raymond township in Maine; and he and his oldest son, William, were thinking of establishing a large livery stable and furnishing regular stage-coach service between Boston and Salem.

Still he was a blacksmith, unrecognized as a kinsman by such relatives as the proud cosmopolitan Derbys and Crown-inshields. Even the old maid and bachelor Mannings, who lived in his neighborhood, probably regarded him as no more than an humble acquaintance who happened to have their name. It is likely that he and his wife were addressed by Captain Richard with the titles "Goodman" and "Goody." But blacksmith Richard was a man of alert mind. There can be little doubt that he knew who in Essex County shared his Manning blood.

That he was ignorant of the public shame two of his great-aunts suffered in 1681 is inconceivable. His own grand-father, at that time on the point of marriage, was an on-the-scene witness of the drama from the beginning to the end. Blacksmith Richard had doubtless heard the story told many times, and had passed it on to his children as a dark family secret.

He must have marveled at the Providence which had brought about a mutual love between one of his daughters and a scion of the Hathornes. For he could not have been unaware of what Major Hathorne and his son the Colonel represented in seventeenth-century Massachusetts Bay. But blacksmith Richard was a practical person living in the present, mindful mainly of property. He gave his blessing to the contemplated union. He saw in Mate Hathorne a mariner of steady habits and ambition. The young man was, moreover, a brother-in-law of the great merchant and shipowner Simon Forrester, now counted among the fore-most capitalists in America.

But Nathaniel could not think of assuming the responsibilities of marriage before becoming a captain. Eager to gain the necessary experience, he set out on December 7, 1796, for a return to the East Indies, as chief mate on the *Perseverance*, Captain Richard Wheatland the master and Simon Forrester the owner. Almost five months passed before the vessel reached Batavia, the first port of call. There had been calms. And there had been days of storms and raging seas, when Nathaniel wrote in his private log such jingles as

> In midst of all these dire alarms
> I think, dear Betsy, on thy charms.

After a week in Batavia harbor the *Perseverance* went on to Manila, which had been opened to American trade the year before by Captain Henry Prince of the ship *Astraea*. Aboard this vessel as supercargo, making observations and teaching navigation to each member of the crew, had been the mathematician Nathaniel Bowditch, Mate Hathorne's second cousin. The *Perseverance*, after extended calls at Canton and Whampoa, started on the voyage home November 29, 1797, passed Java Head December 19, sighted the Cape of Good Hope February 7, left Ascension February 28, and sighted the New Jersey shore April 8. After a stay of a fortnight in New York, the ship got to Salem April 28, bringing 158,000 pounds of tea to Mr. Forrester, who was obliged to pay a duty of $19,000. After a separation of almost a year and a half Nathaniel was once more holding hands with beautiful gray-eyed and raven-haired "dear Betsy."

The circumstances under which he became a captain and thus got himself ready for marriage are unknown, for his activities from the spring of 1798 until the summer of 1801 appear to have been unrecorded. The mariners serving in the East Indies trade during this three-year period were carefully listed. Since his name was not included, the probability is that he spent the time voyaging to the West Indies or the Azores.

His brother-in-law, Captain George Archer, died at sea on the passage from Hamburg in December, 1799, leaving a widow and four small children. A cousin and namesake, the Nathaniel Hathorne who fought in the Revolution, died on the schooner *Eliza* in the harbor of Havana early in 1801. Was the Nathaniel still living also some day to sail from Salem and never return? Or was he to have the good luck his father, Captain Daniel, had enjoyed? In the loneliness of the ocean the young man, thinking of Betsy, must have pondered these questions hundreds of times.

If he was often in Salem during the three years when his movements are unknown, he saw the town's loyalty to the federal government put to the test. It was the period when the famous *Essex*, a thirty-two-gun frigate, was planned, built in a local shipyard, paid for by voluntary contribution, and presented to the United States navy. Heading the list of donors, with $10,000, was Elias Hasket Derby, a Manning relation. Captain Richard Manning, to the surprise of those who knew the old bachelor's miserliness, gave $1,000. The only Hathorne represented among the donors was Colonel John, who gave $200. When an occasion demanded oratory instead of money the Colonel was not wont to trail so far behind. At a great memorial meeting for Washington held in Salem early in 1800 he was a chief speaker.

Finally, on August 2, 1801, Nathaniel Hathorne, designated Captain in the register, was married to Elizabeth Clarke Manning. The couple made their home in the northwest second-floor room of the Hathorne house. The furniture—consisting of a canopied bed with curtains and valances, a secretary, a bureau, a card table, two or three small tables, a looking glass, and chairs—was their own. Theirs too were the andirons, shovel, tongs, bellows, lamp stand, table and bed linen, and twenty dollars' worth of china bowls and dishes. Prominent somewhere in the room, probably on the bureau, were an India punch bowl and pitcher which Nathaniel had had made in Calcutta. One of the small tables was reserved for his pipes, in which he took great pleasure. The tobacco he bought, measured by the yard, was also used for chewing.

If the bride and groom observed a custom which was then popular in Salem, they appeared in their wedding finery at meeting in the groom's church—the conservative First Church—the Lord's day following their marriage. The historic old congregation now had an organ, and the hymns were sung in tune. But the theology preached by the minister, the Reverend John Prince, differed little from that which the Reverend Francis Higginson had taught in a mud-and-log hut on the same site in 1629. Since coming to Salem, Betsy had joined her parents in worshiping at the East Church and was accustomed to Dr. Bentley's radicalism. But in taking Nathaniel as her husband she took also his creed. Under the Reverend Mr. Prince's guidance, she was soon to be an old-fashioned Congregationalist, qualified to acquaint her children with the doctrines of original sin, total depravity, divine election, and a Providence working wonders.

The young couple's honeymoon could not have been gay. Whenever the bride ventured from her room she ran into her mother-in-law, or a sister-in-law, or her brother-in-law Daniel. The mistress of the house, Captain Daniel's widow, had the main chamber all to herself. In summer at her window and in winter at her fireside, it was said, she spent her time waiting for her sons to come home from the sea, as Salem mothers had waited for a century and a half.

Daniel, a bachelor of thirty-three without ambition, had the room he had formerly shared with Nathaniel. He was often in Salem, for the small vessels he commanded rarely ventured farther than Virginia or the West Indies or the Azores. The three daughters left at home were probably crowded into a single chamber. Sarah, nearing forty, the childless widow of John Crowninshield, passed her days lamenting her loneliness and fretting at the Providence which had denied her the fulfillment of marriage. Eunice, three years her junior, had been from girlhood passive and listless. Though Ruth, the youngest, was only twenty-three, she was homely and had doubtless given up hope of ever having a suitor.

The two sisters who lived in homes of their own, Rachel Forrester and Judith Archer, were frequent visitors. The latter was not only a mourning widow of less than two years but also a mourning mother. She had recently buried at the Burying Point her five-year-old daughter Judith. Madam Forrester, still beautiful after the strain of bearing many children, was a woman of tenderness and remarkable gentility. In looking at her portrait one is impressed most by her ladylike mien. But sorrow seems to haunt her face. If the Salem gossip recorded by the diarist Dr. Bentley may be trusted, her husband was often in his cups, and when in such a state was abusive and cruel. It is certain that at the time of her brother Nathaniel's marriage she was greatly concerned over the unbalanced character of one of her sons, Simon junior. It was probably Madam Forrester who saw that Nathaniel's and Betsy's room was comfortably and attractively fitted up.

The newly married pair had four months together. Then, early in December, the time when Salem mariners usually set out for the East Indies, Captain Nathaniel took over command of Elias Hasket Derby's *Astraea* and sailed for Sumatra and Java. Six years before this, Nathaniel Bowditch had made his celebrated voyage of observation on the same vessel. Again the trip required about a year and a half. When in the spring of 1803 the *Astraea* got back to Salem, bearing a heavy cargo of pepper and coffee, Captain Nathaniel discovered that he was the father of a one-year-old daughter.

She was Elizabeth Manning Hathorne, born exactly seven months and five days after the marriage of her parents. Since the age of nine months she had been able to walk, understand all she heard said, and talk. In the seventeenth century she would have aroused grave suspicions. Major Hathorne, or perhaps a minister or elder, would have "labored" with the parents, seeking to discover whether they had consummated their union before the marriage vows were taken. If they had, they were guilty of fornication and could not expect Heaven's favors until they had confessed their crime at meeting and received a whipping or paid a fine. Babies born to a couple less than nine months after marriage were a heavy problem to the early Puritans. But since it was the nineteenth century, Ebe, as the precocious little girl was called, was admired and petted, and the parents were asked no questions.

Once more Captain Nathaniel lingered in Salem until December, and then once more set out for the East Indies. The vessel on this voyage was the ship *Mary and Eliza*. Early in March, 1804, she rounded the Cape of Good Hope, and at the end of April was anchored in Batavia harbor. The Captain appears to have been in a hurry. By June 22 he had made the rounds of the trading ports and had taken on a cargo of sugar, mace, nutmeg, coffee, and camphor, including an adventure for himself valued at five hundred Spanish dollars. He straightway headed for

Salem. On July 4, when he was well past Java Head, he wrote in the log, in the form of verse,

> Strong breezes, frequent squalls,
> Middle part fresh breezes,
> Latter part fresh gales.

When—a little less than four months later—he reached Salem he found out that on this July 4, precisely twenty-eight years after the signing of the Declaration of Independence, his wife, listening to the tramp of parading feet and the patriotic music of a brass band as she suffered travail, had borne a son. The boy was to be the romancer. Spoken of by all who saw him as strikingly beautiful, he had been given the most revered of traditional Hathorne names, the name of his father, Nathaniel.

Providence, it seems, was determined to bar happiness from the Hathorne home. While the women in the household were rejoicing over Nathaniel's seeing his little son for the first time, a dread anxiety was pulling at their hearts. The return from Fayal of the brig *Morning Star*, commanded by Nathaniel's brother Daniel, was overdue. The anguish of uncertainty increased with the days. Finally proof came that the *Morning Star* with all on board had gone down.

The Essex County probate court, meeting in December, 1804, named three, among whom was Betsy's brother William Manning, to make an inventory of Daniel Hathorne's possessions. They reported little besides an interest estimated at $800 in the Hathorne house and books on navigation valued at $62.50. Daniel's other nautical equipment and most of his personal property were lost on the *Morning Star*. He left no will, and the court appointed his nephew, John Forrester, to administer his estate.

The aged Hathorne mother now had only one son to wait for as she sat at her window or by her fire, imagining perhaps her baby Hathorne grandson growing up to be a mariner like his father and uncle. But Captain Nathaniel was not again to give her and his wife the worry of waiting for him to return from a long voyage to India or China. Henceforth he was to confine himself to waters nearer home. Maybe his brother's fate stirred old Mrs. Hathorne and Betsy to exact from him a promise to venture no more to the distant East.

Early in 1805 he took command of the brig *Neptune*, owned by Joseph Peabody, and sailed to Trinidad. He was on his way back to Salem by March 1, interested in what disposal he would make of a private adventure in which he had invested $429. The items composing it, as he listed them in his account book, were six hundred gallons of molasses, two hogsheads of sugar, a case of gin, a half cask of wine, and one ham.

By the beginning of April he was at home, listening to Ebe's flow of talk and watching Natty, as the boy was called, try to creep. The Captain's ability to appraise the quality of textiles must have met with his wife's approval. For on several occasions she sent him to the shop kept by John Scobie to buy cashmere and linen, along with such incidentals as cotton thread and skeins of silk and wool. He usually bought a yard or two of tobacco for himself while on a shopping errand, and one time he purchased a pair of men's gloves, some hose, and a pair of galluses. He no doubt heard impassioned political arguments while he lingered at Scobie's, and perhaps declared with a shipmaster's firmness his great faith in the principles of Thomas Jefferson.

On June 30, 1806, shortly before he left on the *Neptune* for a voyage to Nantes, in France, he and Betsy took the babies to the First Church and had them baptized. Why they waited so long to have this sacrament performed is not clear. Ebe was well past four, and Natty lacked a few days of being two. Precisely two centuries had passed since the baptism in the Bray church in Berkshire of the first American Hathorne.

The year 1807 arrived before Captain Nathaniel returned from France. He was at home from the first of March until the end of June, running up bills to the amount of forty dollars at John Scobie's, charging many yards of tobacco. Then, as master of the brig *Nabby*, he made a voyage to Cayenne in French Guiana. One of his obligations on this trip was to dispose of an adventure belonging to his wife's favorite brother, Robert Manning, a youth of twenty-three. The adventure consisted of twenty-five pieces of "long snow white nankeen," a number of Madras handkerchiefs, pieces of white cambric and "blue cotton cashmere," a fancy silk kerchief, and the leather trunk in which the cloth was packed. The whole, valued at $125, was sold in Cayenne with the rest of the *Nabby's* cargo. But on his return to Salem Captain Nathaniel failed to pay his brother-in-law the money due.

Robert Manning was not the kind to demand payment. He understood fully the gravity of Captain Nathaniel's situation. President Jefferson's notorious embargo on shipping had been proclaimed. The act was a direct threat to the only means Captain Nathaniel had for supporting his family. Since he possessed no savings, he saw ahead the possibility of destitution. The President, he reasoned, would realize the folly and injustice of the embargo and order it lifted within a few weeks. So, encouraged by the mercantile firm employing him, Archer & Andrew, he decided to get the *Nabby* loaded and out to sea before the naval frigates designated to enforce the embargo could arrive and cut off all means of egress. It is likely that in his haste he profited from Robert Manning's aid.

On a day late in December, 1807, he bade his wife and children farewell. The scene could only have been most stressful. He was sure that he would have no difficulty in getting out to sea this time. But what of his next voyage? If the President failed to lift the embargo, the enforcement would by then be complete. There was also concern over the welfare of Betsy, who was expected to be brought to bed on any day with her third child.

Providence favored Captain Nathaniel until he got to Cayenne and exchanged his cargo for molasses, worth $8,675, and cocoa and raw cotton, valued together at $2,000. As soon as the *Nabby* was reloaded, news came that the President's embargo was almost wholly successful, that no vessels were attempting to leave New England ports. There was nothing Captain Nathaniel could do except proceed to Salem and face the uncertainty of the future.

The *Nabby* was no more than two or three days out of Cayenne when the Providence which had been smiling upon the perplexed young shipmaster suddenly turned table and visited upon him a severe malarial chill. Soon his temperature was mounting, and the water he passed became bloody. The mate, realizing the seriousness of the sickness, put in at Paramaribo, in the Dutch colony of Surinam, the nearest port where medical aid could be had.

The physician brought on board the *Nabby* was at first not sure of the type of malaria from which the patient was suffering. But after Captain Nathaniel had been for a day or two in a boardinghouse—kept by an Englishwoman, Hannah Birch—the doctor pronounced the disease to be yellow fever. All, it appears, was done for the sufferer which could be done. But that all was not enough. After as long perhaps as a week of fighting the fever, Captain Nathaniel gave up and died. The precise date of his lonely end—it could not have been later than the beginning of March, 1808—is unknown.

Whether the news of the death reached Salem before the return of the *Nabby* is likewise unknown. All that is certain is that Betsy learned of her widowhood on a day early in April. As soon as the messenger who had brought the news departed, she went alone to her own room. There, in a little bed, slept the baby whom Captain Nathaniel had never seen. It was a daughter, Mary Louisa, born January 9 and baptized in the First Church February 27. Ebe, who a short time before had passed her sixth birthday, was playing in the adjoining room with Natty, who was soon to be four. The mother called for the two to come; and when they walked in she looked at them a long moment and then, facing the boy, said calmly, "Your father is dead." Natty was too young to understand the meaning of the words. But Ebe understood. The scene was to remain vivid in her memory for the rest of her long life.

The elder Hathorne mother now had only her grandson George Archer, beginning his apprenticeship before the mast, to wait for as she spent her days hating the sea. A few months before the death of her younger son in Surinam another grandson, Simon Forrester junior, had committed suicide while returning from the East Indies. Frenzied by drink, he had fastened a weight to his body and plunged from his moving ship into the ocean. All his life he had been wayward and impetuous. There was too much of the primitive Irish of his father in him, said the many Salem Anglo-Saxons who disliked the brash domineering elder Forrester. Harvard College, from which Simon junior was graduated with the class of 1803, had failed to teach him self-control.

In an obituary in a Salem newspaper appeared the statement, "He had long been in habits which could not promise much for his future years."

The mother in the Manning home, sixty years old, was also waiting for one to return from a voyage. He was her son John Manning, born in 1788. Unlike his brothers, all of whom were landsmen, he had felt the lure of the ocean, and at fourteen or fifteen had signed on a vessel as an apprentice seaman. Then he had sailed away, never to be heard of again. But his mother could not make herself believe that he had gone down at sea. She kept his landsman's clothes and all his personal things in readiness for his use, and until her dying day was to hope against hope that at some hour he would come walking in.

Little Natty, the romancer of the future, learned very early of the grief weighing upon the hearts of his grandmothers. Ebe was to tell of how he would make up stories about himself as soon as he could talk. Each would end with the statement, "Then I'm going away, and I'm never coming back."

There must have been times in the year 1808 when the boy's mother thanked the Providence which had spared her husband from the distress she saw around her. Shipmasters who the year before had maintained their families in comfort were now in want. Seamen by the scores with no chance of employment had to beg for charity. Such was the effect of the embargo proclaimed by President Jefferson. While his opponents poured out abuse, calling him "His American Majesty," his supporters—among whom Captain Nathaniel Hathorne had been numbered— argued that only his policies could prevent a French or English war which would be far more costly than the embargo. The Jeffersonians in eastern Massachusetts were in the majority, and at the election that year returned their candidate for Congress, Jacob Crowninshield. Then, when Mr. Crowninshield suddenly died and was replaced by another faithful party man, Joseph Story, they were given a surprise. For, according to none other than Jefferson himself, it was Congressman Story who brought about the repeal of the embargo, early in 1809. There was a connection between the Hathornes and Mr. Story, who was on the eve of his great career as a member of the United States Supreme Court: his sister Mary was the wife of little Natty's first cousin John Forrester, graduate of Harvard College, class of 1801. The worried young Hathorne mother was not the kind to understand political paradox. To her the trouble over the embargo was contradictory entanglement—like life in general as it was now pressing upon her, demanding one sorrowful task after another.

She had her husband's sea clothes to unpack and look at when the *Nabby* got back from Paramaribo. The laundress who washed them had charged fifty-five francs and had been paid by Captain Nathaniel's employers, Archer & Andrew. They of course would deduct the fifty-five francs from the amount they owed the Captain's estate. This came, all together, to $1,086.54.

But the washerwoman's bill was small when compared with other bills which would have to be deducted. Hannah Birch, who kept the boardinghouse in which Captain Nathaniel died, had charged seventy francs. A broker in Paramaribo, named Schwennike, had advanced almost four hundred francs for cash expenditures. The physician had charged eighty-three francs, and the porter wine which he had the patient drink had cost thirty francs. Fifteen francs had to be paid for the permit to bury the body. The undertaker's bill had been almost five hundred francs— for the coffin and the thirty ells of cloth used as a shroud. The sexton who dug the grave had charged more than a hundred francs, and the minister who pronounced the committal had been given sixty francs.

The Captain's death among the Dutch and other foreigners unafraid to demand exorbitant prices had cost his estate almost half of the cash assets. When, on August 1, 1808, Archer & Andrew submitted to Mrs. Hathorne a final accounting, they showed that $513.14 had been paid to settle the Paramaribo bills. The amount remaining, to be paid to the estate, was $573.40.

But Captain Nathaniel had died intestate, and Mrs. Hathorne could not touch a penny credited to him until the probate court acted, naming her the administratrix and appointing appraisers to submit an inventory of the Captain's total wealth. These men—John Watson, Joseph Eveleth, and Jonathan Archer—valued the furniture with which Mrs. Hathorne and her husband had begun married life at less than a hundred dollars. Also included in the inventory were sheets, quilts, counterpanes, the three small beds for the babies, Mrs. Hathorne's flatirons, table napkins, one tea caddy, the Captain's toilet articles, his gold watch and chain (valued at $60), the silver watch and charts he used at sea, his quadrant, his gold buttons and shirt pin, his books (valued at $10), his spyglass, his gun, and a pair of pistols. The appraisers fixed the value of all personal belongings at $338.66. Other assets, the main item being the money due from Archer & Andrew, amounted to $940.89. Debts—including the money due Robert Manning for the adventure he entrusted to Captain Nathaniel in 1807—came to $645.08. When the creditors were all paid, Mrs. Hathorne had, besides personal property, $296.21.

It was with this sum and the interest in the Hathorne home, which could not become dollars and cents while old Mrs. Hathorne lived, that Betsy and her three children faced the future. She saw nothing ahead for them except the humiliation of living as dependents. The Hathorne women with whom she had dwelt for seven years were themselves dependents—upon Madam Forrester. Their close neighbor Richard Manning was, on the contrary, prosperous. He had sold his blacksmith shop, and was giving all of his attention to his successful Salem–Boston stagecoach line and to the thousands of acres of primitive land which he had bought in Maine at a very low price. On the part of the young widow there was no hesitation in adopting the sensible course. With her few belongings and her daughters and son she moved across the two backyards and took up her residence once more under her father's roof.

HERBERT STREET

BY THE beginning of the nineteenth century the streets of Salem had been given permanent names. Main Street had become Essex Street. The central north-south thoroughfare, from which the old town house and all other obstructions except the pump and watering trough had been removed, was Washington Street. The wide avenue extending along the South River, with wharves on one side and mansions of merchants on the other, was Derby Street. Burying Lane had been named Liberty Street, and the lanes on which stood the Hathorne and Manning houses were, respectively, Union Street and Herbert Street.

Salem, half the size of Boston, was ranked among the important American cities, and in the commercial ports of foreign lands was perhaps the best known of all. The white inhabitants, about five thousand males and six thousand females, were still predominantly Anglo-Saxon. The colored, scarcely more than three hundred in number, were Negro with a sprinkling of Indian. The population as a whole was divided into four classes, and the distinguishing barriers were so sharp that it was next to impossible for an individual to rise from a lower class to a higher. Since the period of the witchcrafts, Salemites had come more and more to look upon "money as their god and large possessions the only heaven to covet." By the time the three children of Captain Nathaniel Hathorne reached years of understanding the town was as distinctly plutocratic as it had once been theocratic.

The power of the ministers and magistrates of the seventeenth century was now wielded by the rich whose families had been in New England so long that little was known of their origins. Though it was trade which had brought wealth to these plutocrats, they affected the ways of the English landed gentry from whom they claimed they were descended. Their homes—a number of which were designed by Salem's own gifted architect, Samuel McIntire—overlooked the Common, or were on Essex Street, or Derby Street, or in the northwest quarter on Federal Street, or in the southwest on Chestnut Street. Usually of three stories, sometimes of wood painted gray or white, but most often of red or yellow brick, these mansions were eighteenth-century classic in style, massive, evenly proportioned, and built for the ages. Many of the hipped roofs were bordered by balustrades, glistening white; and some were topped by cupolas, where the owners could ascend and watch for their ships to come in from the Orient loaded with coffee, tea, spices, medicines, and textiles to be sold at enormous profits. At the back of a mansion, separating it from the stables, there was likely to be an acre or two of formal garden requiring the year-long services of two or three gardeners. In designing the front doorways the architects took full advantage of the opportunity to show variety and quiet ornateness. The interior walls were covered with paper brought from China or France and adorned with portraits painted by such artists as Copley, Stuart, and Frothingham. The carpets, the window hangings, the mantels, the furniture, the plate and china stamped with authentic or pretended family crests—all bespoke "the best that money can buy," a favorite phrase of the Salem rich. Their libraries contained many volumes which had been sent to France or Italy to be bound. The books were read. Because of the stress which the rich placed upon the art of manners they spoke the English language surprisingly well, and those who had spent time in foreign countries to advance their trade also knew other languages. In politics most of the plutocrats were Federalists, but some, including the influential Crowninshields, felt that their best interests lay in supporting the Jeffersonians. The correct place for the rich to observe the formalities of worshiping God was the conservative First Church. They themselves had not gone to college, but they were sending their sons to Harvard.

The class they most disdained was the second, made up of the new rich. The few composing this lower order were keen competitors in business. They had been in New England for only a generation or two, and if they claimed gentle descent they were considered pretenders. Chief among them was Simon Forrester, whom the Crowninshields called "old Forrester," with special emphasis on the adjective when he went driving with his wife in the most luxurious equipage which had ever been seen in Essex County. He aped the first class—lived in a mansion on Derby Street, fitted it up in the best taste, had a mural depicting his departure from his home in Ireland painted above the mantel in his drawing room, bought hundreds of beautiful books for his library, and saw three of his sons graduated from Harvard. He informed Salem that he himself had been educated at Cloyne College in Ireland and that a Scotch baron and an Irish earl were among his forebears. Salem was also told that the ancestral seat of the Hathornes, his wife's family, was Wigcastle, Wigton, in Wiltshire, and that the Hathorne coat of arms was "azure, a lion's head erased, between three fleurs-de-lis." Salem's top aristocrats refused to be impressed. Those among them who yielded to the lure of Mr. Forrester's gold and married into his family simply dropped from the first class into the second.

The third social order, several times as numerous as the two upper classes put together, was made up of those whom the rich spoke of as descendants of the English yeomanry. They were mariners, craftsmen, shopkeepers, farmers, and professional men with little money. They constituted a middle class in the town, and in political campaigns were called the backbone of the country. The modest houses in which they maintained their families were situated on such streets as Union and Herbert.

Born on the former and taken to the latter after their father's death, Ebe, Natty, and Louisa Hathorne learned early that there was only one class in Salem which regarded them as betters. This class, to which the majority of the population belonged, was made up of laborers on the wharves and in the shipbuilding yards, common sailors, hostlers and stagecoach drivers, the many engaged in domestic service, and, at the very bottom, the colored, the older of whom had once been slaves. All these workers were paid very low wages, and when there was an election were not averse to selling their votes. They lived in the hollows bordering the North River or across the Mill Pond in the marshy South Fields. Because of the presence of the children of this lowest class in the free public schools, many a middle-class father unable to pay tuition at a private academy allowed his sons and daughters to grow up illiterate. One of the taverns where workers were accustomed to gather and drink ale on pay days was located on an inelegant part of Derby Street a few paces west of the junction with Herbert. When Ebe, Natty, and Louisa ventured out alone to visit their aunt Rachel Forrester, they were told that on reaching Derby Street they must turn eastward without so much as a glance at the creatures going in and out of this den of irrespectability.

After a few visits to their rich aunt's the three children came to realize the great contrast between her luxurious home and their grandfather Manning's simple house. They had not been taken to meeting at the First Church many times before they saw that they were not clothed in the finery other children were wearing. They were still very young when they perceived that their mother and grandmothers were never given the title "Madam" by which Salem's women of wealth were addressed. Ebe, Natty, and Louisa in such way learned that they belonged to the middle class. Still they were told that the Manning blood which ran in their veins was running also in the veins of Salem's most splendid and powerful families. They were also told about the prominence of Major William Hathorne in founding Salem, about the supposed witch's curse pronounced upon his distinguished son Colonel John, and about the bold exploits of their grandfather Hathorne when he was a privateersman during the Revolution. At first the children were perplexed at all the contradictions. Then, with clearer understanding, came indignation, resentment, shame, and, above all, pride. To Ebe and Natty these emotions were to cling and grow stronger with the years. Louisa, carefree and incurious, was too occupied in enjoying life as it came to bother about such matters as class consciousness.

Ebe and Natty even went so far as to assume the attitude of Salem's top aristocrats towards the Forresters. Once Uncle Simon, already an aged man, met Natty in the street and offered him a ten-dollar bill. The boy, in disdain, refused to accept it. "He would have taken the money," said Ebe, "if it had come from anyone whom he thought nearly enough related to have the right to bestow it." But Natty chose to believe the Forresters when they asserted that the Hathorne ancestral seat was Wigcastle, Wigton, in Wiltshire. He himself was to make the claim in his journal, and most of his biographers were to repeat the error.

Even after Richard Manning became the possessor of thousands of acres in Maine, town lots in Portland and Salem, dozens of horses, and a sufficient number of stagecoaches to make daily runs to and from Boston, Marblehead, and Newburyport, he designated himself a yeoman and lived in yeomanly style. Only a man with a superior mind could have achieved his success in business. Yet his tastes and manners remained what they had been during his boyhood on his father's small farm in Ipswich and his subsequent years as a blacksmith. Though two of his children, Mary and Robert, showed ambition, he gave them little encouragement. His library consisted of fourteen volumes, valued at $14. Evidently he felt that he had done enough for the cultural advancement of his family when he purchased for $70 a pew in Salem's East Church. There seems never to have been more than a single servant in his house, and she was one of his wife's poor relations. He kept a private chaise, but it was for his own use in journeying to his estates in Maine. Richard Manning was true to the prime tradition of yeomanry: his one great aim in life was to make more money to buy more land.

His Herbert Street dwelling and the lot on which it stood were valued together at only $2,500. The house was a wooden boxlike structure, oblong in shape, with two full floors and a low-studded third story. The narrow part faced the street, the east end, without a door, being but a step or two from the sidewalk. The grounds, as viewed by a contemporary, were "a tangled mass of vines, herbs, and weeds, a few feet of turf being here and there discernible."

The entrance was on the south side, with the sitting room to the right and the kitchen to the left. There were no curtains for the windows, and the floors, except in the second-story chamber occupied by the master and mistress, were without carpets. The furniture, of the plainest and cheapest kind, consisted of two desks, a secretary, a bureau, several walnut and mahogany tables, three looking glasses, one easy chair, a number of ordinary chairs, six or seven beds, and—the most expensive single item—a "Willard's timepiece" valued at $30. In the cupboards in the kitchen there were two china tea sets, two dozen china plates with blue edges and a like number all white, a dozen wine glasses, a dozen tumblers, and a pair of decanters. There was much pewter—two dozen plates, six "basins," eighteen one-quart mugs, and twelve one-pint mugs. The silverware was valued at $36.30, and there were a dozen napkins, probably used only for company. Among the incidental possessions was "a shower bath worth about a dollar." The total value of the contents of the house—with bed linen, quilts, blankets, and counter-panes counted—amounted to less than $500. Yet the lots Richard Manning owned on Derby Street alone were worth $2,000.

Samuel, the youngest in the Manning household, was seventeen when his sister Hathorne moved in with her three children, enlarging a family of nine to a family of thirteen. With the routine upset, tension was inevitable. While Ebe, Natty, and Louisa were finding out what it meant to belong to Salem's third class, they were also learning the bitter lesson of being dependents. The grandfather and the uncles—William, Richard, and Robert in addition to Samuel—were never, it appears, unkind. Nor were the younger aunts, Maria Miriam and Priscilla Miriam. But there is evidence that the grandmother, past sixty and well hardened, found young children as disturbing as animals. Natty very early became aware of her dislike of dogs. When reprimanded one day for kicking a puppy the boy said, "Oh, he'll think it was Grandma'am." The old woman, obsessed with the idea that her vanished son John would one day come back to her, could not have been conscious of how she envied her widowed daughter and orphaned grandchildren, who knew for a certainty that Captain Nathaniel Hathorne was dead. Mary, the oldest of the Manning brood and the brightest of the daughters, seems to have been the old-fashioned Puritan in the family. She bought a membership in the Salem Athenaeum so that she could get books to read, and for a time kept an afternoon school for the very young. She was physically unattractive, and knew that she was doomed to spinsterhood. Yet her beautiful sister Betsy, three years her junior, had experienced love and maternity. The Hathorne children were to realize in time that they owed a great debt to Aunt Mary. But as their disciplinarian she could not have been a human female if she had not been severe.

Mrs. Hathorne, a woman of little will, submitted to the situation and made the best of things. The tension in the household served to bring her and her children closer together and taught them to be loyal to one another. "Mother was so good and generous that she couldn't keep from spoiling us," Natty was to say. A visitor to the Herbert Street house reported, "Mrs. Hathorne and her family lived upstairs, practicing the greatest economy by taking their meals up there." The mother and the three children slept, it appears, in a single room until Uncle Robert, seeing that Natty was growing up, offered to share his bed with the boy.

Ebe was not only the oldest but the most ingenious of the three. Natty and Louisa formed the habit of abiding by her decisions, a habit they were not to shake off in the years to come. She was the leader in all the childhood adventures. Whenever the town crier rang his bell in front of the Manning stagecoach office at the corner of Essex Street and Union, all three hurried to the scene as if they were going to hear about the end of the world. The aged crier never had more to announce than an auction or the loss of a lady's purse, but Ebe would declare that some day he would surely bring startling news. When old Mrs. Spencer, wearing a sunbonnet and driving a rawboned horse, stopped her cart on Herbert Street and blew her whistle, it was beautiful Ebe, with big gray eyes and raven hair, to whom Aunt Mary or Mrs. Hathorne would hand out a few pennies. Then the children would dash to the cart and buy of the wares Mrs. Spencer made and peddled—sugar rocks, called gibraltars, and molasses sticks, called blackjacks. Perhaps a penny or two would be left over to spend for ginger cakes at a favored cent shop in the neighborhood. Sometimes in their ramblings the children strayed beyond bounds and wandered westward on Essex Street. Then at Ebe's suggestion Natty and Louisa would guess how many people they were going to meet on making the next turn, count the cracks in the head of the wooden bust of Hippocrates which stood outside an apothecary's shop, list the wonders which might be seen from the top of the steeple on the First Church meetinghouse, and give names out of *Pilgrim's Progress* to the horses and oxen drinking from the watering trough beside the pump in Washington Street. Often, when their elders were not looking, the children darted from their front door down to Derby Street, ran past the wicked tavern as they had been told to do, and at the head of the long Derby wharf found a place to stand and watch ships going out to sea and ships coming in. Ebe, envied because of her recollection of their father, was able sometimes to identify a vessel he had sailed, perhaps the *America*, on which he and Captain Jacob Crowninshield had brought the elephant from India.

On the west side of Union Street, directly opposite the Manning stagecoach office and stables, stood a spacious new brick "block." The first-floor side fronting on Essex

Street was divided into shops. The rest of the building formed five or six connecting residences. Living in one of these from the end of 1811 to 1813 was a dentist, who, upon call, also served as a general physician. He was Dr. Nathaniel Peabody, forever moving and always poor. But he was a gentleman, scion of an old Essex County family, and had studied at Dartmouth College. Among his distant Peabody cousins was the merchant Joseph Peabody, who during a prosperous year was likely to pay into the Salem customhouse duties amounting to as much as a quarter of a million dollars. The dentist's oldest daughter, named Elizabeth Palmer but called Lizzie, became much attached to her neighbor Ebe Hathorne, two years her senior. Both girls were in school, and did their lessons together. Lizzie, marked for fame as an American educator, looked upon Ebe as "brilliant," and "thought her a great genius." Natty was to remain in Lizzie's memory "a broad-shouldered little boy, with clustering curls, springing about the yard." The youngest of the Peabody children at this time was Nathaniel Cranch, recently born. Between him and Lizzie were two girls, Mary Tyler and Sophia Amelia. The latter was a pink-and-white tot of three, delicate and spoiled because of an illness suffered while teething. Though Natty undoubtedly saw her and the rest of the Peabodys many times, none of them made an impression upon him. Thirty years later Sophia Amelia was to become his wife, but he was to be unable to recall that he had known her in her infanthood. Ebe on the contrary was to remember well the months the Peabodys spent on Union Street.

Early in 1813 they moved to west Salem, to share the Essex Street house which the second Colonel John Hathorne had occupied until his retirement to the farm on Salem Neck. The present occupant, the Colonel's son William, a licensed shipmaster, kept the cloth shop on the first floor and reserved several of the rooms for his own family. The rest of the house was rented to Dr. Peabody, and there was so much space that his wife, an experienced schoolmistress, hired an associate and turned two rooms into "an academy for young ladies." Mrs. Peabody—both of whose parents, though active patriots during the Revolution, had been born and reared in England—was a gentlewoman and a bluestocking, interested in editing the poetry of Edmund Spenser for American readers. "Her able partner in the academy," said the Salem *Gazette*, "is qualified to teach, for a special fee, drawing, music, embroidery, and the French language."

This was probably the school which Ebe Hathorne wished to attend. But for her and Louisa, in their poverty and dependence, an education without such frills as drawing, music, and French was considered adequate. The schools which the two sisters attended are unknown. Natty was put into the academy taught by Joseph Emerson Worcester, a young Yale graduate, already on his way towards becoming a celebrated lexicographer. The boy had schoolmates who were ready to remind him that he belonged to Herbert Street; and with at least one, whom he pronounced "quarrelsome," he had fights.

Life since their father's death had moved evenly for the three children. But in the spring of 1813 the power of the Providence they heard about every Sunday at the First Church was brought home to them. On April 16 came the death of their grandmother Hathorne, who was nearing eighty. For five years the children had been running across the backyards to pay visits to the sad old woman, who had seen two sons and two sons-in-law fall victim to commerce at sea. Natty when only four or five had sat for hours in her presence turning contentedly the pages of *Pilgrim's Progress*, playing at reading. Before the day set for her funeral arrived, the children's grandfather started on one of his regular trips to Maine. The Salem *Gazette* for April 20 reported: "Died in Newbury, yesterday afternoon, Mr. Richard Manning, aged fifty-nine, a very respectable citizen of this town." He had left home apparently well, and in his bed at an inn in Newbury had been overcome by a "fit of apoplexy." The two deaths just three days apart and the interments—the grandmother's at the Burying Point and the grandfather's at the North Ground, to be known later as the Howard Street Cemetery—filled the minds of the children with fancies of palls and graves and funeral discourses. From someone, probably Ebe, Natty had picked up a gruesome line out of Shakespeare's *Richard III* and shouted it at every opportunity, the line being, "My lord, stand back and let the coffin pass!"

The death of the grandmother meant that the Hathorne estate was at last to be divided and that Captain Nathaniel's widow and children would receive a son's share. The problem of the division was solved by Mr. Forrester, who bought the Union Street house, gave his wife's sisters the right to continue using it as a residence, and paid to Mrs. Hathorne in currency whatever was due her and her children. The amount came to only a few hundred dollars.

In the case of Mrs. Hathorne's father the situation was different. He died intestate. This meant that Mrs. Hathorne was entitled to a share of the profits accruing annually from his extensive holdings. He had made over his stagecoach business to his sons William, Robert, and Samuel; but he had kept his land, the largest parcel being ten thousand acres in the town of Raymond in Maine. Already farmers were buying small portions of this and other properties, providing a steady flow of income. Mrs. Hathorne's share was small. But it was enough to free her and her children from a state of dependency. In dying when and as he did, Richard Manning rendered Ebe, Natty, and Louisa Hathorne an important service.

On November 10, 1813, seven months after the deaths of old Mrs. Hathorne and Richard Manning, an afflicting Providence visited again the Herbert Street home. While on the playground at school that day Natty was accidentally struck on the foot by a flying ball. Many months were to pass before he was again "springing about the yard." The injured foot failed to heal. Ebe said, "It pined away, and was considerably smaller than the other." The physicians consulted—Dr. Peabody and Mr. Forrester's son-in-law Dr. Gideon Barstow among them—helped little. One, probably Dr. Peabody, prescribed a newfangled treatment: Natty was required to stick the stricken foot out a first-floor window while someone from the window above poured cold water on it. The doctors agreed that the boy should get about on crutches, wearing a padded boot to sustain his sprained ankle. But most of the time he lay on the floor before the fire and read. "Everybody thought that if he lived," said Ebe, "he would be always lame."

He was lied to, flattered, pitied, and pampered. Neighbors called to bring toys and things to eat, and to assure him that within a few days he would be leaping and bounding as never before. He overheard them telling one another that he was the finest boy they had ever seen. Many of them he disliked, especially a fat old woman whose homeliness repelled him. He wished to be left alone with his Bunyan or Froissart, and with the household kittens, whose softness and grace fascinated him and Louisa alike. When tired of reading he played with the animals, building covered avenues out of books for them to scurry through. His mother, always weak, yielded to his every whim. Day by day he became more tightly bound by her apron strings, and painful to him was to be the untying.

Among the books scattered about him as he lay on the floor were his reader, speller, grammar, geography, and arithmetic. Every evening Mr. Worcester came and heard him recite his lessons. There was more than the incapacitated pupil to draw the schoolmaster to Herbert Street. The brilliant lexicographer of the future was attentive to Natty's aunt Maria Miriam, then twenty-six. Like her sister Betsy, she was beautiful. But Providence put an end to whatever romance was developing between her and Mr. Worcester. In the May following the accident suffered by her nine-year-old nephew she was suddenly taken sick with a serious throat infection. A few days later old Mrs. Manning knew beyond a doubt that one of her children was no more. Maria's death meant that henceforth the income from the Richard Manning estate would be divided among eight instead of nine. Thus Mrs. Hathorne became a bit richer.

During Natty's months of invalidism excitement over the War of 1812 was running high in Salem. Lying on the floor with his books and kittens, the boy learned the meaning of political dissension. He and Ebe found out that right on Herbert Street there were neighbors no longer on speaking terms—Federalists opposing the war, and Jeffersonians, loyal to President Madison, supporting it. When the bodies of two high-ranking American victims of the defeat inflicted upon the *Chesapeake* by the British frigate *Shannon* off the Marblehead shore were brought under flag of truce to Salem for burial, the churches dominated by Federalists refused the use of their meetinghouses for the elaborate funeral planned by the Jeffersonians. Ebe and Natty no doubt asked many questions when they heard that one of their Hathorne cousins had been ordered to jail for leading Jeffersonians in a riot. He was Colonel John Hathorne's son and namesake, a member of the Harvard class of 1798, the first of the Salem Hathornes to be graduated from college.

Two of his brothers—Ebenezer Hathorne and the Captain William in whose house the Peabodys were still living —were at sea engaged in privateering. In wringing all possible profits from this form of warfare, which was revived with the enthusiasm known during the Revolution, merchants who were Federalists and merchants who were Jeffersonians met on common ground. Surely the Hathorne children were filled with curiosity when they heard their elders read from the *Gazette* about the amazing deeds off the shore of England of their paternal first cousin once removed, Captain Joseph Ropes. But it was not from a mercenary motive that this most spectacular of all American privateersmen of the War of 1812 was preying upon British commerce. Captain Ropes himself declared that the force which led him on from one daring exploit to another was the passion to avenge the death of his father, a fallen privateersman of the Revolution.

For Salem the alarming day of the war came on Sunday, April 3, 1814, a few weeks before the death of Maria Manning. The United States frigate *Constitution*, pursued by two British ships of the line, had found refuge in Marblehead harbor the night before. When the news reached Salem, everybody supposed that the enemy would press in for attack and invasion. Numbers of the rich, owning private conveyances, made plans to flee into the interior. Workers, organized into groups and armed with picks and shovels, were dispatched to strategic places to set up earthworks. All possible aid was hurried to Marblehead. For drawing cannon the Manning stagecoach horses—at rest in their stables, since the day was the Sabbath—were put into service. The British remained at sea, and the expected bombardment never came. Yet the *Gazette* and other Salem newspapers reported the events of the day as if a great battle had been fought and won. Among the citizens of the town specially commended for their worthy aid were William, Robert, and Samuel Manning. Perched on top of the first piece of artillery which a span of their beasts pulled to Marblehead was the sire of the powerful Crowninshields, in his eighty-first year and soon to die. "Old King George C. the First," commoners in Salem were in the habit of calling him. When Ebe and Natty heard their uncle's name associated with the name of this worthy their pride no doubt soared.

At the beginning of the war Ebe, eleven, was absorbed in studying astronomy. Her "lofty" interest had even drawn a bit of gallant mockery from Uncle Robert. But the stress of the times turned the girl to politics. Following the example set by the Mannings, she lined up with the Federalists. Natty, loyal to the Hathornes, declared himself for the Jeffersonians. The brother, expert in bumping about the house on his crutches, and the sister, faithful in fetching books from a circulating library for him to read, must have had many a hot argument. But an event which took place right at the end of the war must have made them wonder about dissension of all sorts. Though Federalists and Jeffersonians hated one another, they had united in hating the British on the April Sunday when Salem expected invasion. That day the patriarch of the town's rich, "old King George C. the First," had straddled a big gun and ridden like a plebeian over the rough road to Marblehead. While Congregationalists ignored Christmas, Episcopalians celebrated the holy fete with elaborate ceremony. Still on December 25, 1814, Federalists, Jeffersonians, aristocrats, commoners, Congregationalists, and Episcopalians joined in sending roasted turkeys and plum puddings to the more than three hundred British seamen crowded on the *Aurora,* a prison ship anchored in Salem harbor. In a card in the *Gazette* the unhappy captives expressed their thanks for "the liberal and generous provisions made for them in commemoration of the birth of the Savior of all." On hearing of this act of charity Ebe and Natty had to conclude that there was no consistency in the behavior of their elders.

A few weeks later the children learned that on the day before this Christmas of 1814 the treaty ending the war had been signed at Ghent. Natty, though still lame, had discarded his crutches. Whatever physician was attending the boy had been too hasty in giving him permission to walk without mechanical aids. He suffered a relapse; and this time, with both his legs in a sort of paralysis, he was worse off than he had ever been. The "old crutches," pieced at the ends to accommodate his augmented height, were again needed. Once more his mother pitied and petted. A strange feeling possessed the boy, convincing him that he would not live beyond the age of twenty-five.

"It was Dr. Time who at last cured him," said Ebe. His uncle Richard, also a cripple, had married into a Maine family and was living on the Manning estate in Raymond. As boarders in the home of one of his neighbors, Mrs. Hathorne and her children spent the summer of 1816. The change served as the climax of Natty's recovery. The boy was not long back in Salem before he was again in school, probably not under Mr. Worcester.

Able to use his legs and feet again, Natty reveled in walking. For him it became, and was to remain, the most pleasant of recreations. Sometimes he and Ebe, also a great walker, tramped out to Salem Neck, past the house to which their elderly kinsman Colonel John Hathorne had retired, and on to Juniper Point. From there the view of Baker's

Island and the ocean beyond was unobstructed. At other times the brother and sister wandered westward, climbed to the crest of Gallows Hill, and recreated in their imaginations the scenes of the witch hangings. Occasionally Natty, all alone, followed the road into Danvers until Hathorne Hill came into sight. Its picturesqueness could not have escaped him, but he appears to have been ignorant not only of its association with his family history but also of its true name.

On one excursion to the Salem Village of the witchcrafts he was accompanied by three or four of his schoolmates. None of them had suffered from a shriveled foot, and they all strode with a firmness of which Natty was incapable. He found himself getting ashamed. Then, half angry, he began to think of ways in which he could show that he too could be superior.

His opportunity came when, on turning back towards Salem, the boys stopped to call on an old woman one of them knew. She was a characteristic crone, and lived in a hovel. Still she was so kind as to make tea for her visitors. While the others drank, Natty set his cup aside, untasted. No one noticed his incivility, and in saying good-bye to the old woman he was as courteous as any of the boys. But they were scarcely out the door when he exclaimed, "She's a witch! And the stuff you drank was witches' broth!" Then, repeating what he had read in Hutchinson's *History*, he told how witches had always liked to live in Danvers and how they got control of those they wished to harm. As he went on he kept repeating, "They always begin by giving a victim witches' broth." The boys, only mildly interested at first, became intent—and then alarmed. Finally they all agreed, "The tea she gave us *did* have a strange taste!" One of them was to say sixty years later, "We slunk home scared to death, and that rascal Nat Hathorne ap-

peared to be the most terrified of the lot. He kept saying
that the old woman had likely had a hand in shriveling his
foot and God only knew what she'd do to him next."

If the older members of the Herbert Street household had
heard of this moral victory, they would have felt a certain
relief. The incident proved that there was no reason to
despair of Nat's ability to recover spiritually from the cod-
dling he had received during his years of illness. But he
probably told no one of his resorting to subterfuge to get
the better of his schoolmates. In religious books, the only
kind he was allowed to read on Sunday, deceit was listed
among the cardinal sins. The boy was too wary to give
Grandma'am and Aunt Mary the opportunity to break
forth with a lecture.

To them he remained a problem. And Ebe was by no
means what they wished her to be. A queer pair were she
and her brother, unlike any Mannings ever heard of, or
Hathornes either. Nat turned the pages of his father's log
books, and penciled comment in the margins, but never
gave a thought to going to sea himself. Though the stables
were full of horses, he had no interest in driving or riding.
He preferred to get into an abandoned stagecoach, which
he called "dead," and fancy himself journeying with the
"ghosts" of the travelers whom it had long since served.
He memorized pieces from books and went through the
skylight up to the roof and declaimed them to space. Betsy,
behaving as a young Salem widow was supposed to behave,
spent most of her time in the confines of her own room.
But Ebe was also in the habit of sequestering herself in some
corner. When anyone came near, she assumed the look of
a bereaved spouse and went on with her reading or scrib-
bling. If cleaning the house depended upon her, the place
stayed dirty. When it was suggested that she do a bit of

mending or darning, she would say, in her superior manner, "It's Louisa who wishes to learn to sew." She and Nat would read all night if not forced to go to bed. Directly above the chamber in which she slept with her mother and sister was the room "under the eaves" in which Nat slept with Uncle Robert. The brother and sister had some sort of pulley outside their windows for exchanging the poems and stories and essays they created. On February 13, 1817, Nat let down a piece called "Moderate Views." It was:

> By passions unruffled, untainted by pride,
> > By reason my life let me square.
> The wants of my nature are cheaply supplied,
> > And the rest are but folly and care.
> How vainly, through infinite trouble and strife,
> > The many their labors employ,
> Since all that is truly delightful in life
> > Is what all if they please may enjoy.

Even Grandma'am and Aunt Mary had to concede that the lines were pretty good for a boy not yet thirteen. Of the pieces which Ebe sent up by the pulley nothing is known.

Three weeks after Nat penned his verses on the golden mean Ebe began her sixteenth year. The girl had her mother's beauty. Many a young man who saw her out walking, or sitting sedately at meeting at the First Church, must have looked upon her longingly. But those with whom she talked found her cold, hard, and painfully proud. Even Nat was in great fear of her intellectuality. At any moment it was likely to come out in sharp cutting words. Only in her ambition was she emotional. Men of her social level in Salem saw that in her great dreams none of them were included, and the aristocrats who were struck by her attractiveness remembered that she belonged to Herbert Street. Dancing, which fascinated Louisa and at least pleased

Nat, appears to have meant nothing to the imperious Ebe. In the year 1817 a widower, John Dike, wooed and won her aunt Priscilla. He was a kind man, a prosperous shopkeeper, and, though the father of a boy of Nat's age and a girl a year or two younger, about as desirable a husband as twenty-eight-year-old Priscilla could have expected. But Ebe considered him common, and let him know that she would never accept him as a member of the family.

The Hathornes since their summer in Raymond had talked much about the wonders of the place. In Salem, Uncle Richard's house would have appeared a modest cottage, but it was so superior to other houses in Raymond that the settlers named it "Manning's Folly." It stood near Dingley Brook, the tree-bordered mile-long stream which connects Thomas Pond and Sebago Lake. Among the outbuildings were Uncle Richard's store and mill. Across the brook, which was spanned by a wooden bridge, Uncle Robert put up a dwelling, a two-story farmhouse of the simplest type. The first occupants were Mrs. Hathorne and her children, who moved in on a day in the autumn of 1818. The letters they dispatched to Salem showed their joy at having at last a home wholly unto themselves.

Grandma'am was hard to please. She had no reason now to complain about lack of space. Only four were left in the Herbert Street house—she, Mary, Robert, and Samuel. William—quite a dandy, but efficient as manager of the stagecoach company—had taken quarters in Salem's best hotel, the Essex House. There he was to remain, a contented bachelor, until his death as a very old man. Robert—the brains of the stagecoach business, the chief administrator of his father's estate, and an ambitious pomologist, with orchards across the North River—was often away from home. Samuel—whose duty it was to see that the stagecoaches were supplied with power—frequently went on trips to buy horses. Old Mrs. Manning, accustomed to a hubbub of activity in the house, found herself fretting about loneliness.

In January, 1819, Robert went to Raymond. Nat, as well as matters of business, required attention. The preceding October the boy had been sent to a boardingschool at Stroudwater, near Portland. He had fought against going, and once there had had no will to draw upon his ingenuity in order to win respect. The only female on the premises, the master's wife, pronounced Nat "a shockingly awkward boy." He tortured himself by assuming that no one loved him, and retaliated by refusing to write letters, even to his mother and sisters. Uncle Richard had finally visited him, and had found him "very homesick." Now he was in Raymond for the winter vacation. "Doleful complaints," wrote Robert to old Mrs. Manning. "No momma to take care of him. What shall I do with him? I think of sending him back to Salem."

How Robert's mother answered his question is unknown. But Nat did not return to Stroudwater. For the rest of that winter and during the entire spring he was permitted to "savagize" in Raymond. Letters came to Herbert Street telling of his skating and fishing and shooting, of boys with whom he had made friends, of the funny things the farmers said when they came to trade at Uncle Richard's store, and of the Mr. and Mrs. Tarbox who froze to death and of Uncle Richard's adopting their little daughter. It was plain to see that the boy, allowed to run free and wild, was very happy.

His mother and sisters were happy too. Ebe was as ecstatic as one of her temperament could be over the splendors of Sebago Lake, and the glorious forests in which she rambled at will, and the views of the distant White Mountains. Louisa's letters told of the goats and chickens, the planting and harvesting, the state of everybody's health, the cow's having a calf, and the "messes of milk" that were churned. Betsy—with a good many mistakes in spelling, though she had once won a prize as a "superior orthographer"—wrote of her sewing, of the Sunday school in which she was teaching a class, and of the eagerness of the scholars to learn. Evidently, in Raymond, Betsy was not the recluse she had been in Salem.

Written between the lines of the communications penned by Ebe and Nat was the exaltation they felt in belonging to the top level of the society in which they found themselves. Raymond was a rough frontier community, but in it they represented the best. Uncle Richard, actually a justice of the peace, was looked up to as the squire of the township, and Mrs. Hathorne was accorded the respect due his sister. None of his neighbors were richer than he. The proud girl and boy for the first time in their lives knew what it meant to keep their heads held high at all times.

In his letters to Salem, Nat said nothing about his solitary nocturnal vigils in huts in the woods. Sometimes after supper he ventured out alone to skate on Sebago Lake or, when spring came, to wander along the shore. Instead of returning home at a proper hour he would stop at some abandoned cabin and build a great fire. There, until near dawn, he would read, or write entries in the diary he was keeping, or listen to the silence, or think his thoughts, dwelling no doubt on his conviction that he must die before reaching the age of twenty-five. It is certain that his mother knew when he was absent from his bed and got from him the truth about these strange unwholesome nighttime experiences. But whatever concern she felt she kept from her brothers. She was adept in shielding her son from the stern discipline Robert believed in. The wise uncle had to be tactful in doing for his nephew what he thought was right.

By the beginning of July he had Nat back in Salem, in a school on Marlborough Street taught by Samuel Archer. At the same time Robert saw that Betsy and the girls stayed in Maine. "I do not know what to do with myself," Nat wrote to Louisa. "I shall never be contented here, I am sure. I wish I was but back in Raymond, and I should be happy." Mr. Archer was noted for the discipline he maintained in his academy, and on Herbert Street the boy could expect no soft treatment. His letters to Raymond were a listing of woes. Grandma'am was starving him, she was so stingy. The only oranges she gave him to eat were rotten, and she was saving the guava jelly "against somebody is sick." She never spoke a pleasant word to him, he claimed, and Aunt Mary was always scolding. "If ever I attempt a word in my defense," he complained, "they cry out against my impudence." But their chiding, he reasoned, gave him "employment in retaliating." In a letter specially dismal he wrote, "Mother, I wish you would let Louisa board with Mrs. Dike if she comes up here to school. Then Aunt Mary can't have her to domineer over. . . . Oh, how I wish I was with you with nothing to do but go agunning! But the happiest days of my life are gone. Why was I not a girl that I might have been pinned all my life to my mother's apron?"

The appeals to Raymond went unheeded. Evidently Mrs. Hathorne had promised Robert that she would not interfere. Supported loyally by old Mrs. Manning and Mary, he faced Nat with the alternative of making progress in his studies or becoming an apprentice to a cutler. The boy got to work with his Latin and Greek, first under Mr. Archer and then under a private tutor, Benjamin Lynde Oliver. The latter, an exacting scholar well on in years, heard his pupil recite conjugations and declensions every morning at seven o'clock. More than once Nat excused himself for writing a short letter to his mother by declaring that he had "ten or twelve lines of Latin to parse and translate." In a letter to Louisa he said, "I have taken to chewing tobacco with all my might, which I think raises my spirits." Uncle Robert kept check on the rise and fall of the "spirits," and saw that some time was allotted to play. Nat at last learned how to swim, went occasionally on horse-buying journeys with Uncle Samuel, served as a clerk for the stagecoach company at a salary of a dollar a week, and, as a special reward for diligence, was sometimes allowed to go to the theatre—once to Boston to see Edmund Kean in *Lear*. The boy still read for the joy of the reading—Spenser, Shakespeare, Milton, Pope, Godwin, Scott, Byron, and such works as Rousseau's *Confessions* and *Héloïse*, the *Newgate Calendar*, and Howell's *State Trials*. When he had leisure moments he still wrote verse, like this :

> And genius is a star whose light
> Is soon to sink in endless night,
> And heavenly beauty's angel form
> Will bend like flower in winter's storm.

After the boy had had a year of hard studying, Louisa came back to Herbert Street. But she had not been there long when Uncle Robert began to fear the effect of her gaiety and passion for dancing upon Nat. So she was sent to stay in the house of her uncle Dike, who had recently lost his daughter, a victim of consumption. Then, after another year, as Uncle Robert grew anxious about the examination which Nat would have to pass in order to enter college, he summoned Ebe to lend a helping hand.

Because of the infrequency of her letters her brother had sent her word that when they met he was going to give her "a kicking." But on beholding her he changed his mind. Indeed, her appearance so dazzled him that instead of addressing her "Ebe" he called her "Elizabeth." She was nineteen, a full grown woman, to be listened to and obeyed. Even when she came in one day "quite hidden" by the wide-brimmed fifteen-dollar leghorn hat which Uncle William had just given her, she was commanding. Knowing that her cynicism would be heaped upon him if he lagged in his studies, Nat worked all the harder. "I fear nothing in life so much as Ebe's ridicule," he was to say.

Uncle Robert succeeded in untying the boy from his mother's apron. When Mrs. Hathorne and her son again met, after a separation of more than two years, she saw a youth to respect rather than a weakling to pity and coddle. Inheritor of her own gray eyes, dark hair, and delicate features, he was extremely handsome. It was at this period in his life that a strange gipsylike old woman stopped him on a road one day and, gazing into his eyes, asked, "Am I looking at a man or an angel?" The inquisitive creature was not seeing male beauty marred by effeminacy.

The reunion with Mrs. Hathorne took place in the late summer of 1821 in Raymond, where Nat spent a few days before going, in Uncle Robert's company, to Brunswick, Maine, to enter Bowdoin College. This institution had been chosen because it was inexpensive, conservatively Congregationalist, not too distant from either Salem or Raymond, and not, as was Harvard, divided between rich students who were aristocrats and poor students who were commoners. After seventeen-year-old Nat passed his entrance examinations and was admitted to the freshman class, Uncle Robert, who had agreed to provide the money necessary for his college education, left for home. Except for vacations spent in Raymond or Salem, Nat's path for the next four years was to diverge from that of the rest of the Hathornes.

Ebe and Louisa rejoined their mother in Raymond in the fall of 1821. With the Hathornes all away the Herbert Street house was very quiet for a year. But late in 1822 Betsy and her daughters came back to Salem to stay. Primitive Raymond, decided Mrs. Hathorne and old Mrs. Manning, was no place for marriageable girls to attract the right sort of men. Ebe, more studious than ever, soon let her mother and grandmother know that a husband was the last thing in the world she was seeking. In temperament Louisa was still a little girl—and such she was to remain.

In 1824, on December 20, Robert Manning, at the age of forty, was married to Rebecca Dodge Burnham. The house to which he took his bride was on Dearborn Street in north Salem, in the midst of his beautiful pear and apple trees. His achievements in developing new species of the fruits were soon to bring him international recognition. He had done what he could for his sister Betsy's children. Their future was in their own hands.

He seems to have had nothing to say when in the summer of 1825 Nat returned from Bowdoin a bachelor of arts and with characteristic Hathorne firmness made it clear that his one ambition was to be, of all things, an author. The young man had already written several tales and possibly part of a novel, and he proceeded to convert his and Uncle Robert's old room "under the eaves" into a study. Neither he nor anyone he knew was able to measure the power of his determination. Only a particular visitant from the beyond could have estimated it accurately—the ghost of his first American Hathorne ancestor. After a lapse of two centuries the history of the Hathornes was repeating itself. Young Nat's will to create beauty in words was precisely such a will as had driven William Hathorne to the New World to assist in the founding of God's State upon earth. Like his great-great-great-grandfather, Nat submitted wholly to the urge which possessed him. In its light, conventions and appearances became as nothing. The young man had no qualms in settling down as a dependent upon his mother while waiting to gain complete mastery of his art and make his bid for the world's awards.

Mrs. Hathorne's income was very small. Yet, passive as usual, she uttered no protest, and saw that Nat was made comfortable and was given the foods he liked—apple dumplings, squash pies, and Indian cakes. Old Mrs. Manning and Aunt Mary were no doubt thinking, "How much better for us all it would be if we had made him a cutler!" Louisa loved her brother so much that to her his wishes were laws. Ebe, who had had pieces published in newspapers, was enthusiastic over the course he had adopted. She too was enthralled by the will to become an author. Now she saw herself and Nat struggling on side by side to success and fame. Except for her there was only one other in all the world from whom Nat could expect sympathetic encouragement. This person was the closest of his college comrades, Horatio Bridge, who belonged to a landed family of Augusta, Maine.

Ebe, living exclusively for the development of her intellect, had become a confirmed recluse. She saw no visitors, studied and wrote until very late at night, rose about noon, had her meals brought to her room by Louisa or Hannah the maid, and took long solitary walks into the country around Salem. Nat, falling sway to her influence as he had done in early boyhood, was soon following like habits. Mrs. Hathorne, in bad health, was often confined to her bed. There were stretches of days when the various members of the Herbert Street household did not once assemble together. What the strange Hathornes were doing in her home appears to have been too much for old Mrs. Manning. It was evidently time for her to give up the ghost.

This she did on December 23, 1826, after a severe spell of the dropsy she had suffered for years.

By the end of the third decade of the nineteenth century several steamships had at various times dropped anchor in Salem harbor, the first having arrived on July 4, 1817. It was obvious that the shipbuilders were from year to year making them safer, larger, and heavier. Also by 1831 steam locomotives were in use on railways in the United States. Salem, dependent almost wholly upon commerce, had a shallow harbor and stood well to the east of the shortest lines connecting other important New England trade centers. The wise men of the town envisioned the possibilities of the new methods of transportation and realized that they were headed for an economic revolution. If Salem survived as a city its heart would be the factory rather than the counting-room.

The shift from commerce to industry might have been gradual and undisturbing, as it was in other American centers. But Providence, as if in chastisement of Salem's money-worshiping aristocrats, saw that the revolution was started with a tragedy comparable only to the witchcrafts in sensationalism. The horrible inciting incident was enacted on the night of April 6, 1830, and the last scene of the denouement was not witnessed until nine months later. Long before the end many of the most effectual of the town's wealthy wielders of power were bowed down with disgrace and shame. Their one aim was to get rid of their holdings in Salem as quickly as possible and begin life anew in Boston or New York or elsewhere.

Robert Manning was among the wise who foresaw the rapid advance of railroads. Though he was still active in the Manning stagecoach company, he was putting most of his savings into his orchards and into the development of a brokerage business he had started. By April 6, 1830, he was the father of two sons and a daughter, all three of whom were to live into the twentieth century. Next door to his home on Dearborn Street in north Salem he had built a cottage. Here the four Hathornes had been dwelling for two years. Aunt Mary and Uncle Samuel were still in the Herbert Street house, part of which was rented to Aunt Priscilla and her husband. Mr. Dike had failed as keeper of a cloth shop, but was making a new start as a dealer in coal. Of the Hathorne aunts only Ruth was left. Old Simon Forrester had died in 1817, leaving his substance—estimated at a million and a half—to his widow and children. He had lived long enough to see another of his sons come to a sorrowful end—death due to fits brought on by alcoholism. Aunt Rachel, a consumptive in her last years, had lingered on until 1823. She left legacies to her sisters, but not a cent to her Hathorne nephew and nieces. Aunt Eunice had died of "apathy" in 1827, and Aunt Sarah Crowninshield from a broken hip in 1829. About the same time Aunt Judith Archer had died in Baltimore, where she had gone to live while Nat Hathorne was in Bowdoin. Aunt Ruth, well past fifty and nearly blind, was alone in the Union Street house. Often Nat or one of his sisters called to read to her.

The will to write, to become a famous author, had possessed Nat more and more since his graduation from college. On April 6, 1830, a sunny Tuesday throbbing with the urge of spring, there was not a man in Salem, not even the most energetic merchant, who worked with Nat Hathorne's diligence. But only Mrs. Hathorne, Ebe, and Louisa knew how the young man labored every day. In 1828 he had somehow got hold of a hundred dollars, and had used the money to guarantee against loss the publishers of his first book, *Fanshawe,* a novel of college life possibly written

in part before his departure from Bowdoin. He had forfeited the hundred dollars, and with very good reason: the
immature work could only have been a failure. It had appeared without his name on the title page, and he was
never to acknowledge that he was the author. Since committing the folly of having it printed he had made great
improvement. One of his essays, the charming "Sights from
a Steeple," was to appear anonymously in the next number
of a popular annual, the *Token*. The editor was holding for
future publication other pieces, including "The Gentle
Boy," a story on the seventeenth-century Quaker persecution in which the first of the Hathornes of Salem had
figured so prominently.

Since the young romancer never spoke of his writing
and had forbidden his mother and sisters to speak of it,
Salem had no way of learning of these achievements. It
is even doubtful whether Uncle Robert, whose articles for
horticultural journals Nat edited and turned into present-
able form, knew of the pieces which had interested the
editor of the *Token*. The few in Salem who were acquainted
with Nat looked upon him as a lazy trifler, with little of
the admirable besides good looks and a gentleman's speech
and manners. One who had been his neighbor on Herbert
Street was to say, "Why, we all thought he was the most
indolent fellow God ever created, loafing about the house,
living on his mother's little inheritance!" An old woman,
a friend of Mrs. Hathorne, ran into him at a fire one night
and scolded him unrestrainedly, ending her abuse with,
"The idea of a strong young man's not going to work as
other people do!"

Nat, a full inheritor of what he called the "granite" of
his Hathorne sires, had ignored the criticism, and had gone
on submitting, day by day, to his will to write. Ebe, as
strong in determination as he, was always by his side to

encourage and help. To just what degree she assisted in the production of his earliest essays and tales was never to be divulged.

If he followed his usual habits on the evening of April 6, 1830, he took a walk after darkness fell and on returning to Dearborn Street sat for a while with his mother and sisters and drank a dish of chocolate. Then he went up to his room, thinking as he retired for the night that the next day would be like any other he had passed in recent months. But Salem was never again to be as he had known it. Before he fell asleep that night the deed which precipitated the far-reaching change had been consummated.

At six o'clock the next morning a manservant in one of the most beautiful of the Salem mansions designed by Samuel McIntire, the residence on Essex Street owned and occupied by the eighty-two-year-old merchant Captain Joseph White, went downstairs to light fires. Captain White, a philanthropic aristocrat worth half a million dollars, had no immediate family. For years his widowed niece, Mrs. Mary Bickford, had kept house for him. Just at this time she was in Wenham, seven miles away, visiting her daughter, Mrs. Joseph Knapp. When the servant entered the east parlor, he felt an unusual chill in the air. Then, to his surprise, he noticed in the back an open window. On attempting to close it he saw that a wide plank had been leaned against the sill from the outside, forming a ramp down to the ground. Fearing burglary, he hastened to the kitchen and talked with the only other servant who had spent the night on the premises, a maid. Together he and she hurried upstairs to report to Captain White, who slept in the southwest chamber on the second floor.

They found his bed a tousled heap of sheets and blankets —all splotched with blood. It was only on second look that they saw their employer's face upturned from the gore-streaked pillow. The forehead and the parts of the cheeks which were free of the crimson smirches bore, beyond a doubt, the pallor of death.

Within a few hours all Salem knew of their horrifying discovery. That afternoon the coroner's report was made public. Captain White had been slain about ten or eleven o'clock the evening before. His skull above the left temple had been fractured by a blow from a blunt instrument, and in the region of his chest there were thirteen deep wounds, made by a sharp dirk or poniard. The motive of the murderer, or murderers, had not been robbery. Several gold doubloons lay on a table by the bed, and valuable plate in the room had not been touched. Papers in a locked iron chest which stood below one of the windows were found to be in order, and the key was in the bureau drawer where, to the knowledge of Captain White's lawyers, it had always been kept. In their office was the deceased's will. The bulk of his estate was to go to his nephew and partner in business, Captain Stephen White, son of a dead brother. The only other near relative living, Mrs. Bickford, daughter of a sister, was to receive a cash settlement of $15,000.

The two heirs sat up with the corpse that night. Captain Stephen White, a merchant and shipowner of great importance, was married to a sister of Justice Joseph Story, of the United States Supreme Court. Another sister of Justice Story was the wife of Nat Hathorne's first cousin John Forrester, who was also at the Essex Street mansion that night to honor the dead. Present too were Mrs. Bickford's daughter and son-in-law, Captain Joseph Knapp, a shipmaster twenty-six years old. He belonged to an aristocratic family of Salem, but since his marriage had maintained a home in Wenham.

Shocked beyond reason, Essex County felt that only a

fiend could have committed such an atrocious assassination. New locks were put on doors and new bars on windows. Firearms and weapons of all sorts were made ready for use. Watchdogs were given special training. Since pedestrians were advised through the newspapers to go abroad only in groups, Ebe and Nat Hathorne ceased their solitary rambles to remote places. Rewards for the apprehension of the guilty were offered by the governor of Massachusetts, the selectmen of Salem, and the deceased's nephew and niece, acting jointly. The Salem council appointed a committee of vigilance, made up of twenty-seven leading citizens headed by the late Simon Forrester's son-in-law Dr. Gideon Barstow, who had represented eastern Massachusetts in the national Congress from 1821 to 1823.

By the time this group was organized for action Essex County was calm enough to view the case with logical discernment. Who besides a madman obsessed with a lust for blood could have committed the murder? It was suggested that since Captain White had made his money out of the African slave traffic a bold desperate Negro bent upon avenging the wrongs suffered by his race was the likely killer. Reasons were offered—especially the unlatched window—for suspecting the two servants who reported the murder to the police. Accusing eyes were even cast in the direction of the dead man's lawyers. Several persons actually argued that Captain White, though eighty-two, had been involved in some sort of a love affair and was the victim of a jealous rival. Some insisted that Mrs. Bickford, away from home the very night of the slaying, was back of the gory business. But she must have found out, said many, that her inheritance was to be only a paltry fifteen thousand, while her cousin, Captain Stephen White, knew that he was to come into a great fortune. It was upon him that the weight of popular suspicion naturally fell.

To charge with the basest of murders a brother-in-law of the most brilliant and most highly esteemed associate justice on the bench of the United States Supreme Court was no small matter. The Salem assassination became a national affair. From Canada to the Gulf of Mexico newspapers ran accounts of "the murder in high place," and far and wide people made wagers on how long it would be before Captain Stephen White would break down and confess.

Then, after almost four weeks, came news even more upsetting than the report of the slaying. A professional criminal had convinced the police authorities of New Bedford, Massachusetts, where he was held in jail on a charge of shoplifting, that he could name the killers of Captain White. His statement had been forwarded to the Salem committee of vigilance, and the man had been brought to Essex County in chains. In Ipswich, in closed court, he had so impressed the examining judges that they had ordered the apprehension of the four he named. It was when they were arrested and lodged in the Salem prison—on Sunday, May 2—that the public heard the story of their accuser and learned their identity. The four were Daniel Chase, of Lynn, Colonel Benjamin Sellman, of Marblehead, and Richard Crowninshield junior and his brother George, both of Danvers.

Crowninshields charged with the awful murder of Captain White! The two young men were grandsons of "old King George C. the First." Their paternal grandmother was born Sarah Hodges Derby. One of their uncles had been Captain Jacob Crowninshield, member of Congress, honored by Jefferson with the offer of the secretaryship of the navy. Another uncle was Benjamin Williams Crowninshield, actually secretary of the navy under Madison and Monroe and at present a candidate for reëlection to Congress on the Jacksonian ticket. An aunt was the wife of Nathaniel Silsbee, a United States senator from Massachusetts. Another uncle was the dashing Captain John Crowninshield, a favorite in Salem, Boston, and New York society. Still another uncle had been the sybaritic bachelor George Crowninshield, builder and owner of America's first palatial private yacht, *Cleopatra's Barge*. After his death the luxurious craft had been bought by the father of the two murder suspects, the elder Richard Crowninshield. In marrying an Irish woman of New York he had defied the Salem caste system. Yet much, if not all, could be forgiven a Crowninshield. After he had spent his patrimony he had known a few hard years —at the period when his sons were emerging out of boyhood. But for a decade now he had been prosperous, manufacturing broadcloth in a mill near the beautiful Danvers farm on which he lived. It was known that his sons, especially Richard, were sowing their wild oats. But there was a difference between the prankishness of youth and crime. Accusing two Essex County Crowninshields of murder in the nineteenth century was what accusing the archangels Michael and Gabriel of heresy would have been in the seventeenth.

While all America gasped with excitement on reading of the charge brought against two grandsons of "old King George C. the First," indignation over their arrest seethed in many a Salem house, including no doubt the houses on Herbert and Dearborn Streets occupied by the Mannings and Hathornes. The blood running in their veins was also in the veins of the Crowninshields. In the latter indeed there were two streams of the Manning blood: the Crowninshields and the Derbys alike were direct descendants of the first Mrs. Anstiss Manning. Then there was the late Sarah Hathorne Crowninshield to take into account. Her husband was an own cousin of the father of the two Crowninshields now held in prison. "But for the grace of Providence," Nat Hathorne probably said, "I myself might now be locked in

jail in the place of my double cousins Richard and George."
It is unlikely that he had ever in his life spoken to either of
them. But in him, as in every New Englander, the ties of
blood were strong. He could not have been unresentful
when he saw two of his kinsmen, however distant, charged
with murder on the evidence of a low shoplifter.

Within a few days another professional criminal entered
the case, an ex-convict of Belfast, Maine. A blackmail letter, a demand for $350 made upon Captain Joseph Knapp,
was received and turned over to the committee of vigilance.
Somehow a good deal of the letter became known to the
public. "The refusal to grant my request," wrote the ex-
convict to Captain Knapp, "will ruin you. Are you surprised
with this assertion? Rest assured that I make it, reserving the
reasons and a series of facts which are founded on such a
bottom as will bid defiance to property or quality. There is
no need to enter a discussion of facts which will harrow your
soul. I am acquainted with your brother Frank and the business he was transacting on April 3. I think you were very
extravagant in giving $1,000 to a person that would execute
the business for you. You see that things will out." While
this communication was the talk of Salem, the Crowninshields were thinking of the best way in which to bring the
authorities to account for accusing Richard and George.

But when, on the basis of the ex-convict's sworn statement, Captain Knapp and his twenty-year-old brother
Frank were charged of complicity in the murder and taken
into custody, Richard and George Crowninshield were not
set free. It was May 26, a Wednesday, when the Knapp
brothers were committed to prison. Seventy-two hours of
black anxiety for Salem's greatest families followed. Then,
on May 29, Captain Knapp, at the advice of his minister, the
Reverend Henry Colman, turned state's evidence and signed
a lengthy confession, which was at once made public.

After seven weeks of speculating the world had a solution to the mystery of the White murder. The instigator was Joseph Knapp. As Mrs. Bickford's son-in-law, he had free access to the White mansion. One day while rummaging through a set of private papers he found what he took to be Captain White's final will, a legal writing which provided for Mrs. Bickford a small legacy and for Stephen White practically all the rest of a half-million-dollar estate. Joseph, ignorant of the Massachusetts laws of inheritance, reasoned that if this instrument were destroyed and the aged man got out of the way before another will could be made Mrs. Bickford would fall heir to at least $200,000. He took into his confidence his brother Frank, six years his junior, and the two laid plans. On April 3, a deal was made with Richard and George Crowninshield. In return for a promised payment of $1,000, they agreed to "blot out" old Captain White. On April 5, Joseph went to the White mansion, stole the will he had seen, and unlatched the window of the east parlor so that it could be opened from the outside. The evening of the murder he was in Wenham with his wife and mother-in-law, and George Crowninshield was with his parents in Danvers. Richard Crowninshield, armed with a dirk and a hickory bludgeon which he himself had turned and weighted with lead, did the killing. During the few minutes required for the deed Frank Knapp was standing guard on Brown Street at the back of the mansion. The next morning, as soon as the news of the murder got abroad, Joseph burned the stolen legal writing—only to find out a few hours later that it was a mere scrap of paper, a memorandum for the dead man's lawyers, who held safe in their own keeping the authentic will. Providence, working with the usual mysteriousness, had seen that the murder was done in vain. Joseph Knapp was left to pay the assassins their hire and live with his consciousness of guilt.

When on May 29, 1830, he fixed his signature to his sworn statement the plutocracy which had been evolving in Salem since the witchcrafts of 1692 came to an abrupt end. On June 12 the American public found out that two scions of one of the country's greatest families were thieves as well as paid killers. That day the Salem police—informed by the Maine ex-convict, whose name was Palmer—discovered in the Crowninshield barn in Danvers a cache of stolen goods. Richard and George were obviously leaders of a crime ring, which included Palmer and the New Bedford shoplifter. The latter, it was certain, could have known nothing of the plans for the White murder. In accusing the Crowninshield brothers and Colonel Sellman and Daniel Chase he was simply trying to get revenge for some sort of underworld double-dealing. Shortly after Joseph Knapp's confession was signed the charges against Sellman and Chase were dropped, and the two were given their freedom.

Richard Crowninshield had the habit of making up verses. If at the proper period in his childhood he had been subjected to the discipline of a wise Robert Manning, he too might have turned out to be a writer. He was just two months and ten days younger than his double third cousin Nat Hathorne. The place of his birth was Liverpool, where his mother had accompanied his father on a trading trip. He was bright and beautiful. His parents, fascinated by his precocity, became his slaves. Whatever he desired, however expensive it might be, he got. By the time he was eight he was known as "the little terror of Essex County," and his parents and uncles laughed at his "wicked escapades." He rebelled at schooling, and remained ignorant of grammar and spelling.

He was fourteen or fifteen when his father entered a period of financial adversity. The boy, following the accepted Crowninshield pattern, went to sea. Serving before the mast, he found out that his name protected him against discipline. By the time he was sixteen he had entered upon his career as a criminal.

In Charleston, when he was near twenty-one, he became engaged to the daughter of a wealthy South Carolina planter. Such a report on his character as that which follows came from Salem: "He is of dark and reserved deportment, temperate and wicked, daring and wary, subtle and obdurate, of great adroitness, boldness and self-command. He has for several years frequented the haunts of vice in Salem; and though he is often spoken of as a dangerous man his person is known to few, for he never walks the streets by daylight. Among his few associates he is a leader and a despot." The engagement was broken.

When he was asked by the Knapp brothers to kill Captain White, he began speaking about how the fee was to be paid, showing at once that he was willing to take on the job. To Joseph Knapp the day after the murder he casually said, "After I had done for the old man, I put my fingers on his pulse to make certain."

The evening of the murder he was at home in Danvers, sitting in the parlor before the fire with George and the rest of the family. Shortly after nine o'clock he said he was tired and was going to bed. Instead he stole out a back door to the stables, saddled a horse, and, carrying his bludgeon and dirk, dashed off for Captain White's mansion in Salem. Before midnight he was back home, in his room on the second floor. He changed into a dressing gown, went downstairs, and found George and his father still before the parlor fire, reading. Complaining of sleeplessness, he said he needed a cup of herb tea, and a servant was summoned to prepare it. His composure was that of a man without nerves. With George's assistance he had established, he believed, an unshakable alibi.

When arrested and imprisoned he maintained his mien of indifference and bravado. "But when he was told of the arrest of the Knapp brothers," said the jailer, "his knees smote beneath him, the sweat started out on his stern and pallid face, and he subsided on his bunk." On June 12, suspecting that Palmer, his henchman in robbery, was lodged in the cell directly below his, he dug through the mortar of the floor with his fingernails and let down a pencil and a piece of paper tied to a string. On the paper were written two lines of verse, which Palmer was supposed to cap if he were really there. The Maine ex-convict, who had turned informer, begged like a terrified child to be transferred to another wing of the prison.

On the morning of June 16, the jailer found Richard Crowninshield's body hanging at the end of a handkerchief tied to the bars of his cell. The assassin for hire had been dead for ten or twelve hours. On his bunk were papers proving that during the two or three days preceding his suicide his spirit of defiance had been almost crushed by the concept of sin and retribution which he had inherited from his Crowninshield, Manning, Williams, Hodges, and Derby ancestors. To his father he wrote: "These are the last lines from your undutiful son, who has disregarded your chaste moral precepts—always bountifully bestowed upon the unfortunate being who will ere you receive this cease to exist. My last request is that you have my body decently buried, and have it protected from the dissecting knife. May the blessing of God rest upon you. Farewell." To George, over whom his will had been complete, he wrote: "Dear brother, may God, and your innocence, guide you *safe* through this trial. Had I taken your advice I would enjoy life, liberty, and a clear conscience. But I have not, and perceive my case to be hopeless. Therefore, I have come to the determination to deprive them of the pleasure of beholding me publicly executed, as after I am condemned they will not give me the opportunity. May God forgive me! George, this is an awful warning to you. And I hope it will be the means of reforming many to virtue. Albeit they may meet with success at the commencement of vice, it is short-lived, and if they persist they will meet with a similar fate to mine. Oh, George, forgive me for what I have caused you and others to suffer on my account! My last benediction rests upon you. A long, a last, adieu." But the old Puritan urge, absorbed in childhood, never quite triumphed. The one other paper found in the killer's cell was a hymn of hate addressed to the guardians of the law:

> Ungrateful wretches, why do ye crave
> The life our heavenly Maker gave?
> Why shut us in these gloomy cells,
> Where only brooding sorrow dwells?
> Detested fiends, be banished hence,
> Among your kind go boast your sense—
> Where imps of hell and devils roam,
> Go forth and find your native home.

Those acquainted with Richard Crowninshield had insisted from the time of his arrest that he would neither openly confess bludgeoning and stabbing Captain White nor die by a hangman's rope.

For the trial of Frank Knapp, which began July 12, Daniel Webster was appointed by the state to serve as special prosecutor. Many in Salem were never to forgive the great orator for "straining the law and making an accomplice in a murder a real principal." Whatever means was adopted, Webster won a conviction, and on August 20 heard Frank Knapp sentenced to die. The hanging took place at nine o'clock on the morning of September 28 "at the north end of the Salem prison in the yard." Several thousand spectators, including a few women, witnessed "the melancholy exit."

At Frank's trial Joseph at last showed that he was not entirely devoid of honor. Since he had turned state's evidence, he was supposed to appear as a witness against his brother. In refusing to do this, he forfeited the state's promise of impunity. Placed on trial in November, he was easily convicted. His "melancholy exit" took place on December 31, with as many as five thousand looking on, fewer women this time.

America expected to read also of the execution of George Crowninshield. But at his trial, held early in 1831, the defense lawyers proved an alibi and the state had to yield. "Not at all cast down by what had taken place, walking arm in arm with a girl," George was seen a few months later by Nat Hathorne.

It is possible that Nat wrote several reports on the trials for the Salem *Gazette*. Certainly the accounts of the executions in that newspaper bear marks of his style. The editor was acquainted with his skill. In the *Gazette* towards the end of 1830 two of his stories appeared anonymously—"The Hollow of the Three Hills" on November 12 and "An Old Woman's Tale" on December 21. The former, which tells of a witch's revelations to a sin-ridden woman, could have been suggested by Joseph Knapp's wife and mother-in-law, both of whom were strongly suspected in Salem of "being privy" to the plot which culminated in the murder. The latter story, probably written long before 1830, is in all likelihood a variation of the old legend of the Hathornes of Bray as it had been preserved through six generations of their Salem descendants. To give it novelty Nat used an indeterminate ending, as Washington Irving had done with pleasurable effect in "The Stout Gentleman."

Nat Hathorne drew directly from facts in the White murder in creating his most successful humorous story, "Mr. Higginbotham's Catastrophe." He was to recall the case in the sunniest of his novels, *The House of the Seven Gables*. He never penned more sprightly letters than those in which he pictured the reaction of Salem towards the tragedy.

In the light of these facts one might suppose that down in the romancer's subconsciousness, the source of his art, there was cruelty. The truth is that he was only human, wise, and proud. He would never have asked for Providence to visit upon his town the distressful events of 1830. He was to be as secretive as the rest of Salem about the White murder, which in bringing shame upon the Crowninshields also brought shame upon him, who was of their own flesh and blood. But since the tragedy came, crushing the power of the class by which he and those dear to him had always been scorned, his satisfaction went deeper than he could have consciously realized. Not again in Salem would a Richard Crowninshield be able to hide himself behind his name and follow a criminal course unhindered by the law. Not again would those who belonged to streets like Herbert meet discrimination at every turn. Not again would the prevailing order entice a man to bury his soul under a pile of gold. Nat Hathorne intuitively saw all this; and within his heart of hearts, unperceived by his outward awareness, the comic spirit stirred.

"THE SCARLET LETTER"

AS LATE AS March 30, 1826, when the romancer scratched his name on a windowpane in the Herbert Street house, he was still using the traditional spelling *Hathorne*. By the year of the White murder he had changed to the more phonetic *Hawthorne*, as the Corwins had changed to *Curwen* and the Endecotts to *Endicott*. The romancer's mother held on to the *Hathorne*, but Ebe and Louisa followed their brother in inserting the *w*. It is possible that he had seen the name written *Hawthorne* in seventeenth- or eighteenth-century records. He appears never to have gone to the trouble to have his reversion to the old spelling formally legalized.

While he was acquiring the knowledge and skill by which he was to make the name Hawthorne the most distinguished in Salem annals, the town was undergoing the change precipitated by the White tragedy. Benjamin Williams Crowninshield was defeated for Congress in the election of 1830, and within a few years he and most of the other Crowninshields were out of Salem. During the same period the most powerful of the Derbys departed. Some of the aristocrats who were hanging their heads in disgrace drifted to distant places. Harvard-trained Phippen Knapp, brother of the two who were executed for the murder of Captain White, migrated to the Southern frontier town of Montgomery, Alabama, to spend the rest of his long life as rector of an Episcopalian parish. The romancer—laboring with his sister Ebe in recreating the New England which Major Hathorne, the first Colonel John, Captain Joseph, and Captain Daniel had known—had little time to think about the economic and social revolution taking place about him. Gradually he was perfecting his art; and gradually—through the *Token*, the *New England Magazine*, and other periodicals—he was winning readers. But none of his pieces were as yet subscribed Hawthorne. The changing Salem remained ignorant of his work as an author. To his neighbors he was still a shameless good-for-nothing.

Early in the fall of 1830—a few days before the hanging of Frank Knapp—Uncle Richard Manning died in Raymond. He had no children, and his estate went to his widow. Possessed also of lands deeded to her by her father, she was not long in remarrying. Her new husband, François Radoux, had come to Maine from France by way of Canada. He had fought at Waterloo as an officer under Napoleon.

In 1832 Hawthorne and his mother and sisters, after four years on Dearborn Street next door to Uncle Robert, moved back to Herbert Street. The Dikes had gone to live in a house of their own on Andover Street, and Aunt Mary needed assistance in caring for Uncle Samuel. This likable judge of horses, a forty-year-old bachelor, was suffering from hemorrhages of the lungs. He resisted the "hectic" to which he had fallen prey until November 17, 1833. Two or three days later his relatives gathered once more for a burial in the Howard Street Cemetery. In his will, filed for probate January 7, 1834, he was styled "Gent." All his brothers and sisters except Priscilla Dike were named for bequests. To Mrs. Hathorne went one half of his interest in his father's estate, and each of her children got a legacy of $100. He had transferred his membership from the East Church to the First Church. The pew he held in the latter went to his sister Mary.

Hawthorne had joined him on several horse-buying expeditions—to New Haven, and into New Hampshire.

Traveling alone on summer trips during the decade of the 1830's, the romancer got acquainted with the White Mountains, central New York along the route of the Erie Canal, Niagara, the Berkshire Hills, Martha's Vineyard, and Maine in the vicinity of Augusta. Observations made on these journeys—by stagecoach, rail, and boat—were recorded in notebooks and drawn upon for descriptive sketches, essays, and tales. During this beginning period in his career as a writer Hawthorne was adhering to a set program: he was giving artistic expression to New England's past and present picturesqueness.

He picked up interesting lore from his history-minded second cousin Susanna Ingersoll, whom he nicknamed "the Duchess." She was a niece of the second Colonel John Hathorne. In 1804, when she was nineteen, her father, Captain Samuel Ingersoll, and her one brother to reach manhood, likewise a mariner, died of yellow fever on the same ship while returning to Salem from Guadeloupe. Then her only sister died—and her mother, from whom she had heard many a curious story of early Puritans. Susanna, committed to spinsterhood, became a recluse in the dilapidated Turner Street mansion which was to be known as the House of the Seven Gables. Conspicuous in the parlor was an antique carved seat, to be commemorated by Hawthorne in *Grandfather's Chair*. Miss Ingersoll was not alone in the roomy old dwelling. Living with her was a protégé, Horace Conolly, six years younger than Hawthorne. For a period preceding Horace's birth his father was Miss Ingersoll's gardener. When Salem heard that the recluse had adopted the boy to bring up as her own, gossips whispered, "She has a better reason than appears on the surface for doing that!" Horace, now a dissatisfied Episcopalian clergyman with a parish in a poor section of Boston, had been educated at Yale. It was while Hawthorne was on a trip to New Haven in 1828 that he and Horace met. Since then the romancer had spent much time in the Turner Street house. He liked "the Duchess," and was profiting greatly from her yarns about old Salem.

He seems never to have met Colonel John Hathorne, who died at his farm on Salem Neck on December 24, 1834, at the age of eighty-five. Just six weeks earlier the old man had lost his wife, to whom he had been married for sixty-two years. From their son Ebenezer—a mariner, a privateersman in the War of 1812, an adventurer in the West and Mexico, a clerk in the Boston customhouse, and a Jacksonian Democrat of the most radical variety—Hawthorne found out that they had left interesting documents relating to family history. The shopkeeper Captain William Hathorne, their one other son still living, had transferred his business to Lynn in 1831. Among his offspring was a Hathorne specimen almost as rare as the romancer—a Baptist minister, the Reverend William Herbert Hathorne.

Horace Conolly—Hawthorne's cousin by adoption, if not, as certain gossips insisted, cousin by blood—was superficially brilliant, loquacious, spoiled, and unreliable. Miss Ingersoll lived on the income from her inheritance. But it was small, and from the point of view of the Salem aristocrats she was definitely of the social class to which Hawthorne belonged. Her main moral support was her pride, which Horace shared to the full. He seems to have spent more time in Salem than with his Boston parish. In time he was to renounce the ministry and become in turn a physician, a loafer, and a drunkard. Often of an evening he and another friend to whom Hawthorne had become attached, David Roberts, turned up at Herbert Street to play cards. Roberts, a Harvard graduate and a rising lawyer, was to become mayor of Salem. But his family belonged also to the town's third class.

On the evenings when Hawthorne was host to his friends, Louisa assisted him in entertaining. Aunt Mary, the only Manning left in the Herbert Street house after the death of Samuel, was so tired when darkness came that she went to bed. She did not know as yet that she had a cancer. Mrs. Hawthorne and Ebe were, as usual, "invisible entities."

Louisa was nearing thirty. Love and marriage might have freed her from her little-girl habits. But if she had ideas when she greeted Conolly and Roberts, she was far afield. Both were misogamists. As to Hawthorne's true attitude towards involving himself in wedlock, no one at this time could speak. He rarely came back from one of his summer trips without a report on a flirtation. Intellect-ridden Ebe, who believed that marriage would interfere with his development as an artist, was worried at times. But, to her relief, she always found out that her brother in claiming himself enamored was merely making comedy.

The card players were a merry quartet when they got well into their games of whist. Louisa, called "the Empress" on these occasions, was naturally gay. The gin that was drunk lifted the spirits of "the Emperor," who was Hawthorne, "the Cardinal," who was Conolly, and "the Chancellor," who was Roberts. Frequent and witty must have been the gibes at the Salem aristocrats whom the scandal of the White murder had bowed low.

The bond connecting Hawthorne and Roberts was in the main political. A great day for both was June 26, 1833, when their revered leader, President Andrew Jackson, visited Salem. At the hour of Old Hickory's arrival, said Ebe, Hawthorne was on the streets to shout welcome. It was difficult for her to fancy her brother doing such a thing as yelling.

When she saw how he was attracted to his cousin Nancy Forrester Barstow's little daughter Elinor, she should have known that he would never get control of his full powers as an artist until he had children of his own. He was devoted to the beautiful Elinor, and saw much of her. "He liked little girls," Ebe reported, "but he said he didn't think boys worth raising." Elinor was the model for the child in "Little Annie's Ramble." Once she came to see Hawthorne, and, in tears, told him that she had heard somebody call him an infidel and that she believed he was, since he never went to church. "He took her on his knee," wrote Ebe, "and comforted her—told her that he was not an infidel, and that he did go to church when he happened to be elsewhere than in Salem on a Sunday."

The Sabbath as well as other days was for him a workday. Between the fall of 1830 and the beginning of 1837 more than a hundred of his essays, stories, biographical sketches, and descriptive pieces appeared in periodicals. For a good part of 1836—when he was living in Boston in the home of the one-time popular verse satirist Thomas Green Fessenden—he edited the *American Magazine of Useful and Entertaining Knowledge*, and, with Ebe's assistance, wrote most of the matter making up the monthly issues. On giving up this work, for which he was never fully paid the paltry salary promised, he came back to Salem, and, collaborating with Ebe, wrote within a few weeks *Peter Parley's Universal History*. Thousands of copies of this sketchy schoolbook were to be sold, but Hawthorne's pay was only $100, which he turned over to Ebe entire. The title page bore neither his name nor hers. His anonymity was not broken until March, 1837, when a collection of his stories and essays appeared. It was the first edition of *Twice-Told Tales*. Among the eighteen pieces contained in the volume were "The Gentle Boy," "Mr. Higginbotham's Catastrophe," "The Gray Champion," "Wakefield," "The Wedding Knell," "The Minister's Black Veil," "The Maypole of Merry Mount," "Dr. Heidegger's Experiment," "The Hollow of the Three Hills," "The Great Carbuncle," and "David Swan"—all of which critics of the future were to acclaim as masterpieces. American readers at last got acquainted with the name Nathaniel Hawthorne. But the country was beginning to feel the pinch of an economic depression: few were able to buy such luxuries as books of fiction. Though *Twice-Told Tales* was praised by the reviewers, Hawthorne remained poor. The Salem newspapers ran notices of the publication and complimented the Herbert Street author. Still his neighbors kept alive the rumor that he was a trifler.

In Salem newspapers in the summer of 1835 appeared the advertisement: "Dr. Peabody has removed into Charter Street, third house from Central Street, and continues to operate on teeth, according to the latest improvements. In addition to animal teeth, he can furnish mineral teeth of the best quality from a single tooth to a whole set. Teeth powder and English teeth brushes. Also beetle-nut teeth powder, just imported and esteemed superior to any other." More than twenty years had passed since this dentist—and, on occasion, general physician, now homeopathic—had lived on Union Street, a neighbor of the Mannings and Hathornes. He had moved to Boston in 1824, had remained there until 1828, and then had come back to Salem, to a house "near the water" on Court Street. The angular three-story dwelling in which he installed his family in July, 1835, was adjacent to the historic Burying Point, beginning to be known as the Charter Street Cemetery. From the first-floor windows of the east side of the house one could reach out and touch tombstones. The lugubrious place, only three short blocks from Herbert Street, was to be pictured by Hawthorne in the opening chapters of the unfinished *Doctor Grimshawe's Secret.*

Dr. Peabody and his bluestocking schoolmistress wife were proud of their daughters, all three of whom were intellectual and ambitious. Lizzie, a teacher since the age of sixteen, had for several years also done secretarial work for the Reverend William Ellery Channing, the celebrated Boston Unitarian, whose sermons were eloquent expositions of the philosophy known as Transcendentalism. For a year now she had been assisting one of his disciples, Amos Bronson Alcott, master of the Temple School in Boston. Another disciple of Mr. Channing, the Reverend Ralph Waldo Emerson, had taught Lizzie Greek. Mr. Emerson, now without a parish, was living in the village of Concord, giving the final touches to his soon-to-be-published *Nature,* a compendium of Transcendental ideas. Lizzie believed that in the new philosophy, which stressed the divine origin of intuition and the ascendancy of mind over matter, man had at last found truth. In full agreement with her were her sisters, who had recently returned from Cuba. In this island of everlasting summer they had spent three years on a plantation, Mary as a governess and Sophia as an invalid in quest of health. Sophia had been for years a perpetual sufferer from a severe nervous headache. "The grip of an iron hand upon my poor brain," she called it. Her father insisted that it was the aftereffect of the allopathic drugs dosed out to her when as an infant she was ill from teething. The tropical warmth of Cuba had given her the only surcease from pain she had known in many years. But on the stormy voyage back to New England "the iron hand" had renewed the grasp. Now in the house on Charter Street she had her meals alone, for the noise eaters made in using knives and forks caused "the hand" to grip all the harder.

Since Salem's frequent east winds had a like effect, she rarely ventured outdoors. She had converted her sunny third-floor room into a studio, and spent most of her days painting. Washington Allston had spoken well of her talent for drawing and for combining colors. She had even succeeded in selling a few of her pictures. In the evenings she read—perhaps in French, with ease, or in German or Italian, with difficulty. Visitors, usually bringing flowers, called frequently. With her almost thirty years and her invalidism, she scarcely dared to dream of a prince charming.

Despite her Transcendental optimism and her belief in a great law of compensation operating throughout the universe, she must have felt at times that a malicious Providence was hounding her brothers. The Peabodys had been living on Charter Street less than a year when news came that Wellington, the youngest in the family to survive childhood, had died of yellow fever in Louisiana. He was a black sheep, a failure as a student and afterwards an unhappy wanderer on sea and on land. "He was nursed at my breast," said Mrs. Peabody, "when I was anxious and worried. That's why he's unstable." He had not been long in his grave when George, who was four years Sophia's junior and the brightest of the brothers, joined a group of Boston athletes in a long distance running contest. He came in first in a race from Roxbury to the Massachusetts State House. But the feat was too much for his endurance. Soon he was confined in a room in the Charter Street dwelling, a victim of consumption of the spine. Until 1839, death was not to deliver him from the torment he suffered. Providence had made an unaspiring plodder out of the oldest boy in the family, Nathaniel Cranch, born two years after Sophia. He married early, and then settled down to pass most of the hours of his long life mixing and selling homeopathic medicine in a Boston dispensary.

About the time of the publication of *Twice-Told Tales*
Lizzie Peabody turned up at Charter Street for a visit with
her parents, sisters, and sick brother George. She had not
seen a copy of the new book, but she had found out that
it contained pieces she had read in periodicals and was the
work of a Salemite designated on the title page as Nathaniel
Hawthorne. She dismissed as the possible author each of
the Hathorne men she knew or had heard about. They
were too "lacking in manners" to write the prose she had
admired in "The Gentle Boy." The one among them who
bore the name Nathaniel was, moreover, notorious for his
laziness. The author of *Twice-Told Tales*, she concluded,
was using a pen name. Then it occured to her that the
book could have been written by none other than her
amazingly ingenious childhood companion Ebe Hathorne.
Convinced that her deduction could not be false, she called
at Herbert Street to express congratulations and renew
the old intimacy with Ebe.

The caller saw only Louisa, who made clear the truth
about the authorship of *Twice-Told Tales*. With characteristic lack of tact Lizzie said, "If your brother can write
like that, he has no right to be idle." Louisa replied, "My
brother is never idle."

This interview, awkward as it was, led to friendly intercourse between the Herbert Street and Charter Street families and thence to what a Hawthorne descendant was to
call "the brookside angling" of the three Peabody sisters.
Hawthorne—as handsome as Lord Byron to Lizzie, as re-
freshing as a breeze in springtime to Mary, and as magnetic
as amber to Sophia—was the prize to be hooked. Almost
two years passed before it was certain that Sophia, freed
of the grip of "the iron hand" when in Hawthorne's presence, was to be the catcher. However Lizzie and Mary

might have felt at the start, they submitted joyfully to their sister's victory, especially when they realized that the love which had come into her life was restoring her health. Lizzie was to remain single and attain fame as a trainer of the young, while Mary was to be the wife of the celebrated educator, Horace Mann.

Ebe—whose beautiful eyes, low laugh, and long tapering fingers impressed Lizzie—was for many months unaware of the real purpose of "the brookside angling." Finding the brilliant Peabody sisters intellectually congenial, she called on them, received them at Herbert Street, took walks with them, accompanied them to the home of a Salem bluestocking for "Transcendental Saturday evenings," and exchanged with them books, pictures, flowers, and rare seaweeds. But when at last she sensed that her brother had lost his heart to the invalid Sophia she returned to her seclusion—disappointed in him, apprehensive over his future, and embittered at what appeared to her to be the deceit of the Peabodys.

Hawthorne was born to lean upon someone, and his years of illness in childhood had made him all the more dependent. Since his graduation from Bowdoin, Ebe had been his main prop. It was she above all others who had kept him submissive to his will to write. Now she found herself displaced.

She could only look on while he abandoned his aim to become "the artist of the beautiful" and turned his energies towards earning enough money to get married. Spurred on by the aggressive Lizzie Peabody and aided by his associates in the Democratic party, he succeeded in obtaining a position as gauger in the Boston customhouse. During 1839 and 1840—the last two years of President Van Buren's administration—he weighed salt and coal, lived in miserly manner in the home of the lawyer and littérateur George

Hillard, dispatched lush love letters to Sophia, and wrote little for publication besides *Grandfather's Chair* and *Biographical Stories for Children*. The former of these juveniles was brought out by a principal Transcendental publisher, none other than Lizzie, whom all the Peabodys after the death of George joined at 13 West Street in Boston. In this building, a favorite gathering place for Transcendentalists, were the family living quarters, the doctor's dental office and dispensary, Sophia's studio, and Lizzie's editorial office, press rooms, and bookshop. Hawthorne managed to save out of his salary as a customhouse employee about a thousand dollars. Most of this money he lost in 1841 when, still under the influence of the Peabodys, he used it to buy membership in the colony which a group of economics-minded Transcendentalists were establishing at Brook Farm in West Roxbury. Once settled there he believed that he had found a home to which he could bring his bride. But after seven or eight months of milking cows, piling manure, seeding the fields, cutting hay, and living in the closest contact with his visionary fellow colonists he decided that Brook Farm was no place for a man of his individualistic nature. Great must have been Ebe's satisfaction when he returned to Salem.

He got back to Herbert Street in time to see Aunt Mary Manning die of the cancer which had tortured her for months. If he expected to inherit something out of her substance, he met disappointment. Her will provided that the income from her real estate was to go to her bachelor brother William as long as he lived and afterwards to Ebe, who was left also all personal belongings.

Hawthorne, despite frustrated hopes, was determined at whatever cost to marry and establish a home. He counted upon a partial refund of his investment in Brook Farm, and in time he was to go so far as to sue for it in the courts.

Twice-Told Tales, enlarged to two volumes, was soon to be reissued, and he made himself believe that his royalties would be considerable. Most of all he built his hopes upon the promise of John O'Sullivan, editor of the *Democratic Review,* to which he had contributed six pieces in 1838. "All the tales and essays you write," said Mr. O'Sullivan, "I'll buy and print." Hawthorne felt that he was at last in position to take unto himself his adored Sophia as wife.

Though the engagement had existed since the end of 1838, his mother and sisters did not hear of it from his own lips until June, 1842. When at last he spoke, Mrs. Hathorne said, "We've known a long time." She gave to the proposed marriage her "fullest blessing and concurrence." Louisa uttered no protest. Ebe at least led her brother to believe that she would be sympathetic. But only a woman deeply hurt by defeat and determined upon estrangement could have written the ironic congratulatory letter which she addressed to Sophia.

On July 9, about a month after the letter was dispatched, the marriage took place at the Peabody home in Boston. No relative of the groom witnessed the ceremony.

Three months later, when Robert Manning—at the age of fifty-eight—died of palsy, Hawthorne retaliated. He was unable to attend the funeral of the uncle to whom he owed his education, because, he said, he had the potatoes and apples to harvest, a guest to entertain, and "a literary matter to be completed." He and Sophia had gone straight from the marriage altar to the Old Manse in Concord. Their love, they fancied, had converted the gloomy gray house into Paradise. Lost in happiness, they had no past and no future. Hawthorne described their ecstatic present in a tale entitled "The New Adam and Eve." He had written to Louisa the day after his marriage that he would neither give up his own relations nor adopt others. He appeared unheedful of that promise on the occasion of Uncle Robert's death. Yet in the letter in which he made weak excuses for not attending the funeral he did say, "Something must be done for the children."

Robert Manning's widow found it unnecessary to look beyond her Dearborn Street home for help. Though the eldest son, named for his father, was only fifteen, he was a reliable support, altogether different from his dreamer cousin, Nathaniel Hawthorne. The lad had grown up in his father's orchards, and did so well in following in his father's steps that after only a year he won a prize for an exhibition of pears at an Essex County horticultural fair. He too was to become a famous pomologist. In the democratic Salem which was in the making no family was to be more respected than the Mannings of Dearborn Street—two sons and two daughters. Rebecca, the youngest, born in 1834, was to live unmarried, until she was near ninety-nine, and many a biographer was to profit from her amazingly vivid recollections of her illustrious cousin Hawthorne.

Six weeks after the death of Uncle Robert, came Thanksgiving Day. Only three of the Mannings of his generation were left to celebrate the time-honored Puritan fete—Mrs. Hathorne, Mrs. Dike, and Uncle William. Whether the reunion was held at Herbert Street or Dearborn Street, it was a sad occasion. Mrs. Hathorne had half expected that her son and daughter-in-law would be present. But Hawthorne and Sophia had decided that it would be profanation to leave their Paradise for their first celebration of Thanksgiving as man and wife.

The only servant they could afford, an inexperienced Irish girl named Mary O'Brien, knew little about cooking. Sophia—"by the mere force of instinct, having never been taught," said Hawthorne—had roasted the five-pound turkey, steamed the plum pudding, and baked the pumpkin pies. Certain pieces of the china in which the Irish maid served the delicacies were a gift from Hawthorne's mother. They had been brought from Canton by Captain Nathaniel Hathorne, and bore the initials NH. As the husband and wife feasted, thanking Providence for their bliss, they fancied themselves earth's first man and woman and Mary O'Brien their attending cherub.

There were no flaming logs to look at while they ate. The Old Manse was warmed by airtight stoves, which consumed a fraction of the fuel required in fireplaces. They gave out comfort, but they were miserable machines, these money-saving heaters. Pizwizzen, the stray cat which had been adopted, had leaped to the top of one when it was hot, and was still limping with badly burned paws. Hawthorne had nothing to smoke after the feast was ended. The household purse had grown so light that he was depriving himself of cigars. The turkey for the Thanksgiving celebration was the smallest and cheapest procurable. Still Sophia had done a lot of adding and subtracting of accounts before permitting herself to purchase it. Hawthorne had been so submerged in honeymoon happiness that he had turned out little for Mr. O'Sullivan to buy and print. Not a cent of the Brook Farm investment had been recovered, and the royalties from the new *Twice-Told Tales* were almost negligible. Hawthorne had written to his Boston friend George Hillard, "Surely the book was puffed enough to meet with a sale. What the devil is the matter?"

Necessity demanded a change in habits at the Old Manse. During the winter and spring following the Thanksgiving of 1842 Hawthorne wrote tales for the *Democratic Review* at the rate of one a month and also found time to write a few pieces for other periodicals. Sophia worked too, painting her conception of Endymion, wondering, as she decided upon colors, whether she might dare ask a hundred dollars for the finished picture, without a frame. She knew that she would have to be very persuasive if her husband, with his pride, allowed her to sell one of her creations. Every month bills had to be paid, and there was hardly ever enough money. Still the Old Manse, as Hawthorne and Sophia pictured it in letters, remained Paradise.

On their first wedding anniversary, July 9, 1843, the heavenly benediction which they had felt upon the place was withdrawn. They had planned to make of the day twenty-four hours of bliss. But Providence intervened. A young woman, unknown to either Hawthorne or Sophia, chose that very day to drown herself in the Concord River, and the spot she decided upon was near the Old Manse. That evening Hawthorne joined the men who were searching for the body. Most of them were weathered yeomen, indifferent to the grimness of the task in which they were engaged. As they poked with poles and pitchforks among the reeds and rushes, they kept up a flow of earthy talk. When at last they found the body and drew it to the surface, Hawthorne witnessed the awful ugliness of death. The pitchforks had torn away most of the clothing, and the young woman, who in life might have been pretty, was bloated with water and smirched with mud. The sight produced upon Hawthorne an impression he was not to forget. He felt that Providence had set a blight upon his and Sophia's Paradise. Henceforth he was to refer to the place as simply the Old Manse.

When the Thanksgiving Day of 1843 came Sophia was in the sixth month of pregnancy. With her body grown unshapely, she no longer danced to the tunes of the music box which Henry Thoreau had brought to the Old Manse. Now of an evening she sewed while Hawthorne read aloud from Spenser or Shakespeare. When she would hold up a tiny sleeve, he would stop and ask, "And for whom, pray, is that?"

For the Thanksgiving celebration of 1844 he took his wife and the first fruit of their love, a nine-months-old daughter named Una, to Salem. From Boston they traveled in the cars, which had been in operation for six years.

Since Aunt Mary Manning's death and Hawthorne's marriage Mrs. Hathorne and her daughters had had the Herbert Street house all to themselves. They had made no attempt to relieve the sombreness of the rooms. To Sophia the place was "Castle Dismal." But on the Thanksgiving Day of 1844 little Una brought in a bit of gayety. "I've never before seen a baby with so perfect a body!" declared Mrs. Hathorne. The child was carried across the two back yards to the Hathorne house on Union Street for a visit with Aunt Ruth. Not until 1847 was death to deliver from loneliness and near-blindness this sixty-six-year-old spinster, the last of the generation of Hathornes to which the romancer's father belonged. Timidly holding Una in her lap, she exclaimed, "Little Nat's little girl!" When the baby was taken back to Herbert Street, dinner was announced. To the surprise of Sophia, who had somehow heard that Hawthorne had never in his life eaten a meal with his mother, all the family gathered at table. Sophia attributed the change in custom to Una's presence in the house. Ebe, who had fault to find with the writing Hawthorne had done since his marriage, must have held back her sarcasm that day. According to all reports, no sour words marred the happiness of the reunion.

On the Thanksgiving Day of 1845 Hawthorne, Sophia, and Una were again in Salem. For a month the Herbert Street house had been their home. The circulation of the *Democratic Review* had dropped so low that Mr. O'Sullivan was no longer able to pay for contributions. Hawthorne had edited Horatio Bridge's *Journal of an African Cruiser*, and was sharing the royalties. They were insufficient for the support of his family. He had been unable to pay rent in Concord, and had been obliged to borrow money in order to buy food. He and Sophia, forced to dismiss their servant girl, had themselves performed the labors of nursery and kitchen. Hawthorne had not permitted the sale of Sophia's "Endymion," but he had accepted gratefully the things to eat sent by a neighbor. Now, with his wife and child, he was under his mother's roof, looking to his political friends for deliverance from his distressful situation.

Mr. O'Sullivan had proved to be a frail financial prop. But he had remained a force in the Democratic party, and was doing all in his power to obtain for Hawthorne some sort of government post. Active also in the romancer's behalf were Horatio Bridge and another old Bowdoin friend of still greater influence, Franklin Pierce, a recent United States senator from New Hampshire. Since a Democrat, James K. Polk, was in the White House, the chances for Hawthorne were good. He knew that one seeking a political appointment had to know how to wait. But in this time of need he found it indeed difficult to exercise patience. Sophia was again pregnant. To Horatio Bridge he wrote, "What a devil of a pickle I shall be in if the baby should come and the office should not!"

During the long anxious winter he vowed over and over that if he succeeded in securing a position which paid an adequate salary he would never again write to sell. But before freeing himself for good from his cursed will to weave words into patterns he had one more commitment to fulfill. The pieces he had written in Concord and a number of earlier tales still uncollected were to be reprinted in two volumes with the title *Mosses from an Old Manse*. The pub-

lishers, Wiley and Putnam of New York, had in their hands
all of the copy except the introduction, which was as yet
unwritten. Again in "the chamber under the eaves" where
he had mastered his art, Hawthorne got busy with what
he thought would be his last task as a professional man of
letters.

Shut in a room on the floor below was Ebe, so much "the
invisible entity" that Sophia never saw her. On the occasions
when she and her brother met she appeared "frozen." Just
now she was absorbed in translating the tales of Cervantes.

She was dissatisfied with her brother's Concord stories,
even with such pieces as "The Birthmark," "The Artist of
the Beautiful," and "Rappaccini's Daughter." These tales
—splendid but, it must be admitted, precious—were born
out of the union of Hawthorne's mind with Sophia's. Great
art, Ebe contended, springs only from a mind which is
wholly unto itself. She believed that unhappiness on the
part of the creator is necessary for the creation of a master-
piece. She insisted moreover that her brother had to be in
Salem, breathing the Salem air, in order to attain high accom-
plishment.

Whatever might be the value of her theories, it is certain
that "Young Goodman Brown," written prior to April, 1835,
is the strongest tale in *Mosses from an Old Manse*. It presents
an unforgettable picture of a New England witches' Sabbath
and brings out with great force the truth of universal guilt.
The idea had probably been suggested by Ebe, who in
turn had found it in a tale by Cervantes, "The Conversation
of the Dogs." By the beginning of 1846 she had doubtless
come to distrust the ability of her brother to regain control
of the power he had wielded in writing "Young Goodman
Brown." But Hawthorne—working, she might have said,
under the proper conditions—soon showed that he was
still an artist worthy of her full respect. His introduction

to *Mosses from an Old Manse* belongs among the world's great informal essays.

A few weeks after it was finished President Polk appointed Hawthorne "surveyor of the district of Salem and Beverly and inspector of revenue for the port of Salem." On April 20, 1846, the new surveyor presented himself for duty at the customhouse on Derby Street. His salary was $1,200 a year, four times as much as he had earned during his most lucrative twelve months in Concord.

He did his work with his accustomed thoroughness. But there was little to do. The day for merchant ships light enough to sail the shallow waters of Salem harbor was almost ended. The economic revolution, which had been moving in strides since 1830, had already made the town more industrial than commercial. For every man of trade who departed a dozen factory workers came in—usually Irish or French Canadian. Such cargoes as Hawthorne was called upon to evaluate were petty. Still, as he well knew, years would pass before Salem would cease to exist as a port of entry. Through the kind offices of his friends, he held a sinecure, with ample remuneration. For the first time in his life he felt affluent.

Sophia, pregnant and anxious, was unhappy in the house which she knew as "Castle Dismal." Besides, Herbert Street was not a fitting address for a surveyor of customs. The collector, General James Miller, lived in the great mansion on Derby Street formerly occupied by Benjamin Williams Crowninshield. Hawthorne looked around, and soon found quarters on fashionable Chestnut Street, in the dwelling where the late celebrated linguist John L. Pickering had lived. By the end of May Hawthorne and Sophia, with a maid to care for Una, were in their new home. They must have taken only three or four rooms, for they began at once to complain about limited space.

Early in June, in anticipation of her confinement, Sophia went to her mother's house in Boston. There, at two o'clock in the morning on June 22, the second of the Hawthorne children was born. It was a boy, and the name, already chosen, was Julian. He was a dark baby, with black hair and brown eyes.

O'Sullivan, Bridge, and Pierce had argued for the Salem surveyorship for their literary friend on the grounds that it would leave him free to spend his afternoons at home writing. But during his sixteen months on Chestnut Street, Hawthorne was sunk in uxoriousness and fatherhood. He had a good excuse to offer to his friends. The only place he had for writing, he said, was the nursery. And how could he open up his portable mahogany desk and concentrate on a tale or essay when Julian, lying in his cradle three feet away, was likely at any moment to break into a lusty shriek? The slight sale of his *Mosses from an Old Manse*, despite the beautiful introduction and such pieces as "Young Goodman Brown" and "Rappaccini's Daughter," made him all the more determined to keep his back turned upon the literary life. During the year following the birth of his son he perhaps derived a certain pleasure from regarding his urge to put words on paper as a folly of the past.

But by the summer of 1847 his old will to write was once more demanding action. It was at this time that the Manning heirs finally disposed of the house on Herbert Street. In searching for a new home for his mother and sisters Hawthorne found on unfashionable Mall Street a vacant dwelling roomy enough for them and also for his own family. The place was rented, and all moved in—Hawthorne and Sophia with the babies and nurse on the first floor and Mrs. Hawthorne, Ebe, and Louisa on the second. That left free the third floor, the front chamber of which Hawthorne converted into a study. He could no longer tell his friends that the nursery was the only place he had for writing.

A detached stairway made it possible for Ebe to get down to the street without encountering Sophia. Still there was friction. Una, nearing four, loved nothing better than to go upstairs alone for a visit with her grandmother and aunts. All three adored the child. Ebe liked to give her good things to eat, and on one occasion held out a piece of candy, probably a gibraltar or a blackjack.

"Mama won't let me eat that," Una said.

"Eat it anyway," Ebe said. "You don't have to tell her what you do up here."

Una ate—and when she got downstairs she talked. Indeed, she repeated to her mother every word Aunt Ebe had spoken. The outcome was that the child was no longer allowed to go unaccompanied to the second floor.

Hawthorne, possessed of the fear of the writing desk which every author feels after a period of literary inactivity, perhaps told himself that he could not get down to work because it took all his energy to keep peace in the Mall Street house. Weeks passed before Sophia could report to her mother that he was spending his afternoons in his study.

On July 4, 1848, Sophia and the children were in Boston, where they had gone for a visit of a week or two in the Peabody home. Hawthorne joined them for the holiday, and stayed until late in the evening to see the fireworks. When he got back to Mall Street, after midnight, he was surprised to find Ebe waiting for him in his own sitting room. She said that she had a matter to discuss with him— possibly the problem of finding a publisher for her translations of Cervantes. She added that she would like to have him accompany her on a ramble into the country the next afternoon. He was delighted at the prospect of an outing with his old-time walking partner, and before going to bed he wrote of it to Sophia. "Perhaps," he said in concluding the letter, "she will now make it a habit to come down and see us occasionally in the evening."

He was hoping for too much. Towards her sister-in-law Ebe was to continue to maintain an attitude of complete aloofness. But the coldness which she had manifested towards her brother since his marriage had at last given way to sympathy.

He needed her support. He must have felt in the summer of 1848 that he needed to make use of his every possible resource as a man of letters.

The preceding autumn Longfellow's *Evangeline* had been published. By now readers throughout America were weeping over the haplessness of Gabriel and Evangeline, the lovers of Acadie. Longfellow and Hawthorne had been classmates in Bowdoin, but a close friendship between the two had not developed until 1837, when the poet's highly commendatory critique of *Twice-Told Tales* was printed in the *North American Review*. Hawthorne now returned the favor by praising *Evangeline* in the Salem *Advertiser*. Reviews equally enthusiastic were appearing in newspapers all over the country.

The more of them Hawthorne read the more resentful he must have become—not at Longfellow but at himself. His friend Horace Conolly had heard from a woman of Nova Scotia the story of the Acadian lovers, and had in turn related it to Hawthorne, urging him to develop it into a romance. But Hawthorne was not interested. Then one day, when he and Conolly were at dinner with Longfellow in Cambridge, Conolly related the story a second time. "May I use it for a poem?" Longfellow asked. "You may if Hawthorne doesn't want it," Conolly replied. Again Hawthorne said that the story did not appeal to him. But he immediately realized his mistake, and as soon as he and

Conolly were out of Longfellow's house he began to revile himself. "He was the maddest man I ever saw," Conolly was to say. Now, in the quiet of his study, puzzling desperately over every story idea that occurred to him, Hawthorne was no doubt again a victim of self-scorn. The fame which his Bowdoin classmate was reaping from *Evangeline* might have been his but for his folly in arriving too quickly at a decision. Only by employing all his powers and creating a tale better than the tale of the lovers of Acadie could he hope to undo the injustice he had done to himself. Providence was confronting him with a challenge.

It is likely that Ebe was to a great extent responsible for the return of his thoughts to the channels in which they had flowed when he brought into being such stories as "The Gentle Boy" and "Young Goodman Brown." Lizzie Peabody had asked that he contribute an essay to her *Aesthetic Papers,* to be published in 1849. The piece he chose to write for her was "Main Street," a picture of life in seventeenth-century Salem. Much of the matter was drawn from Joseph Barlow Felt's *Annals of Salem,* with which Hawthorne had been familiar since the appearance of the first edition in 1827.

As his mind teemed with images relating to the Massachusetts Bay of his earliest American ancestors, he was in all probability haunted by two pictures which had been flashed before his inner eye when he first read Felt, if not before. One picture showed two young women sitting on repentance stools in the Salem meetinghouse on a lecture day in 1681 each with a paper marked INCEST pinned to her cap. The other picture was that of their supposed common lover, their brother, an outlaw roaming the forests of Maine, tortured by his conscience if he was guilty, incensed over Puritan injustice if he was blameless. In pre-

senting the pictures Felt had withheld names. That Hawthorne knew the identity of the two sisters and the brother
can hardly be doubted. The effect which this dark Manning
family secret produced upon the romancer's emotions could
only have been penetrating and most poignant.

While he was in his middle twenties he had touched upon
the theme of incest in "Alice Doane's Appeal," a tale of
witchcraft which won Ebe's approval. But Hawthorne at
forty-five realized that a story intended to win wide public
favor must be based on a love which was natural and beautiful, like the love in *Evangeline*. In another of his tales,
"Endicott and the Red Cross," first printed in the *Token*
for 1838, he had introduced a woman who was forced to
wear upon her breast the letter A in punishment for the
crime of adultery. He had found out that Massachusetts
Bay magistrates had several times decreed such a punishment.
Could nineteenth-century readers be made to believe that
among the wearers of the shameful A there was one whose
adulterous behavior deserved to be condoned? If he could
win sympathy for the marked woman by showing that her
illicit love was heaven-given and therefore above any moral
code, he could fashion her into the heroine of a romance.
His kinswomen tagged INCEST must not be mentioned.
But while he was tracing the actions of one punished as they
were punished, the two unfortunates would remain before
his mind's eye, reminding him constantly, as they sat in
shame on their repentance stools, of the unnaturalness and
cruelty of seventeenth-century Puritans.

The most eloquent defense of illicit love which Hawthorne could have known was a book he had got acquainted
with in an English translation in his boyhood. It was Rousseau's *Julie; ou, La Nouvelle Héloïse*. "My brother read it
because he was told he shouldn't," Ebe said. He had un-

doubtedly read it in the original several times since. During July and August, 1848, he held in his possession the copy in French which belonged to the Salem Athenaeum.

Rousseau's aim in writing *Héloïse* was to show how a deep and beautiful attachment between a man and woman may be frustrated by the conventions of a highly complex society. The scene is eighteenth-century Switzerland. The main drama is an experiment conducted by M. de Wolmar, a rationalist so dominated by mind that his heart is dead. He has entered into a marriage of convenience with Julie d'Étanges, a rich aristocratic woman half his age, and she has borne him children. He knows that before becoming his wife she was the paramour of her tutor Saint-Preux, a young sentimentalist of great brilliance and charm but too humbly born and poor to sue for the hand of a gentlewoman. The aging husband knows too that his wife has lost little of her passion for her former lover. Curious to determine whether her intellect can control her emotions and keep her faithful to her marriage vows when she is faced with temptation, M. de Wolmar invites Saint-Preux to his château and throws him and Julie into daily contact. Though all the old fires flame anew in the hearts of the lovers, they behave in the absence of de Wolmar as they do in his presence. He feels that his experiment has resulted in a triumph for rationalism until Julie, ill from exposure after rescuing one of her children from drowning, dies because she has lost the will to live.

Hawthorne found in *Héloïse* the plot for *The Scarlet Letter*. He shifted the drama to seventeenth-century Boston. M. de Wolmar became Roger Chillingworth, Julie d'Étanges became Hester Prynne, and Saint-Preux became Arthur Dimmesdale. Puritan conventions—far more artificial and merciless than the conventions of eighteenth-century Switzerland—determined the altering of situations. Hawthorne adopted without modification the theme of *Héloïse*, the tragedy of love in a denaturalized society.

Much of his philosophy, moral and political, had been drawn from the great Swiss sentimentalist. In tale after tale he had pictured man's inhumanity to man as resulting from a denial of the natural affections. He had shown repeatedly in his fiction that to him the chief of sinners was the heartless person of power who, to satisfy an intellectual curiosity, leads victims into suffering and studies their writhings. He had presented the type of character exemplified by Rousseau's rationalist de Wolmar in such stories as "The Bosom Serpent," "The Birthmark," and "Rappaccini's Daughter." If—as appears most likely—he wrote "Ethan Brand" late in 1848, he added to his gallery of portraits one more reproduction of M. de Wolmar before undertaking the creation of Roger Chillingworth.

By the beginning of the summer of 1849 Hawthorne must have had *The Scarlet Letter* complete in mind. "If a book is great," said Ebe, "the author is in mental pain when he writes it." Upon her brother that summer Providence visited an avalanche of anguish, despair, and grief. A Whig, General Zachary Taylor, had been in the White House since March 4, and on June 8 Hawthorne was dismissed from his post in the Salem customhouse. Though he was only a victim of the political spoils system, he chose, in his desperation, to believe that his loss of employment was due to a local Whig coterie made up largely of aristocrats who had survived Salem's social change. All of his lifelong resentment at these privileged rich boiled with a vengeance as he faced again the poverty he had suffered in 1845. At that time his mother had shared her all with him and his family. This time she was fatally ill. Her death, hastened no doubt by worry over his unhappiness, came on July 31. The little she left went to Ebe and Louisa. Hawthorne was penniless. But Sophia had saved a few dollars out of household expense money, and George Hillard sent a purse, contributed by friends who wished to remain anonymous. Hawthorne was assured against want for at least a few months. But in accepting money from well-wishers whose names he did not know he did harm to his pride. Moreover he was tossed between the animosity he held for certain Salem Whigs and the grief he felt over the death of his mother. It was while he was in this state of mind that he wrote *The Scarlet Letter*.

He had long ago found out that as an "artist of the beautiful" he possessed a sure means of escaping wretchedness. Shut in his study for hours every day with only his fancy for companion, he could forget the room below where he had recently knelt by the bed of his dying mother. He could forget that Sophia—never so beaming with Transcendental sunniness as in these troublous days—was down on the first floor painting screens and lamp shades to sell in order to bring in a few extra dollars. As his fancy transfigured his little Una into little Pearl, he could forget that his children were eating what amounted to the bread of charity. He could forget sad-eyed broken-in-health Louisa, who had gone to live with Uncle Robert Manning's widow on Dearborn Street. He could forget Ebe, who was writing from the boarding place she had found in Beverly, "I can lose myself in the woods by only crossing the road, and the air is very pure and exhilarating, and the sea is but a mile distant." Still, as his fancy led him over the lanes and cow paths of seventeenth-century Boston, he never forgot what Ebe more than any other had helped him learn, his duty to himself as an artist. The story flowed from his mind to the paper with remarkable ease.

When the work was done, he was dissatisfied. The tale was too sombre, he thought. His plan was to publish it in a volume with several tales of a lighter character. But he had won two new props, the Boston publishers James T. Fields and William D. Ticknor. They easily convinced him that they should issue *The Scarlet Letter* as an independent volume.

The date of publication was March 16, 1850. Though the first edition, consisting of two thousand copies, was exhausted within ten days, the book was not an outstanding commercial success. Yet at all times during the century since its appearance there has been a group of the best critics ready to pronounce it one of the world's great novels, the highest achievement ever attained by an American writer of fiction. Beside it *Evangeline*, but for which it might never have been begun, is watery and *Héloïse*, upon which it was modeled, is formless and, as a novel, amateurish.

The Hawthornes had been in Salem two-hundred-and-thirteen years when *The Scarlet Letter* was published. It had taken that long for one of them to attain supreme mastery in any field. How Major William and his son Colonel John would have been "wounded in their hearts" if they had known that their name was at last to be raised to high honor by a descendant who was a "wanton gospeler," the teller of a tale which was a satire aimed at their kind!

A GREAT NAME

IN PICTURING Salem in the introduction to *The Scarlet Letter* Hawthorne was more venomous than truthful.
The indignation manifested by certain citizens of the town
was justifiable. Some went so far as to threaten the romancer
with physical violence. Writing to Louisa from Boston
shortly after the appearance of the book, he said, "I should
come and see you, but cannot endure the idea of returning
to Salem just yet. It would be tempting Providence to incur
another risk of being tarred and feathered."

Every day more readers were becoming familiar with the
name Hawthorne. Once again the romancer was confident
that he could make a living with his pen. This time he was
encouraged by Mr. Fields and Mr. Ticknor, both of whom
were effectual men of business.

Hawthorne had said in the introduction to *The Scarlet
Letter* that he did not wish his offspring to take root in
Salem. The new home he and Sophia chose was in the hills
of western Massachusetts. Before the end of May, 1850,
they were settled in a farm cottage near the village of
Lenox, with a Negro servant, whom they knew as "Mrs.
Peters," to look after the children. Though the "little red
house" was plain, the views of the mountains—Bald and
Monument to the south—were splendid. At the foot of the
slope on which the cottage stood stretched the blue waters
of Stockbridge Bowl. To get down to the lake one had to
pass through a thicket of underbrush. Soon Hawthorne,
Una, and Julian were calling this miniature jungle "the
tanglewood."

In moving westward Hawthorne followed in the steps of many a kinsman. Only four blood relatives bearing his name were left in Salem. Sixty-year-old Ebenezer Hathorne, shaking with palsy, had at last married but had begotten no children. He was living, in the style of an ordinary yeoman, on the Salem Neck farm which he had inherited from his father, the second Colonel John. Louisa, sufficiently restored in health to write her usual cheerful letters, had been accepted by the Mannings of Dearborn Street as a member of the family. The remaining two Hathornes still in the town of their forebears were also old maids—both named Ruth. One, a faithful worshiper at St. Peter's Church, was a granddaughter of Captain Daniel's brother William. The other, listed as insane in at least one Essex County record, was probably a great-granddaughter of Captain Benjamin Hathorne, youngest son of the judge of witches, the first Colonel John.

Ebe had found a permanent boarding place with the family of Samuel Cole, a farmer who lived in the district of Beverly known as Montserrat. "When I first came here," she said, "I was sick, and Mrs. Cole used to come up, bringing an armful of wood, and sit down upon it and stare at me and tell me I was in a consumption. I disliked everything, especially herself, so much that I felt quite indifferent whether I were or not. I longed to tell her, but refrained, that when I was buried I desired the coffin put out a window, to get me out of the house as soon as possible." Ebe was not in such a doleful mood when she resumed her work. After a few months with the Coles she was writing to her brother, "I have been very busy with Cervantes's tales. I want to consult you about what I think about a few necessary alterations when you come."

Louisa visited the Hawthornes in Lenox, but Ebe did not see her brother from the time he departed for western

Massachusetts until he came back east to live. He was too occupied during his year and a half in the "little red house" to keep up a frequent correspondence with his sisters. Each of them received copies of the two books he wrote while there, *The House of the Seven Gables* and his first collection of classic myths for child readers, *A Wonder-Book*. Certain critics of the future were to see greater artistic merit in the juvenile than in the romance. Yet Hawthorne considered *The House of the Seven Gables* superior to *The Scarlet Letter*. To Louisa the last book he wrote was always the best. Ebe remained the discerning judge. It appears that all she had to say of *The House of the Seven Gables* was, "My brother does his best only when he works in Salem."

A day specially happy for Hawthorne and Sophia was May 20, 1851, when their third child was born, a girl named Rose. Una was already past seven, and Julian was nearing five. Writing of the new member of the family to a friend, the father said, "Mrs. Hawthorne has published a little work which still lies in sheets, but makes some noise in the world; it is a healthy miss, with no present pretensions to beauty." To Louisa he wrote, "She is the brightest and strongest baby we have had." It was evident that her hair was going to be even redder than Una's.

Sophia was forty-two and Hawthorne was forty-seven. They looked upon the baby—Rosebud they called her—as the child of their aging years. "She is the last we shall have," Hawthorne said. Sophia had nursed Una when she and her husband were facing want. She had nursed Julian when she saw Hawthorne pretending that he was content to settle down permanently as a customhouse drudge. Now she was nursing Rosebud while her husband was following happily the course which Providence had marked out for him and while she herself was well and carefree. If there was truth in Mrs. Peabody's theory that the mental attitude a mother holds when she is nursing an infant has much to do in shaping its character, then Rose had a better chance than either Una or Julian of growing up to be strong-minded and stable.

In the letters which Sophia wrote to members of her family in the autumn of 1851 she alluded to the colds which were bothering her husband. The chill mountain air was, she said, the cause. Her sister Mary—Mrs. Horace Mann, who lived in West Newton, a suburb of Boston—replied that in November she and her boys would join Mr. Mann in Washington, where he was serving as a representative in Congress, and that the Mann residence in West Newton, centrally heated, was at the disposal of the Hawthornes during the winter. They decided at once to quit Lenox and go to the house of warmth.

An incident which happened the first evening they spent in the new place augured ill for their move. In the excitement of getting settled Sophia and everybody else forgot about Rosebud until they heard her shrieking in the parlor. When they rushed in they found that she had crawled back of a sofa to inspect the glittering pipes which gave out the warmth and had got her fingers scorched.

It was impossible for Hawthorne to like his brother-in-law Mann. On noticing that the romancer smoked, the educator had said, "I as a gentleman, Mr. Hawthorne, must tell you that I no longer respect you as I did." With the Manns everything had been the bettering of the Massachusetts public schools, and now it was the freeing of the black slaves in the South. Even their sons were little abolitionists. As Hawthorne looked about his new home, reminded at every turn of Horace Mann's determination to make human existence severe, he felt that he either had to lose himself in his work or get away.

No longer complaining of colds, he wrote his novel of

Brook Farm, *The Blithedale Romance.* Whatever comment
Ebe made after reading the book was not recorded. She
could only have been alarmed at her brother's marked
decline as an artist. In time most critics were to agree that
The Blithedale Romance is a weak work except for the
passage which pictures the retrieving of the body of the
suicide Zenobia from the waters of the upper Charles. Hawthorne had written this scene while remembering with
astounding vividness how he had assisted in recovering from
the Concord River the body of the unknown woman who
drowned herself near the Old Manse on his and Sophia's
first wedding anniversary.

On May 16, 1852, Hawthorne wrote to Louisa, "The
whole family of Manns, great and little, have come here;
and you may readily believe that we are anxious to get
away." The place they went to was their own, a dwelling
and twenty-two acres of land in Concord, purchased all
together for $1,813. At the back of the house were a bluff
and a little forest, and in front, across the Concord-Lexing-
ton road, stretched a meadow. Hawthorne and Sophia
named the place the Wayside. While she busied herself
looking after repairing and painting and papering, he began
the writing of *Tanglewood Tales,* a second collection of
classic myths for child readers. He believed he was in the
home where he would spend the rest of his days turning
out volumes for Mr. Fields and Mr. Ticknor to print and sell.

He was not to finish *Tanglewood Tales* until the following
spring. Then he was to live through another interlude of
literary inactivity—an interlude preceded by events which
brought surprise, excitement, and sorrow.

The Democrats in their convention at Baltimore the
summer of 1852 nominated Franklin Pierce for the Pres-
idency. His name was placed before the convention by the

delegates from Virginia: he was the choice of the proslavery interests in the country. A campaign biography of such a candidate had to satisfy his backers. It must moreover be highly popular. Still the author of *The Scarlet Letter*, mindful of the possible reward, deliberated only one day before deciding to turn his talent to the writing of a vote-winning book on his old Bowdoin friend's life and times.

He had scarcely begun the research when Providence struck with the first sorrow—a punishment, said certain abolitionists, for his loyalty to the party which stood for slavery.

He had invited Louisa to come to the Wayside for a visit. She answered that nothing could make her happier. But a few days later she wrote that Uncle Dike had offered to take her to Saratoga and Albany, and then on a boat down the Hudson to New York. She felt that the trip would benefit her health, and had decided to accept Uncle Dike's invitation. She would come to Concord immediately after her return to Salem.

Hard at work on the Pierce biography, Hawthorne, said Sophia, seemed ill at ease, apprehensive of some disaster that was approaching. Late on the afternoon of July 29, just two days before the third anniversary of his mother's death, it came. The *Henry Clay*, the Hudson River boat on which Mr. Dike and Louisa were sailing, was in sight of New York when fire broke out amidship. Immediately the entire central section of the vessel was in flames. Mr. Dike, on an open deck at the prow, was cut off from Louisa, who was resting in a cabin towards the stern. As the blaze sped backward, sweeping all before it, she saw that she must jump into the water or be burned to death. She made the leap and was drowned, while Mr. Dike was rescued. That night her body was dragged from the Hudson, identified, and made ready for shipment to Salem for burial.

Why had the awful spectacle which Hawthorne witnessed the night of his first wedding anniversary made upon him so deep an impression? Why had he written with such power in *The Blithedale Romance* of the recovery of the body of the drowned Zenobia? One of his early stories, "Mr. Higginbotham's Catastrophe," had been based on the idea that events cast their shadows before as well as after. Transcendental Sophia, dwelling often in her thoughts upon the notion of timelessness, could see truth in the idea. As for Hawthorne, he was numb from shock after hearing of his younger sister's horrifying end. His one aim was to finish the biography of Pierce as quickly as possible and then get away to the Isle of Shoals for a few days of the loneliness of being among strangers.

In November, with Hawthorne's vote-winning book helping to a degree, Franklin Pierce was elected President of the United States. On meeting him shortly after the results of the election were known Hawthorne said, "From the bottom of my heart I pity you!" Again, as Sophia observed, he had premonitions of a disaster which would touch him at least indirectly, and was scarcely surprised when he heard early in January of a dire visitation of Providence upon Mr. and Mrs. Pierce. Accompanied by their only living child, a boy of eleven, the two took the cars in Boston to return to their home in Concord, New Hampshire. The train had gone only a short distance when there was a wreck. The car in which the Pierces were riding was thrown down an embankment. Neither the future President nor his wife was hurt, but a falling beam struck their son, killing him instantly. Pierce had the presence of mind to throw his greatcoat over his wife's face and shut out sight of the child's crushed head. This bright lovable boy, as Hawthorne knew well, was the pride of Pierce's life, the chief reason for his ambition.

Shortly after Hawthorne learned that his reward for the campaign biography would be the highly lucrative consulship at Liverpool, news of another grievous stroke of Providence reached the Wayside. The affliction this time was the death of Sophia's mother.

Still there was the gayety of anticipation at a Boston wharf on that July 6, 1853, when Hawthorne—passing the second twenty-four hours of his fiftieth year—embarked with his wife and children for the voyage to Liverpool. The ship was the Cunard steamer *Niagara*. Una and Julian soon found on a lower deck the cow which would provide milk for the passengers during the voyage and the coops that were noisy with the chickens which would be killed and eaten. The British minister to the United States, bound for Halifax, was among the passengers. Also on board was William D. Ticknor, of the publishing house which now had the writings of Nathaniel Hawthorne on the shelves of booksellers throughout America.

Before embarking Hawthorne had posted a letter to Ebe saying that he was going to send her money. In writing the biography of Pierce (it must be pronounced altogether fulsome) he had once more, in his desire to benefit those he loved, placed in pawn his artist's birthright. Probably the question on Ebe's mind was, "Can he ever again redeem it?"

The next time Ebe saw her brother, seven years later, she undoubtedly observed what his Concord friends had not noticed—the strands of gray in his long dark hair and the look of worry in his eyes. His "Italian moustache," so called because he had grown it in Italy, failed to conceal the lines about his mouth. He was more worn than a man should be at the age of fifty-six.

For four years he had labored in the American consulate in Liverpool, traveling back and forth each day from his home across the Mersey in Rock Ferry, where there was no school suitable for his children and no capable governess to teach them. He had made far less money out of the office than he had anticipated. But he had paid back, with interest, the purse which unknown friends, through the agency of George Hillard, had made up for his benefit in 1849. Sophia had rejected her father's plea for money, saying that her husband had a relative of his own, meaning Ebe, to support. But Hawthorne, without his wife's knowledge, had seen that old Dr. Peabody was free from want during his last days. Hawthorne had lost a considerable portion of his savings in a bad investment, and he had been quixotic in granting financial aid to unfortunate fellow Americans.

The earnings from the consulship had also been sufficient for him to take his family to Italy for a sojourn of nineteen months. He had intended to write while there, but had spent most of his time in studying monuments of architecture, sculpture, and painting and in meeting congenial English and American expatriates, among whom was a Salemite, the sculptor and poet William Wetmore Story, a son of Justice Joseph Story and nephew by marriage of Hawthorne's cousin John Forrester.

The stay in Italy had ended with the blow from Providence which had broken the vigor of the romancer, filled him with anxiety, and marked him for an early death. On an afternoon in November, 1858, shortly after he had established his family in Rome for the winter, Una and the American governess whom Horace Mann had sent over to teach the children went to sketch in the Coliseum and stayed too late. Both caught the Roman fever. While the governess recovered quickly, Una's malarial attacks kept returning throughout the winter and early spring. In April the fifteen-year-old girl lingered for days on the dividing line between life and death. Finally the fever left her—through a miracle, thought Sophia, who believed that no other person so severely afflicted had ever recovered. Una was not entirely on her feet until the end of May. Now, back in America, Hawthorne knew that the oldest and the most winning of his three children was not what she had been before her illness.

During the desperate days when it seemed that she would surely die Mr. and Mrs. Pierce had come to Rome, traveling to forget the loss of their son and their four years of trial in the White House. "Why, what a stout boy Julian has grown!" exclaimed Pierce—with a catch in his voice—at his first sight of Hawthorne's twelve-year-old lad. The ex-President's concern over Una had appeared to be as grave as that of the girl's father.

Hawthorne had returned to England for his last year abroad. At Redcar during the summer of 1859 and later at Leamington he had written the final draft of his Italian romance. The book had been published in London under the title *Transformation* and in Boston, by Ticknor and Fields, as *The Marble Faun*. It was protected by copyright in both the British Isles and the United States, and thousands of copies had been sold. But the critics had been severe. Ebe probably agreed with those who claimed that Hawthorne had too often lost his story in description. But she could hardly have had patience with the many who said that the tale lacks a satisfying explanation of the heroine's shadowed past. Certainly Ebe did not overlook the emphasis which the author had placed upon Guido Reni's supposed portrait of Beatrice Cenci. Hawthorne had at last introduced into one of his major works the grave theme of incest.

On the occasion of his first visit to Ebe after his return from Europe it is likely that he and she alluded to the fact that not one with their name was left in Salem. A short time after the death of Ebenezer Hathorne, in 1858, his home on Salem Neck had gone up in flames. Many private papers had been saved, but not the documents relating to family history which Hawthorne had intended some day to examine.

On his way back from Montserrat he possibly lingered in Salem for a few hours. At the Essex House he might have seen his uncle William Manning, past eighty, still a contented bachelor. Hawthorne might have called at Dearborn Street for a talk with Aunt Rebecca, Uncle Robert's widow, none of whose children were as yet married. There might also have been a visit with the Dikes, neither of whom appeared more elderly than Hawthorne himself.

Before the first summer after his return to the Wayside was ended his concern over Una again became acute. The girl appeared to be suffering from a relapse of the Roman fever. It was thought that the Concord heat was responsible, or, as Ebe supposed, the Concord air. Una did not face death this time, but, from the point of view of her father, she faced worse—mental derangement. After her recovery he was unable to rid himself of the terrible fear that at some unexpected moment her mind might crack beyond repair.

While she stayed at home the winter following, studying with tutors, Julian went to Mr. Sanborn's academy and Rose to a public school. Every member of the family found it difficult to get readjusted to America and Concord. The Wayside was in turmoil all day long. Hawthorne was having a tower built, to serve as a study, and it seemed that the carpenters would never finish the work. With the constant sawing and hammering and the upset state of things, he had a good reason for not concentrating on the English romance which had been in his mind, in a vague state, for several years. One day when a friend inquired about his health he answered, "I feel pretty damned miserable, thank God!"

With the outbreak of the Civil War and Lincoln's call for volunteers he said, "I'm sorry I'm too old to fight and glad that Julian is too young." In a letter to Horatio Bridge he wrote, "Though I approve of the war as much as any man, I don't quite understand what we are fighting for, or what definite result can be expected." Being a Democrat, he believed that different leadership was needed in Washington. If only Andrew Jackson were alive! "Wherever the old hero is," said Hawthorne, "he would undoubtedly rather be on earth at this crisis."

His interest in the war in no way crowded out his anxiety over Una. By the summer of 1861 his worry was alarming his wife. In a letter written to him in July—while he and Julian were on an outing in Beverly, often in Ebe's company —Sophia said: "Of all the trials, this is the heaviest to me— to see you so apathetic, so indifferent, so hopeless, so unstrung. Rome has no sin to answer for so unpardonable as this of wrenching off your wings and hanging lead to your arrowy feet. Rome! And all Rome caused to you!"

Later on that summer, after women throughout the country had begun knitting for the soldiers, Ebe at last visited her brother in his Concord home. She had exchanged letters with Una during the entire period the family were in Europe, and the preceding July she and Julian had got well acquainted on berry-picking excursions. But to ten-year-old Rose, Aunt Ebe was at first mystifying. One said of her, "She has sufficient strength of character to upset a kingdom." So she soon won Rose. She took her into the woods back of the Wayside and pointed out wonders the child had never dreamed of seeing. Then she taught her how to knit. Rose was always to remember her aunt in a brown mohair dress sitting in the light of a lamp giving directions to illustrate the stitches as she "knitted titanically."

One afternoon she, Hawthorne, and Una took the walk to Walden Pond. At once Ebe sought out the place where Thoreau's hut had stood. A depression grown up in weeds and saplings, and a few scattered stones and boards, were all that marked the spot. From one of the trees which had shaded the doorway Ebe plucked several leaves to press and take back to Montserrat. Within a few short weeks Thoreau was to be confined to his bed in his sister's house in Concord, a victim of consumption. Hawthorne and Sophia still had the music box he had brought to the Old Manse during their honeymoon. It played as well as ever the tunes to which Sophia had danced in her bridal happiness, and would soon go back to the lender, to bring to him perhaps a bit of pleasure as he lay dying. He was the one Transcendentalist for whom Ebe felt a sympathy. He and she alike knew the meaning of "indulgence in fine renouncements." She was, above all, unmystic. Still that afternoon at Walden Pond, where Thoreau would never again see spring come up, she felt, she said, his benediction.

There was a boat, and Una took the oars to row her father and aunt to the opposite shore of the mirrorlike pond. When they were in the center, the girl suddenly stopped, raised the oars out of the water, and said in a calm deliberate voice, "It is very deep here—and very dangerous." Hawthorne and Ebe pretended that they were lost in contemplating the surrounding foliage, which they could see whether they looked up or down. After a long minute Una resumed rowing, and soon reached the landing place. What in the girl's mind could have stirred such a statement at such a moment? In hinting weeks later at how this question bewildered her Ebe added, after a pause, "I think I could swim, or float, upon calm water."

She had not been many months back in Montserrat before letters from the Wayside made her realize that it was her brother rather than her niece who was headed for quick collapse. Still he kept up a brave front. In the spring of 1862 he made a trip to Washington and wrote wittily of his observations in an essay for the *Atlantic Monthly*. His sketches on England, begun in the *Atlantic* for October, 1860, were continued through August, 1863, and then published as a volume with the title *Our Old Home*. Against the protest of both Fields and Ticknor, Hawthorne dedicated this work to Franklin Pierce. There was the ring of the courage which had produced *The Scarlet Letter* in his declaration: "If Pierce is so exceedingly unpopular that his name is enough to sink the volume, there is so much the more need that an old friend should stand by him. If the public of the North see fit to ostracize me for this, I can only say that I would gladly sacrifice a thousand or two of dollars rather than retain the good will of such a herd of dolts and mean-spirited scoundrels." In the fall of 1863 he kept Julian braced to pass the Harvard entrance examinations. But he found it impossible to fix his mind upon what he wished to make of his English romance, which was in time to be given to the world in four varying fragments. Then by the beginning of 1864 Ebe was getting reports of his suffering from insomnia, nosebleeding, dysentery, and deafness. All these ailments were symptoms of the "apathy" which had overcome Aunt Eunice and possibly other Hathornes whom Ebe had seen die.

No one could persuade her brother to consult a physician. He who had always leaned upon someone was at last looking to Death for help.

Providence might have spared him the terror he experienced on a morning early in April, 1864. Mr. Ticknor, thinking that an easy journey by boat and the cars would help in checking his decline, took him on a trip southward. In New York the two spent several days at the Astor House, and Hawthorne felt well enough to write letters. Ticknor caught a cold while there. But when a doctor assured him that he was not too ill to continue the journey he and Hawthorne went on to Philadelphia. There the cold turned into pneumonia, and in a hotel room on the morning of April 10 William D. Ticknor died. None of his family and none of his close friends, except Hawthorne, were at his bedside.

When Hawthorne got back to Concord, looking more like a ghost than a man, he greeted his wife with the question, "Oh, why couldn't it have been I instead of Ticknor?" Sophia at once wrote appealing letters to Mr. Pierce and Mr. Fields. The latter saw that Hawthorne was given a medical examination. The conclusion of the physician, Oliver Wendell Holmes, was, "The shark's tooth is upon him." No better treatment could be prescribed, said Dr. Holmes, than the trip with Pierce to the New Hampshire mountains which had been planned.

The two friends, close to one another for forty-three years, traveled by the cars from Boston to Concord, New Hampshire, past the spot where Pierce had seen the life of his little boy instantly blotted out. His wife had helped him bear that blow. But the preceding December he had lost her, and now, said Sophia, no living person was nearer to his heart than Hawthorne.

At Concord the travelers changed from the cars to Pierce's private carriage, driven by a coachman who had been instructed to go slow and avoid all bumps. By roads over which Hawthorne had journeyed with Samuel Manning, the horse trader, they moved northwestward.

On the afternoon of May 18 they found themselves nearing Plymouth, the gateway to the White Mountains. Breaking a silence which had lasted for an hour or more, Hawthorne asked, "Did you see Thackeray when he was in this country?"

Pierce, surprised at the question, which was remote from the topics they had talked about during the day, hesitated. When he did speak, answering in the affirmative, he saw that Hawthorne was not listening. There was more silence, and all at once Pierce recalled that Thackeray had died the preceding Christmas Eve. Then Hawthorne said, very slowly, "But there is another thing—we must all go, we must all go."

In his sleep, very early the next morning, in the Pemigewasset House, a huge wooden resort hotel adjacent to the Plymouth railroad station, Hawthorne went. When Pierce packed his dead friend's belongings to take back to the Wayside, he ran upon a worn pocketbook. Inside was found a single object—a picture of Pierce himself.

Still Pierce was so unpopular in New England in that year 1864 that he was not honored with a place among the pallbearers at Hawthorne's burial in Concord on May 23. Ebe remained in Montserrat that day. To Una she wrote: "Happy are those who die and can be at rest! It is not desirable to live to be old."

When the proper number of days had passed Sophia's friends received by mail her elegy on her husband, written in a highly poetic prose and elegantly printed on a single page. If Ebe saw a copy she probably thought, "Like Cicero after the death of his daughter Tullia, Sophia was weighed down with grief until she began to think of the pretty things she could say about it. "

Ebe knew that her brother, from the moment he realized

the gravity of his illness, had wished the release of death. To someone at some time he had said, "Heaven grant that I may never see sixty. Age is so unlovely, I dread the thought of a decline. Life should be all beautiful." Heaven had heeded his plea just in time. He would have seen the undesired sixty if he had lived only forty-five days longer.

In Montserrat Ebe was not quite the recluse she had been in Salem. Mr. and Mrs. Cole won her, and she won them. They accepted her as a fixture in their home, as they did the pump, or the cats, or the fire in the parlor before which she read to them in the evening. They could have reckoned time by her habits. By eleven o'clock in the morning they heard her stirring in her room, perhaps talking to herself. At noon she was downstairs for dinner. She lingered at table, eating methodically and conversing boldly, often acidulously, on whatever topic was suggested. By two she was ready for her walk, hot or cold, wet or dry—a ramble which sometimes took her in sight of Hathorne Hill in Danvers. The nature she observed in the woods or by the roadsides or on the seashore was forever revealing to her new forms, new colors, new odors, and new sounds. By five in the winter and by six in the summer she was back with the Coles, for tea and a bit of reading aloud in the parlor. Then she went up to her room, and until long past midnight her lamp was lighted.

Sometimes on Sundays she was downstairs by ten, dressed for meeting. It was whispered in Beverly that she was an infidel. Yet all sorts of religious services attracted her, even Methodist and Baptist "revivals." Occasionally on a Sabbath day, perhaps by walking, she got over to Salem's First Church, where she and four generations of her paternal forebears had been baptized. Those who knew her personal habits were in dread that she might forget and start talking out loud to herself during sermon.

The letters she wrote in her room at night were her "visits" to her relatives. These carefully thought out and sincerely penned communications show that she was keenly aware of what was going on in the world from which she held herself aloof. Few women of the time were better informed on current events. She had long ago renounced her ambition to write for publication. Years had passed since she had given up her idea of seeing her translations of Cervantes in print. Her greatest interest now was in the published writings of others, especially her contemporaries. Her room was always piled with newspapers and magazines, sent by this friend and that; and in circulating libraries in both Beverly and Salem she was a familiar figure.

When she read Harriet Beecher Stowe's claim that Lord Byron was guilty of incest with his half sister Augusta Leigh, she studied the charge with a lawyer's precision. Having arrived at a conclusion, she wrote: "In Trelawney's *Recollections of Byron and Shelley* there is an unfinished letter to Mrs. Leigh, which Trelawney found in Byron's papers after his death. The letter is entirely inconsistent with Mrs. Stowe's story. I think it could not possibly have been written if what Mrs. Stowe says had been true. Mrs. Leigh seems to have been the medium of communication between Byron and his wife. Mrs. Stowe is an author by profession, therefore the plain truth is not to be looked for from her. She must write what people will read, and in her mind she habitually mixes up fact and fiction. I dare say she does not know them apart. All the time she was in England she was thinking of making a book, or as many books as she could. Then she never followed Dr. Johnson's advice, perhaps never heard of it, 'Clear your mind of cant.' Her Byron article is full of cant, and, besides all the rest, she is a Beecher. And what Beecher can live without excitement—without creating a sensation? As to Lady Byron, she appears to be one of those people who cannot discriminate between sins, but think one as likely to be committed as another—or rather, who think every departure from their own particular rule of right is a sin so enormous that the person guilty of it would hesitate at nothing."

Aunt Rebecca Manning, or one of her daughters, once urged Ebe to buy a new dress. Ebe said: "Do you not think I had better buy the books I want than the dress you say I ought to have? Besides the cost, the making of the dress will be a trouble to me, whereas the reading of the books will be a comfort."

Such luck as her grandfather, Captain Daniel Hathorne, enjoyed seemed to follow Ebe. Just three months after the death of her brother, who had replaced her mother as a chief support, Uncle William Manning died. The income which he had received from the trust set up by his sister Mary now went to Ebe. This, combined with the small amount coming in quarterly from some sort of legacy which she shared with her brother's heirs, was to be enough to satisfy her needs for the rest of her life.

Una and Rose visited her from time to time, and letters were exchanged frequently between Montserrat and the Wayside. Ebe knew well what was going on in the house where Sophia was now the head.

Julian had almost finished his freshman year in Harvard at the time of his father's death, and Mr. Pierce saw that he was sent back the next fall. But the young man was unstudious. He showed too plainly that he had never been subjected to rigorous mental discipline. From the end of his second year in Harvard until the autumn of 1867 he loafed at home, pretended to read philosophy, boasted of what he would do if he were a student in Heidelberg, and fell in and out of love. Then he went back to Harvard—

apparently again with Mr. Pierce's help—to study civil engineering in the scientific school.

Rose's education, never sufficient to enable her to spell correctly, was picked up at schools in Concord, in Lee (not far from Lenox, her birthplace), in Lexington (at Dr. Dio Lewis's "gymnastic institute"), and in Salem. It was in the fall of 1867 that she went to the town of her ancestors to attend a "select academy for young ladies" on Chestnut Street. By this time Sophia had spent or lost in a bank failure the money left by her husband and also the $1,200 received from the *Atlantic* in 1866 for twelve installments of his *American Note-Books*. Rose's year in the Salem school was a gift from Sophia's cousins, Mr. and Mrs. George Bailey Loring, friends of Mr. Pierce.

Una, Ebe's chief informer, remained at the Wayside all this while, reading "history and the literature suggested by it," keeping up with her Latin and music, teaching calisthenics to a class of children, and going every Sunday to service at Concord's Unitarian Church. But the even flow of her life was broken early in 1868 when she fell in love with Storrow Higginson. The young man—a direct descendant of the Reverend Francis Higginson of Salem—had studied for the ministry and had served as a chaplain in the Civil War. But on returning to his home in Boston he had abandoned a churchman's career. Now he was looking forward to living a life of adventure, and talked of going to South America. Little appears to be known regarding his relations with Una except that she said yes to his proposal of marriage and then—when she was persuaded that he was unworthy— broke the engagement.

The experience of frustrated love was almost too much for Una. Sophia's great desire was to get the girl into a new environment, far removed from the Concord gossips, who, it is known, were whispering about her lack of mental balance. It was Julian who suggested the way out. He was dissatisfied with Harvard's scientific school and was arguing that only in Germany, at the Dresden Polytechnic, could he get the training which would fit him properly for the profession of civil engineering. Sophia had little money. But she owned the Wayside. She owned also a mass of unpublished Hawthorne manuscripts and the journals she herself had kept in Europe.

So, early in the fall of 1868, after the publication in book form of Hawthorne's *Passages from the American Note-Books*, Ebe learned that the Wayside had been sold, that Mr. Fields was to bring out successively her brother's *Passages from the English Note-Books* and *Passages from the Italian Note-Books*, and that Putnam of New York was to publish Sophia's own *Notes on England and Italy*. On a day in early October, Una and Rose, and possibly also Julian, came to Montserrat to bid Aunt Ebe farewell. Even Una seemed excited over the life they were all going to lead in Dresden, where expenses would be half what they were in Concord.

The three—Una twenty-four, Julian twenty-two, and Rose seventeen—sailed from New York with their mother on October 20.

Ebe disapproved of the move. To her, Massachusetts—including even Concord—was good enough for anybody. When she was told once that it was impossible for Una to thrive in New England she said, "My private opinion is that whoever cannot do that need not live at all."

What her nieces failed to state openly in their letters she was able to read between the lines. In this way she found out that Sophia in going to Europe ran into troubles far greater than those from which she had fled.

For months all went well in Dresden. Julian, as pleased with the Polytechnic as he had expected to be, studied with an interest which would have surprised his Harvard professors. Rose, living in a boardingschool where the discipline was hard, practiced the piano faithfully and, to the joy of her mother, manifested an exceptional talent for drawing and painting. Una, usually accompanied by Sophia, spent most of her days in the art galleries. All three of the eager young learners worked diligently to master the German language.

But by the summer of 1869 Julian was dissatisfied. Acting upon impulse, he returned to America—"for a visit," he said. In New York he was offered a position in the municipal department of docks. He accepted it, renouncing for all time his aim to finish his engineering studies.

Before his departure from Dresden the Hawthornes had crossed paths with another American family residing there, the Lathrops. They were three—Mrs. George Alfred Lathrop and her sons Francis Augustus, twenty, and George Parsons, eighteen. The mother met all of Sophia's standards for gentility. The boys were handsome, precocious, and socially interesting. Moreover there was about them the aura of the romantic. Their father, formerly a physician but now a man of business in New York, was a distant cousin of Dr. Holmes and of another friend of the Hawthornes, John Lothrop Motley, the historian. Dr. Lathrop had been trained in the College of Physicians and Surgeons in New York, and on getting married had gone to the Sandwich Islands to practice his profession and also to serve as United States consul. The voyage into the distant Pacific, lasting for months, had taken him and his bride around Cape Horn, and Francis was born at sea. George was born in Honolulu, where the Lathrops had remained until about 1860. Then they had returned to New York. Francis and George had been well educated. Each in his own way was highly aesthetic, and gifted. Francis was a painter, sufficiently talented to attract the attention of Mr. Whistler and Sir Edward Burne-Jones. George had had verses printed in an American magazine, and fancied himself developing into a great poet.

By the late spring of 1870 the Hawthornes and Lathrops were seeing much of one another. Then the Franco-Prussian War broke out and drove both families to England. Sophia and her daughters settled down in London. Francis Lathrop, accepted as a protégé by Mr. Whistler, also chose to remain there. But his mother and brother sailed for New York to rejoin Dr. Lathrop. In the autumn George entered Columbia College as a student of law.

Francis appears to have been a misogynist, living exclusively for his art. To women he was no more than an intellect. George, possessed of a manliness far in advance of his years, appealed to them emotionally.

After his departure for America, if not before, Sophia surely saw that Una, though seven years older than he, loved him as she had once loved Storrow Higginson. At the same time Sophia must have observed that George was in love with Rose.

Again and again, as the mother shuddered at the thought of George's return to London, she must have asked herself, "What would Mr. Hawthorne have done?" The little woman—getting old, but still with the body which even Ebe declared shapely—wore herself weary taking Una to teas, exhibitions of paintings, and lectures. Rose, absorbed in her studies in the South Kensington Art School, seemed to be a less perplexing problem.

Sophia's anxiety was made all the heavier when, near the end of 1870, she heard that Julian had suddenly got married to a girl with a name altogether out of keeping with either Hawthorne or Peabody tradition, the name May Albertina Amelung. The mother could only hope that her son had not rushed into a bad marriage. Even she, always ready to make excuses for his weaknesses, was not blind to his tendency to act without forethought.

But it was Una and Rose for whom she said she wished to live when she broke under her worries five weeks later. She had been in bed near a fortnight when the doctor in attendance pronounced her illness typhoid pneumonia. For days her daughters, aided by two maids, watched over her. The headaches she had suffered before her marriage came back, and once more noises threw her into awful pain. Yet there were hours when she was cheerful and optimistic. She held out until the coming of the first crocuses. Then, on March 3, 1871, she joined her husband in death. It was a Sunday, and on the following Friday came Una's twenty-seventh birthday. On Saturday the burial took place, in Kensal Green, near the grave of Thackeray.

George Lathrop, driven by his passion for Rose to give up his study of law and go back to England, was either in London at the time of the funeral or a few days later. If Sophia had lived a month or two longer, she would have seen Rose yield to his wooing. Then Sophia would have been called upon to care for her older daughter during another period of mental collapse—"Una's calamity," Aunt Lizzie Peabody called it. If Sophia had survived until the autumn she would have seen Una well again—but not in the state of mind to go to St. Luke's, in Chelsea, on September 11 and witness the marriage of Rose and George. Then Sophia would have read letters from Julian denouncing Rose, letters starting the feud which was to continue for years between Julian on one side and Rose and George on the other.

Ebe apparently had no objections to George Parsons La-throp as a husband for her younger niece. But she was out of patience with the couple when she found out, at the end of the year, that they had sailed for America, leaving Una all alone in London. As to her older niece, Ebe said, "I think Una is the best person of the name—born to the name, I mean—that I ever knew; for I cannot claim the merit of amiability for the Hawthornes as a race." In insert-ing the phrase, "born to the name, I mean," Ebe was of course thinking of her mother.

Una had recovered from her "calamity," and was not lonely. Among her many associates in England was Robert Browning, with whom the Hawthornes had been friendly in Italy. When Una lay in Rome almost lifeless with the Roman fever, Mr. Browning and his wife—the latter now long dead—had visited her. Since her mother's death she had had in her possession a portion of the unpublished Hawthorne manuscripts, and before the end of 1871 she and Mr. Browning, working together, got one version of the English romance ready for printing. It appeared in 1872 as *Septimius Felton*, first as a serial in the *Atlantic*, and then, in August, as a volume.

By this time Julian, with his wife and the one child she had borne him, was again living in Dresden, in a position to offer Una a home. In his second year in the New York department of docks he had written a short story, and it had been published in *Harper's Weekly*. He had then begun a novel, entitled *Bressant*. He had learned the power of the Hawthorne name in the offices of magazine editors and book publishers, and he was an inheritor of his mother's articulateness. Writing, he had decided, was for him a ready-made profession. So he had resigned from the New York municipal service, and, confident that he could live by his pen, had gone back to inexpensive Dresden.

Soon after arriving there he finished *Bressant*, and it was serialized in *Appleton's Journal*. Ebe read it and, in strong language, expressed disapproval. But before its appearance as a volume her nephew was under contract for another novel, *Idolatry*, published in 1874. This was the year Julian moved to London, with his family enlarged by another child or two.

It was also the year of Una's first visit back to the United States. Late in May she spent a day with Aunt Ebe in Montserrat. She brought her a dressing gown, ready to wear, except that it was too long. Julian's wife—who was familiarly called Minnie—had sent a pair of quilted satin slippers, trimmed with swansdown. "They suit me exactly in size," said seventy-two-year-old Ebe, after getting them on her feet. "But how I should look with them! They're too fine, and must be kept for show."

Una had spent several days with her sister and brother-in-law in their home in Cambridge. George, who was making the most of his connection with the family of Nathaniel Hawthorne, was assisting William Dean Howells in editing the *Atlantic Monthly* and writing in spare moments. Ebe had read his "Helen at the Loom" in the *Atlantic* and considered it a poem of high order. "I have great hopes for George," she said. But Una—whose infatuation for him was definitely dead—could not have been optimistic about his future. She had certainly observed that neither he nor Rose was happy. Their life together had become a series of quarrels and reconciliations.

Within a month or two Una was back in London, engaged in the settlement work which had occupied much of her time since her mother's death. Frequently, after a day of viewing the misery of London poverty, she refreshed her spirits in the carefree atmosphere of Julian's and Minnie's home, where she was always welcome. She had inherited the

Peabody optimism. Still she had her hours of melancholy, hours when her religion—she had become an Anglican Catholic communicant—was her only comfort.

In 1876 she made a second visit to the United States. Rose was now pregnant, and between her and George there appeared to be harmony. But there was trouble in another direction to distress Una. Julian, who was collecting material for a definitive biography of his father and mother, was enraged at George's writing and publishing *A Study of Nathaniel Hawthorne*. The calling of names back and forth across the Atlantic was at the most bitter stage at the time of Una's arrival in the United States. Ebe, resentful over certain statements George had made in his book, had sided with Julian. But when she heard that Rose was going to have a baby she wrote to her with all the old affection. Rose, who was standing staunchly by George, replied, "Your severe criticism of my husband hung like chains about my hands, and I could not bring myself to write to you. Your sweet letter has made me feel more than ever how much happiness is lost by family dissension."

During her stay in Rose's home Una met Albert Webster, another young man ambitious for recognition as a writer. Once more her emotions ran away with her, and for the third time in her thirty-two years she was in love. Albert— interested mainly, it appears, in her name—asked her to marry him and she said yes. To everybody except her it was clear that the young man was in the last stages of consumption. George, perhaps unwittingly, gave him the idea that the climate of the Sandwich Islands was all he needed for a cure. So he and his fiancée parted, he to go westward to San Francisco and Honolulu and she eastward to England.

A few weeks later, when she was at Julian's house near

London, she received a message stating that Albert had died on shipboard several days out from San Francisco. "Ah, yes!" she exclaimed, as if she had known all along that happiness was not for her. A few days before, when in the brightest mood, she had written to Aunt Ebe. She was making her wedding dress with her own hands, she had said. Ebe on hearing of Albert's death declared, "Una cannot go on from day to day, as I have always done, when there was no reason why I should not, finding interest and a moderate degree of pleasure in what did not at all concern me personally. Neither is she particularly fond of reading."

Una's disappointment this time brought on a collapse which was physical rather than mental. Her hair turned completely white, and the least physical exertion caused fatigue. In the late summer of 1877 she went to an Anglican convent near Bray and Binfield, in the region of England where her paternal ancestors had dwelt. It was said that she was there for a retreat. But it was believed that she was seeking admission into the convent as a postulant. One day she suddenly grew very weak. A message was sent to Julian, but before he arrived she was no more. She was buried in Kensal Green, beside the grave of her mother.

So passed the most unlucky of all the unlucky Hawthornes, she who had served as the model for little Pearl in *The Scarlet Letter*. Hawthorne—under the spell of Rousseau—had seen her as God's highest creation, a darling of nature wholly untouched by erroneous custom. She was dead of the same malady which had killed her father—the malady to which he might never have fallen prey but for his worry over her misfortunes.

Her end served to increase the gossip which had been passed to and fro since the rift between Julian Hawthorne of London and George Parsons Lathrop of Boston became public. "The real reason for Julian's resentment," said many of the talkers, "is that George jilted Una and then won Rose." Innuendoes had even appeared in print.

The issue of the New York *Tribune* for June 25, 1879, carried a letter by George Parsons Lathrop. His purpose in writing it, he said, was to correct "some romantic flights of imagination lately published concerning the Hawthornes." He denied that he had ever been engaged to Una, and told the story of her engagement to Albert Webster. Then he wrote, "Finally Miss Una Hawthorne did have an attack of insanity in London, having also had one ten years before."

At the time George wrote this letter he had just passed through a period of great trial. After the birth of his and Rose's little son—named Francis Hawthorne and called Francie—he had bought the Wayside so that the child might grow up in the country. Then he had lost his position on the *Atlantic*. For months he had been unemployed—months when he and Rose experienced such poverty at the Wayside as Hawthorne and Sophia had known at the Old Manse. Finally George had been called to the editorial staff of the Boston *Courier*. This was the journal with which he was associated when his letter to the *Tribune* was printed.

As Ebe read it she must have felt that she had had enough. But Providence was not yet ready to spare her from observing family sorrows and quarrels.

In February, 1881, little Francie, four years old, took pneumonia, and within two or three days was dead. George and Rose, to ease their grief with new scenes, somehow got together enough money for a trip to Europe. In London they were well received by Julian, whose consideration for their bereavement crowded out for the time being all bad feeling. While they were abroad Rose stayed in England

and George traveled in Spain, gathering material for his *Spanish Vistas*.

Julian had already made plans to return to America, where, as Ebe said, his children—there were now seven—would not "grow up all crusted over with English prejudices." He had not been long back in his native land—living at the Wayside, paying rent to George—when he announced the publication of *Doctor Grimshawe's Secret*, another version of Hawthorne's English romance.

George and Rose, who had returned from their trip and were living in New York, had seen the manuscript of *Doctor Grimshawe's Secret* and considered it too formless to be printed. Rose said in a letter to Aunt Ebe: "Julian's shocking notice in the papers has been a great grief to me. His dishonesty has been a heavier blow than mere cruelty could have been." George—again in a letter to the New York *Tribune*—wrote of the announced volume: "It cannot be truthfully published as anything more than an experimental fragment." Once more the press commentators were stirred to make news out of the Hawthorne-Lathrop feud.

Ebe could do nothing to bring about a reconciliation. Besides, she at last had problems of her own to bother about. She was eighty, and all the relatives she had grown up with were dead—Aunt Rebecca Manning, Uncle Dike, and Aunt Priscilla Dike. But to her the disturbing blow was the death of the Coles. When the new owners of the house in which she had lived for three decades came to take possession, she convinced them that she was as much a part of the place as the parlor chimney. They let her stay, and she continued to follow her usual habits. But her walks were not so long as they had been in the old days, and the reading of a book now took a lot of time.

There were also, as usual, the little annoyances. In a letter which she wrote to somebody after she had become an old woman she said: "I must not forget to tell you that the name Montserrat has been changed to Centreville; we were, formerly, to the great disgust of all the dwellers in this region, except myself, called Ratters; now we are Villens—Centre-Villens; an appellation full good enough for people who are so wanting in taste and ingenuity as to be dissatisfied with a good old name, and yet unable to find a tolerable new one."

She remained well until a day or two after Christmas, 1882. Then she fell sick—with measles, it was said. The ailment, whatever it was, consumed all her strength. A few minutes after 1883 began she departed from the life towards which she had been for many a year only a curious spectator.

She was not the last with her name to be buried in Salem. When she was near her end a middle-aged shipmaster, Captain William Hollingsworth Hathorne, settled in a house on Boston Street with his wife and daughter. He had fought under Farragut at Mobile Bay, and had served as United States consul in Zanzibar. His death came in 1886, and he was buried in the Harmony Grove Cemetery. All that appears to be known of his wife and daughter is that they sold the Boston Street house and left Salem. The Hathorne family line to which he belonged has not been determined.

MOTHER ALPHONSA

A FEW MONTHS after Aunt Ebe's death Rose and George sold the Wayside. Since their return from their 1881 trip to Europe they had lived in nomadic fashion, mainly in New York in the vicinity of Washington Square, where George's mother, widowed in 1877, had a home. With the Wayside no longer a responsibility, Rose and George bought a plot of ground on Post Hill Place in New London, Connecticut, and erected on it a residence of their own odd design. Once settled there they were near enough to both New York and Boston to maintain personal contact with publishers and editors.

Even before Francie's death Rose had earned money with her pen. Now that she had no child to look after she did more writing—tales and poems of mediocre quality, bought because of her name. It was a writing Hawthorne trio—Julian, Rose, and George. Scarcely a month passed when something by at least one of them failed to appear in an American magazine. And during the decade of the 1880's they published about twenty books—fiction, poetry (Rose's *Along the Shore*), biography (Julian's two-volume *Nathaniel Hawthorne and His Wife*), criticism, and travel (George's *Spanish Vistas*). The three had no false notions about the quality of the fiction they were producing. Once George, when mellow from drinking, said to a friend: "I firmly believe I might be a good novelist did I not have weighing upon me the enormous Hawthorne prestige. How am I to live up to that standard? It gets me all paralyzed. Everybody says, 'George Lathrop? Ah, yes! Hawthorne's son-in-law.' I recognize that it has done me good, but it also crushes me. What could I not have been except for that?"

His and Rose's quarrel with Julian over *Doctor Grimshawe's Secret* was in time forgotten. Newspaper columnists waiting for the opportunity to make comedy again out of the Hawthorne-Lathrop feud were to be disappointed. Julian, Rose, and George—to all appearances—were at last at peace.

Julian's house—usually somewhere on Manhattan in the winter and at Sag Harbor, Long Island, in the summer—must have been a noisy jolly place to visit. Everyone wondered how many Hawthornes he and Minnie would add to the list. Finally, when their brood numbered nine, they called a halt.

Julian was no doubt grateful for the silence of Rose and George during the attacks on his *Nathaniel Hawthorne and His Wife*. The ugly portrait of Margaret Fuller which the book presents stirred up trouble. The passage which tells of Hawthorne's challenging a supposed philanderer to a duel puzzled all who had personally known the romancer. Some claimed that this episode was plain fabrication on Julian's part. Still *Nathaniel Hawthorne and His Wife*, though marked with inaccuracy and the tendency to sensationalize, was to be accepted in time as a monument in American biography.

The quarrels and separations between Rose and George had grown more frequent with the years. George's love for his wife was his very existence. It is no wonder that when he was parted from her he sought to forget his misery in drink.

Incompatibility between the two was inevitable. At the time of the marriage Rose undoubtedly thought herself in love. But even then, in her early womanhood, a force too consuming to admit of wifely devotion smouldered within her. It was a dominating sense of duty, a feeling of obedience to destiny, an inner power, beside which her father's will to write was weak. Among her paternal forebears only Major William Hathorne, led by the vision of God's State upon earth, could have understood fully the strength of her spiritual energy. Her position in marriage was as tragic as George's. She had dreamed of excelling at music, painting, and literature. But her real urge, of which she was only vaguely aware, was not to find expression in the arts. She was a frustrated woman. For driving George to alcohol she blamed her quick temper and sharp tongue. Between a parting and a reconciliation her anguish was no doubt as keen as her husband's.

Towards the end of the 1880's she and George, during a period of marital tranquillity, found themselves discussing religion, especially Roman Catholicism. Their motive appears at first to have been little more than curiosity. Rose had had a halfhearted Unitarian rearing, and George was less than a halfhearted Episcopalian. Yet both were potentially religious. The more they investigated, the more interested they became in the Roman Catholic faith. Somehow they were convinced, possibly from reading Cardinal Newman, that even the most extreme agnostic has latent within him a sense of believing, as definite as the sense of seeing or hearing. Rose and George came to want this sense of believing as they had wanted nothing else in life. If they could find where in their minds it was hidden and could bring it to the fore, they would be able, they concluded, to solve the problem of their marriage and their every other problem. They talked with Roman Catholics, including their Irish servant girls. Then they received instruction from Catholic churchmen. Their lives became a prayer for faith.

In March, 1891, newspapers throughout the country announced that George Parsons Lathrop and Rose Hawthorne Lathrop had been received into the Roman Catholic Church.

George at the time was attracting attention because of his prominence in the fight to secure for writers a more just copyright law. The shift of a Puritan Hawthorne to Roman Catholicism would have been exciting news at any period. So the conversion of Rose and George was given extensive comment in the press. It was made the subject of editorials, some commendatory, some mildly critical, and some abusive. Certain former friends wrote to Rose and George boldly charging them of changing their religion in order to gain a new type of publicity. But the Lathrops had that for which they had prayed, and what was said of them could have meant little.

Working together they organized in New London in 1892 the Catholic Summer School of America. Then they collaborated in writing a history of the Order of the Sisters of Visitation. This work was published in 1894 with the title *A Story of Courage.*

But George and Rose Lathrop had never been intended to labor together as man and wife. In the new light which faith had brought, Rose saw that compassion was the only emotion she could feel for the man who had tried for a quarter of a century to possess her heart. When George faced the truth and realized that as Catholics he and Rose were farther apart than they had been as Protestants, he reverted to his old means of escape from unhappiness—alcohol. Rose held on to the appearances of marriage until late in 1895. Then, with the full permission of the Church, stated in writing, she left George, never to entertain again any thought of a reconciliation.

As she traveled northward from New London for a retreat in a convent near Wellesley Hills, she pitied her husband, as she pitied the whole worried world. Often before her mind's eye in recent months had been, she was to say, the pictures of the poor in her father's writings. Why were there so many of these pictures? Why had Hawthorne been impelled by a power stronger than himself to walk in the slums of Liverpool and observe the pains of poverty? One passage in the *English Note-Books* impressed Rose especially—the description of a visit Hawthorne made to the children's ward of a Liverpool workhouse. One "wretched, pale, half-torpid little thing" he saw there took "the strangest fancy" to him. It appeared to be about six years old, but whether boy or girl Hawthorne did not know. A yellowish matter running from the child's eyes was, he was told, the result of scurvy. He had never seen, he said, a creature he was less inclined to fondle. Then he wrote: "But this little sickly, humor-eaten fright prowled around me, taking hold of my skirts, following at my heels, and at last held up its hands, smiled in my face, and, standing directly before me, insisted on my taking it up! Not that it said a word, for I rather think it was underwitted, and could not talk; but its face expressed such perfect confidence that it was going to be taken up and made much of, that it was impossible not to do it. It was as if God had promised the child this favor on my behalf, and that I must needs fill the contract. I held my undesirable burden a little while, and after setting the child down, it still followed me, holding two of my fingers and playing with them, just as if it were a child of my own. It was a foundling, and out of all humankind it chose me to be its father!" And Hawthorne added, "I should never have forgiven myself if I had repelled its advances." Why did the image of this "humor-eaten fright" haunt Rose? This question she was unable to put aside.

After ending her retreat at the convent in Wellesley Hills she stayed on in that town, the guest of an old friend. Every morning at seven she was back at the convent for Mass. During the day she thought—and read what she could find—about the saints who had alleviated the sufferings of those who were dying of incurable diseases. Of deep significance to her was what she learned about St. Rose of Lima, a Dominican tertiary who represented, to the utmost, self-denial in the flesh. Rose Hawthorne had not known until she was eight or ten that in Rose of Lima she had a patron saint. Also significant was what she read of the work of French and Belgian religious societies devoted to the care of the incurable sick. But most important of all, as she was later to declare, was what she learned of the services which Father Damien had rendered to the lepers of the Pacific island of Molokai.

Who among all the American sufferers from disease were most deserving of pity and help? This was the question which was uppermost in the mind of Rose Hawthorne Lathrop during the winter and spring of 1896.

In her girlhood she had probably heard her father or Aunt Ebe tell of the horrible death from cancer of her great-aunt Mary Manning. In 1887 she had seen her friend Emma Lazarus die of that disease. She felt now that she knew why she had been drawn to this Jewish woman, with whom she had at one time contemplated traveling for a summer in Europe. She had been impressed, she believed, not by Miss Lazarus' interesting mind, and not by her talent for writing verse, but by her charitableness towards those of her race who were victims of pogroms in Russia and Poland. When cancer laid her low, she was given the most expensive care. Yet her suffering had been extreme. Then Rose had seen another person die of cancer, a New York seamstress who had sewed for her. This young woman had no money, and no family. The only place for her while she awaited her end in agony was New York's charity hospital on Blackwell's Island, where the care was notoriously brutal.

By the summer of 1896 Rose knew that she would spend

the rest of her life bringing such comfort as she could to the indigent whom cancer had claimed for death. Her future had been determined, she believed, by a decree of Heaven. The powerful force long dormant within her, rendering marriage to George Lathrop a failure, was at last fully awake. For the third time in three hundred years a Hawthrone was in the control of a mighty will. Rose was never to struggle against it, nor make compromises, as her father had done. The granite within her was the granite of the sire of the Salem Hawthornes. The seventeenth-century Puritan and the nineteenth-century Roman Catholic believed alike that the urge propelling them into strange courses had been planted by God. Their submission to it was alike wholehearted.

During the unusually hot summer of 1896 Rose worked in the cancer ward of the hospital at 106th Street and Central Park West in New York. It was a huge round room with a pillar in the center, and reminded her, she said, of a great tent. The beds, with the heads against the walls, formed a circle of pain, despair, and death. The first task assigned to Rose was to dress the sores of a patient whose face was half eaten away. Almost overcome by the horrible cancer odor, she trembled and cringed. But she did the cleansing and the bandaging. The hard beginning was what she needed for self-control. Afterwards she rebelled at no duty, however loathsome it might be.

She had been admitted into the hospital for a training period of three or four months. Before that time expired she had learned how to care for cancer patients of all sorts. She had also made observations which filled her with indignation. One considered too far gone to benefit from medical treatment might be allowed to stay in the hospital if able to pay the high prices charged. If he had no money he was sent away, and the responsibility of the hospital authorities ceased the minute he was taken out the door. No effort was made to build up the morale of the incurables. They were plainly told that they were going to die. More than once Rose's temper flared up, and bitter words came in an outburst. If she had held them back she would have felt that she was committing a sin. The hospital authorities were glad to see her leave.

From the writings of Jacob Riis and others she had learned of the degradation of New York's lower East Side. It was on Scammel Street, one of the most squalid thoroughfares in this overpopulated poverty-ridden district, that Rose Hawthorne Lathrop, in December, 1896, set up her first center for the care of incurable victims of cancer. The place was a flat of only two or three rooms, filthy and foul when Rose found it, but clean, and bright with yellow paint, after she had been living there, all alone, for a few days.

She had sent for newspaper reporters and photographers before finishing the renovation. She wanted the public to see pictures of the elegant Mrs. Lathrop holding mops and paint brushes. Every story she allowed to go into print had to say something of her need for funds. She made much of the fact that she would treat only the cancerous who were incurable and indigent.

Her husband, living alone in a flat on 57th Street, was also sought out and interviewed. His statement was that his wife's charitable work had his full approval and sympathy.

To his friends—who, it appears, were supplying the money on which he was living—he told a different story. Since his wife's leaving him, he said, he had been nervous, tense, restless, and utterly unable to complete "any important literary work." Two or three years after his conversion to the Roman Catholic faith he had dramatized *The Scarlet Letter* for a musical setting by Walter Damrosch. Early in the spring of 1896, while Rose was in Wellesley Hills, the opera was sung with success, first in Boston and then in New York. The critics had been specially kind to the librettist. But the praise meant little to George. With Rose gone nothing remained for him—except alcohol.

Gifts came to Scammel Street—as Rose had known they would. She had used her Hawthorne name for a feeble career as a writer. Now she was using it for a purpose which would win, she believed, her father's happiest approbation were he alive. But the newspaper publicity, which was kept up with regularity, not only drew supporters. It came also to the attention of the sick who might benefit, and Rose found that the little Scammel Street flat was altogether inadequate.

In March, 1897, she moved into more spacious quarters on Water Street. This was the year of the publication of her one book to escape oblivion, her *Memories of Hawthorne*. She had probably got it ready for printing at odd moments. Every penny of the royalties she received from the volume went into her relief work.

On both Scammel Street and Water Street she was in the parish of the Church of St. Rose of Lima. Every morning she attended the half-past-six Mass. When she rented the flat on Scammel Street she had not known to what parish she would belong. That it had turned out to be St. Rose's was not, she insisted, due to coincidence.

Volunteer nurses and helpers, offering hours when they were free, had been coming to Rose from the time they heard through the press what she was doing. They found her enthusiasm magnetic. By the spring of 1898 several women were ready to follow in her steps in dedicating their lives to the work.

Chief among them was Alice Huber, of Kentucky. She had been reared a Catholic, and was deeply religious. By profession she was a painter, and for several years had taught art in New York. It was March 5, 1898, when Miss Huber came to Water Street to begin her long career as Rose's leading assistant.

Precisely a month and two weeks later, at the Roosevelt Hospital in New York, George Parsons Lathrop passed away, the victim, said the newspapers, of a "complication of kidney and heart disease." Rose had been notified of the fatal turn in his illness, but he was gone before she could get to him. Only his mother and brother, the latter now widely famed as a painter of murals, were at his bedside at the end.

The funeral was held at the Church of the Paulist Fathers on April 22. That evening Rose wrote in her diary: "My beloved husband died on April 19th, about half an hour before I reached him. I had made seven offerings of Holy Communion on the first Fridays for the entire conversion of my husband to God and to holiness. As I stood beside his body, soon after his death, the beauty and nobility and the exquisite gentleness of his life, and the eloquence which breathes from the unbreathing being of one who has died in the Lord, spoke plainly to me of his virtues, and the welcome our Lord had given him into His rest. My own soul was trembling in the dark uncertainty of all unworthiness. Yesterday, early, his soul came, I am sure, to console me in his loveliest way of forgiveness."

Within a fortnight she was in the mood to say, "Have last evening, for the first time since George's death, felt courage, and am very cheerful, *in Christ.*" For the rest of 1898 she was praying that George "might be received into Heaven on Christmas Day." When that day arrived she was convinced within her heart that "he was in bliss." "God rest his beloved soul," she wrote in her diary.

By the spring of 1899 she and her helpers—calling themselves Servants of Relief for Incurable Cancer and wearing a gingham habit which certain newspaper reporters saw as Puritanlike—were well-known figures on New York's lower East Side. Their work had so expanded that they were once again as cramped as they had been on Scammel Street. So a new place was found, and purchased—a house on Cherry Street. The name adopted was St. Rose's Free Home, after St. Rose of Lima.

Hitherto the Servants of Relief had had no official connection with the Church. Now that George was gone Rose was free to become what she had undoubtedly long aspired to be, a Dominican tertiary, like her patron saint. On September 14, 1899, both she and Miss Huber were received into the Dominican Order as novitiates. For more than a year they continued in that status. Then, on December 8, 1900, they were given the Dominican habit. Thus Rose Hawthorne Lathrop and Alice Huber became lay sisters, the former with the name Mary Alphonsa and the latter with the name Mary Rose. And thus the Servants of Relief passed under the surveillance of the Church.

Finding themselves by the summer of 1901 once more handicapped by lack of space, they bought a second house —a rambling wooden building of many rooms in the village of Sherman Park, Westchester County, New York. The new place was given the name Rosary Hill Home. As head of two houses, Sister Alphonsa automatically became Mother Alphonsa.

The residents of Sherman Park, fearing that cancer was contagious, at first resented the presence of a group of victims of the disease in their midst. But Mother Alphonsa won her Westchester neighbors, as she had won others. She had not been long in Sherman Park when, in honor of her and her father alike, the name of the village was changed to Hawthorne.

In 1912 St. Rose's Free Home was moved to a building on Jackson Street erected by the Servants of Relief themselves at a cost of $150,000, all obtained through gifts. This new house, equipped to care for as many as seventy-five patients at a time, was under the direct supervision of Sister Rose. Mother Alphonsa was in personal charge of Rosary Hill Home in Hawthorne, where the capacity was about forty beds. By the end of this year 1912 the Servants of Relief had treated, all told, 1,045 persons afflicted with cancer in the last stages—652 Catholics, 363 Protestants, and 30 Jews.

On April 4, 1913, Mother Alphonsa was called upon to perform the most humiliating family duty which had ever befallen the lot of a Salem Hawthorne. In company with a sister—one, it is certain, who was not too much needed at either St. Rose's Home or Rosary Hill—she traveled to Washington. Her mission was to beseech the President of the United States, Woodrow Wilson, to grant a pardon to her brother, who had been since March 26 "convict No. 4,435" in the Federal Penitentiary in Atlanta, Georgia.

During her years of building the Servants of Relief into one of the noblest organizations ever conceived by an American, Julian was busy making the money necessary for the care of his enormous family. He had to see many, many thousands of his words in print in order to educate the seven of his nine sons and daughters who had survived infanthood. To make the sentences flow he had only to sit before his typewriter and start touching the keys. Within three weeks in the year 1897 he wrote a novel, *A Fool of Nature,* and with it won a prize of $10,000 offered by the New York *Herald*. At that time he had been publishing for twenty-five years and had more than forty books to his credit—history, biography, travel, and criticism, in addition to fiction. He had served in various editorial positions, and had lectured —on such subjects as the occult. The people who paid money to hear celebrities speak and who bought the books which publishers issued by the hundreds every season were gulls, Julian felt, and he was always ready to supply what he thought would attract them.

Some of his literary transactions caused his friends to raise their eyebrows. For instance, in 1886, when he was serving as an editor of the New York *World*, he called on James Russell Lowell and asked for a series of articles, offering $1,000 for each. The elderly Mr. Lowell, who had recently relinquished his post as United States minister to Great Britain, said that he did not wish to assume any immediate journalistic commitments, and then spent an hour talking confidentially with the son of his friend of earlier days. When Julian got back to his office he wrote up the interview, restating all Mr. Lowell had said. It was featured in the *World*, filling six columns. Mr. Lowell revered honor too highly to keep quiet. In commenting on the episode in a letter printed in a Salem newspaper Aunt Lizzie Peabody wrote: "Julian's error, I think, was mainly due to a most unfortunate characteristic, namely, an abnormal impetuosity of temperament, preventing all reflective self-criticism; a fault that has led him into all the mistakes of his literary and practical life."

Despite the fact that a journalistic assignment sometimes gave him the opportunity of visiting a land as distant as India, he was often bored with his profession as a man of letters. He was forever dreaming of a way to escape from the rut in which he found himself. But he spent his money as fast as he made it, and was obliged to stick to the drudgery of putting down words on paper. New York got on his nerves. Once he made plans to buy a yacht and maintain it as a permanent home for his family. He could have a tutor on board to teach the children, and he was able to write anywhere. Minnie, his wife, was enthusiastic over the idea of drifting from port to port. But Julian abandoned the plans when he found out that no yacht was to be had at the price he could afford. There was nothing he could do except continue the literary life in New York and wait for another dream.

In August, 1908, a Salem gentleman with whom he was on speaking terms received from him a letter. It was typewritten—on light yellow stationery bearing the letter-head: "Julian Hawthorne, Author, Journalist, Historian." The friendly message was an invitation to buy stock in a company which, it was said, was operating several gold and silver mines in Canada. Julian was serving the company as a "special commissioner." Others serving in the same capacity were Josiah Quincy, of Boston, and Dr. William James Morton, of New York. The former, a member of the illustrious Quincy family of Massachusetts, had been assistant secretary of state under President Cleveland and, from 1895 to 1899, mayor of Boston. The latter was a famous neurologist, son of the Boston dentist who discovered the value of ether as an anesthetic. In concluding the communication Julian said: "For my own part, in going into mining, I revert to the profession for which I was educated. While awaiting the job, I took up literature to fill the interval." That interval, as the Salem gentleman to whom the letter was addressed must have known, had lasted for a full thirty-five years.

Letters of like nature went to persons with savings all

over the country—including such modest earners as army officers and schoolteachers. The company also issued printed prospectuses, all of which were written by Julian Hawthorne. Since such men as he and Mr. Quincy and Dr. Morton were associated with the company, no one seems to have doubted its solidity and integrity. The public bought shares—to the value of $3,500,000.

When months passed into years and no dividends were paid, many of the investors became alarmed. Finally the questionable conduct of the company was called to the attention of the United States attorney general. An investigation was ordered, and it was found that not one of the mines which the company operated had produced gold or silver in paying quantity since 1900. The identity of the individual who had enticed Hawthorne, Quincy, and Morton into the company also came to light. He was a slick promoter, Albert Freeman, at home in high social circles and aware of the effect upon the public of "big names."

He, Hawthorne, Quincy, and Morton were all indicted for using the United States mails for fraudulent purposes. On November 27, 1912, they appeared for trial before a federal court sitting in New York. The argument of the government was that the four defendants were common "green goods men," conscienceless "bunko steerers," the "most notorious gang of swindlers that had ever infested New York." In a summing up, one of the prosecuting attorneys said, "We all know that some of these men bear honored names. Theirs is the greater crime, for they have prostituted them. The penitentiaries are full of men with honored names, which they have used to defraud others." The lawyers for the defense took the stand that their clients had believed from the start to the end in the gainful productivity of the mines and had, to their knowledge, acted at all times in the fullest honesty. The witnesses were so numerous and the testimony so detailed that the trial lasted until March 12, 1913.

Then the jury deliberated nearly twenty-eight hours before handing in verdicts. Albert Freeman, found guilty on twenty-three counts, was sentenced to imprisonment for five years. Hawthorne and Morton were each found guilty on seventeen counts and sentenced to imprisonment for one year, their terms to start with the day of the beginning of the trial, the preceding November 27. Josiah Quincy was acquitted.

When Julian heard his sentence pronounced, said the newspapers, a slight frown appeared upon his face. But when he left the court building to go to the Tombs—guarded by a marshal, to whom he was handcuffed—he walked with a vigor which belied his sixty-seven years.

It was on Easter Sunday, March 23, that he and Dr. Morton, in the custody of marshals, set out for Atlanta. One of his early prison experiences reported by the newspapers came on April 1. The occasion was a concert given at the Federal Penitentiary by the University of Georgia Glee Club. Julian had discarded the tweed suit, red necktie, and golf cap in which he had traveled southward, and had on the regulation prison garb with the number 4,435 prominent on the breast. The young singers on the platform had seen in recent weeks so many newspaper snapshots of the notorious son of the author of *The Scarlet Letter* that they spotted him without difficulty. With his drooping moustache only slightly gray and a look of alertness in his brown eyes, he appeared nearer forty than sixty-seven. The first half of the concert was devoted to comic college songs, and at the end of each Julian laughed and applauded with spirit. But in the course of the second half, which was given over to sentimental nostalgic numbers, he broke down and wept.

It was just three days after this concert that his sister and her companion made the trip to Washington. On arriving at the White House, Mother Alphonsa announced who she was and asked to see Mr. Wilson. When she was assured that an interview with the President that day was impossible, she said, "Then I'll speak with someone who will report fully to him the purpose of my visit."

The official she saw was the President's secretary, Joseph P. Tumulty. The two talked for an hour, and again and again Mother Alphonsa repeated, "My brother is only technically guilty. I know that he really believed in the mines." Finally, Mr. Tumulty told her to wait while he spoke to the President. When the secretary came back to her a few minutes later he had a verbal message from Mr. Wilson, a message which was not made public. Reporters had found out that Mother Alphonsa was at the White House. So when she and her companion walked out the door they ran into a group of correspondents, all of them begging for a statement. This Mother Alphonsa refused. But the press stories on her call to the White House mention without exception the look of encouragement on her face as she and "the wild-eyed little nun" accompanying her took a carriage to drive back to the railroad station.

In the meantime editorial writers throughout the United States were commenting on Julian Hawthorne's conviction. His father, several said, had claimed in the introduction to *The Scarlet Letter* that the Hawthorne family had never to his knowledge been "disgraced by a single unworthy member." How had it come about that this great good man's own son was dragging the family honor in the mud? A cynical answerer to this question wrote, "The fault lies with our money-mad age. Julian Hawthorne has exemplified that no man is proof against the lure of quick wealth."

It was the paradox in the situation of the Hawthornes which impressed a number of the commentators. How was it possible that Mother Alphonsa, who had proved herself a saint, and Julian, who had been convicted of low swindling, could be sister and brother, the offspring of such a man as Nathaniel Hawthorne and such a woman as Sophia Peabody? At least two of the editorial writers recalled a sentence from *The House of the Seven Gables*, "Life is made up of marble and mud."

Julian's enemies among the columnists had a heyday. "Nathaniel Hawthorne and his writings helped to make Salem famous," said one, "but it took Julian Hawthorne to put the easy marks of Harvard in the limelight with his classy literature on gold mines that existed only in his fertile brain." One exclaimed, "How much better it would have been if Julian Hawthorne had written one Scarlet Letter instead of all those yellow ones!" Another said, "Mr. Julian Hawthorne should escape from prison with enough local color for two plays and a best seller." One asked, "Though Julian Hawthorne is said to be chafing at his confinement in Atlanta, is there any good reason for releasing him?"

Evidently President Wilson, in spite of whatever encouragement his secretary might have given Mother Alphonsa, saw none. Julian Hawthorne, as he himself said, served his time "to the uttermost limit allowed by the law." His period of incarceration amounted all together to seven and a half months, which he spent editing *Good Words*, the prison paper, and writing poems for the New York *Times* on such topics as the release from mental pain which he and his fellow convicts experienced while watching a game of baseball or while hearing Caruso sing "Ridi, Pagliaccio" and "O Paradiso" when on a visit to the prison. It was good behavior which made the diminution of Hawthorne's term legally obligatory.

Dr. Morton, whom Julian spoke of as "a friend of a lifetime," left the prison with him. In response to a petition presented by many citizens and physicians of New York, President Wilson on December 10, 1913, granted a pardon to the neurologist, thus restoring his civil rights and making it possible for him to continue the practice of his profession. "No such action," said the press report, "was taken as to Hawthorne because the necessity was not as acute."

Julian wished no pardon. The acceptance of one would have been, he maintained, an admission of guilt. To the end he avowed his innocence, insisting that the mines were precisely what he said they were in letters and prospectuses. Again and again he declared that but for the scandal which broke the company the investors would be enjoying profits. All this he made clear in *The Subterranean Brotherhood*, which tells briefly of his experiences in Atlanta and then presents in detail an argument for the abolition of penal servitude as a punishment for crime. Next to his biography of his father and mother, it is his most interesting book.

But it was not a best seller. It was issued in 1914, when the great war which had broken out in Europe was absorbing the public interest. In the rush of world-shaking events Julian Hawthorne and the shame he had brought upon his family name were forgotten. He and Minnie (their children, several of whom were married, had homes of their own) went to California to live. Again he depended upon his pen for support, turning out book reviews and syndicated articles on sundry subjects.

In 1910 the Hawthorne Memorial Association was organized in Salem. The aim of the men and women back of it was to honor with an appropriate monument the memory of Nathaniel Hawthorne, whom Salemites had at last come to recognize as the greatest of their town's many great sons and daughters. By the end of 1925 the Association's goal was attained.

When Hawthorne walked westward on the left side of Essex Street from the Manning stagecoach office, he first crossed Union Street and then, in turn, two narrow lanes. By 1925 the houses between these lanes had been razed, and the space thus cleared had been converted into Hawthorne Boulevard, a wide avenue split by a beautifully landscaped stretch of garden. At the northern end, between Essex Street and the Common, a large hotel had been built, called the Hawthorne. A hundred paces south of the hotel, in the center of the stretch of garden, a colossal bronze statue of the romancer had been set up. The erection of this monument was the Association's particular responsibility. The sculptor was Bela Lyon Pratt.

Two days before Christmas, in 1925, the unveiling ceremony took place. By a quarter past two an immense crowd was assembled in the East Church, of which the romancer's Manning grandparents had been parishioners in the days when Dr. Bentley was the minister. The exercises were opened with organ music, played by Joshua Phippen, bearer of a name associated with Salem's onetime powerful aristocracy. The orator of the day was Alden P. White, bearer of another aristocratic Salem name. In the procession from the East Church to the monument came first the ushers, then a group of the romancer's grandchildren and great-grandchildren, then the officials of the Association and other notables, and finally the crowd.

To thunderous applause, said the Salem *Evening News*, one of the romancer's great-granddaughters unveiled the statue. It represents the subject as few in Salem ever knew him. He is seen as he appeared in his last years, when, tired and worried, he wore the "Italian moustache" to conceal

the lines of age about his mouth. He is seated, and has taken
off his little round hat, thus revealing to the full his high
forehead and long hair. One of his hands is resting casually
on the head of his cane, which stands between his knees.
He is looking southward, in the direction of the sea. A few
rods to his left, beyond a parochial school maintained by
the Roman Catholic Church of the Immaculate Conception,
are the Union Street house where he was born and the
Herbert Street house in which he grew up. An equal distance to his right, up Charter Street, is the Burying Point,
where lie his great-great-grandfather Colonel John Hathorne, his grandfather Captain Daniel, his aunt Rachel
Forrester in a sepulchre with her millionaire husband, other
miscellaneous Hathorne kindred, and old Governor Bradstreet, with the Latin inscription on the sarcophagus which
marks his tomb long since effaced by the elements and time.

If the Hawthorne descendants who came to Salem that
December day left Hawthorne Boulevard at the conclusion
of the unveiling ceremony and drove in a motor car eastward on Derby Street, they passed on their left the customhouse, where the romancer had worked while giving every
second thought to the creation of *The Scarlet Letter*, and
on their right the wharves, where many a Hathorne shipmaster had dropped or weighed anchor. If the descendants
continued eastward, they were soon in Salem's Polish quarter. If on reaching Turner Street they made a right-angled
turn and drove the short distance to the South River, they
saw on their right the house and garden where Hawthorne
had spent evenings with Cousin Susanna Ingersoll and Horace Conolly. The old mansion, now owned by an organization of settlement workers and known as the House of the
Seven Gables, might have appeared to the descendants a
far more fitting Nathaniel Hawthorne memorial than the
Bela Lyon Pratt statue.

If in returning to the center of Salem they took the Essex Street route, they came again to Hawthorne Boulevard and then, on their right, to the mansion where old Captain White had been murdered. In the building adjacent to it on the west, the Essex Institute, they might have found a vast amount of data relating to the history of their family. If they were obliged to stop for lights when they reached Washington Street, they saw on their left, as they waited, the last of four successive meetinghouses built on the site where their ancestors from generation to generation had gone to thank God for a safe arrival in the New World, to discuss means for defending themselves against the Indians, to hurl insults at Quakers, to view penitents on repentance stools, to question supposed witches, to pray for the return of their men and boys who were gone to sea, to speak defiance to Britain's tyrannical kings, to praise Heaven for the democracy of the American union, and to weigh in their hearts the manifold problems besetting modern life. On that site the progenitors of the living Hawthornes had listened to as many as thirty thousand sermons, delivered by ministers whose theology ranged from the most rigid Calvinism to a Unitarianism stripped of dogma. For two years this last meetinghouse on the time-honored site had been given over wholly to commerce, and the First Church parishioners had worshiped at a sanctuary in a residential quarter.

If the descendants when well past Washington Street turned into southwest Salem, they came to Hathorne Street and Hathorne Place, both of which, lined with trees, extend on land which once formed part of Major William Hathorne's Mill Pond farm. If the descendants drove on into Danvers, they possibly traversed the quarter known locally as "Hathorne, Mass." Nearby is Hathorne Hill, on the summit of which stands a principal building of the hospital for the insane maintained by the state of Massachusetts.

Neither Hawthorne's son nor his daughter was present at the unveiling of his statue. Julian, still in California, had lost Minnie early in 1925 and was already, at the age of seventy-nine, married again. His new wife—a New Yorker, born Edith Garrigues—was a painter, and had been for a time his secretary. Mother Alphonsa, replying to an invitation sent by the president of the Hawthorne Memorial Association, wrote that she was prevented by illness from attending the unveiling. She said in concluding, "I beg you to realize that I feel more than I can express, as the daughter of a beloved father," and signed the letter "Rose Hawthorne, Mother M. Alphonsa Lathrop, O.S.D."

Her last great work for the Servants of Relief for Incurable Cancer was the erection of a fireproof building to replace the wooden house which had served Rosary Hill Home for a quarter of a century. The construction was already under way at the time of the unveiling of the Hawthorne statue, but Mother Alphonsa did not live to see the work entirely completed. On July 9, 1926, early in the morning, she died in her sleep, at the age of seventy-five. The day was the eighty-fourth anniversary of the wedding of her father and mother.

Julian, longer-lived than any known paternal ancestor, was well on June 22, 1934, when he reached the age of eighty-eight. A few days later he was stricken with an illness from which he readily recovered. But the second week in July he suffered a relapse, and this time he was too feeble to bear the strain. He died at his home in San Francisco on July 14. Just three hundred years had passed since William Hathorne was made a freeman in the town of Dorchester in Massachusetts Bay.

Edith Garrigues Hawthorne, Julian's widow, died on January 5, 1949, bringing to an end the seventh generation of a great American family. At the time of her death precisely a century had passed since her father-in-law, whether at his office in the Salem customhouse or in his Mall Street home, was turning over in his mind the images and concepts to which he gave expression in *The Scarlet Letter*.

BIBLIOGRAPHICAL NOTE

I N assembling the material for *The Hawthornes* I found that certain works were as indispensable to me as were encyclopedias and biographical dictionaries. These works are as follows: *New England Historical and Genealogical Register*, published quarterly in Boston since 1847; *Essex Institute Historical Collections*, begun in Salem in 1859, issued irregularly for about a decade and since then quarterly; *Essex Antiquarian*, a quarterly published in Salem 1897–1909; *Vital Records of Salem . . . to the End of the Year 1849*, published by the Essex Institute (Salem, 1916–25); Joseph B. Felt, *Annals of Salem* (2d ed., Salem, 1845–49); Sidney Perley, *The History of Salem, Massachusetts* (Salem, 1924–29); and *Visitor's Guide to Salem*, compiled under the auspices of the Essex Institute (Salem, 1937).

The reader should bear in mind that though these works are not always cited below, facts drawn from them are scattered throughout *The Hawthornes*. The reader will observe that in all groupings works are listed chronologically.

THE HAWTHORNES IN ENGLAND

1490–1650

The legend of the Hawthornes is an enlargement of synopses found in Charles Kerry, *The History and Antiquities of the Hundred of Bray* (London, 1861) and in manuscripts (privately owned, now in preparation for publication) relating to the American descendants of Ralph Staverton of the Manor of Shiplake in Bray. The historical matter on the early Hawthornes of Bray is from these two sources and also from the following works: Henry F. Waters, *Genealogical Gleanings in England* (Boston, 1901); "An Account of the First Reunion of the Descendants of Major William and John Hathorne Held at

Salem, Massachusetts, June 23, 1904," *Essex Institute Histori-cal Collections*, XLI (1905), 72–92; *The Four Visitations of Berkshire*, ed. W. H. Reynolds, *Harleian Society Publications*, Vols. LVI and LVII (1907–8); and the third volume of *The Victoria History of the County of Berkshire*, ed. William Page and P. H. Ditchfield (London, 1923).

The matter on the Puritans of Dorsetshire and their migration to the New World is from John White, *The Planter's Plea* (London, 1630); Arthur Wilmot Ackermann, *Reverend John White of Dorchester, England* (Boston, 1929); and Francis Rose-Troup, *John White, the Patriarch of Dorchester* (London, 1930). For the facts on Endecott, I depended upon Lawrence Shaw Mayo, *John Endecott* (Cambridge, Mass., 1936). My sources for the facts on Higginson are Francis Higginson, *New England's Plantation* (London, 1630), and Thomas Wentworth Higginson, *Life of Francis Higginson* (Boston, 1891). I took certain details from the writings of John Winthrop: *Winthrop's Journal*, ed. James Kendall Hosmer (New York, 1908); *Winthrop Papers*, published by the Massachusetts Historical Society (Boston, 1929–47); and Robert Charles Winthrop, *Life and Letters of John Winthrop* (Boston, 1869). Miscellaneous information on the Puritan migration was drawn from Charles Edward Banks, *The Winthrop Fleet of 1630* (Boston, 1930) and from George Findlay Willison, *Saints and Strangers* (New York, 1945).

MAJOR WILLIAM HATHORNE

1607–1681

For the over-all picture of life in Massachusetts Bay in the seventeenth century I used the works named above by and about Higginson and Winthrop and also the following works: Cotton Mather, *Magnalia Christi Americana*, ed. Thomas Robbins and Lucius F. Robinson (Hartford, 1853); Thomas Hutchinson, *The History of the Colony and Province of Massachusetts-Bay*, ed. Lawrence Shaw Mayo (Cambridge, Mass., 1936); Alexander Young, *Chronicles of the First Planters of the Colony of Massa-*

chusetts Bay (Boston, 1846); Daniel Appleton White, *New England Congregationalism* (Salem, 1861); Brooks Adams, *The Emancipation of Massachusetts* (Boston, 1887); George E. Ellis, *The Puritan Age and Rule in the Colony of the Massachusetts Bay* (Salem, 1888); Daniel Wait Howe, *The Puritan Republic* (Indianapolis, 1899); James Truslow Adams, *The Founding of New England* (Boston, 1921); Samuel Eliot Morison, *Builders of the Bay Colony* (Boston, 1931); and George Francis Dow, *Everyday Life in Massachusetts Bay in the Seventeenth Century* (Topsfield, Mass., 1935).

The matter on Dorchester, Massachusetts, during the years when Major Hathorne was a resident is from Roger Clap, *Memoirs 1630* (Boston, 1844); James Blake, *Annals of the Town of Dorcester* (Boston, 1846); and *The History of the Town of Dorcester, Massachusetts*, compiled by a committee of the Dorchester Antiquarian and Historical Society (Boston, 1859).

The details for the picture of life in seventeenth-century Salem were taken from Felt's *Annals*, Perley's *History*, and the following works: C. H. Webber and W. S. Nevins, *Old Naumkeag* (Salem, 1877); Charles S. Osgood and H. M. Batchelder, *Historical Sketch of Salem 1626–1879* (Salem, 1879); James Duncan Phillips, *Salem in the Seventeenth Century* (Boston, 1933); Frances Winwar, *Puritan City* (New York, 1938); *Visitor's Guide to Salem; Essex Institute Historical Collections;* and *Essex Antiquarian.*

From many, many allusions and brief notes in the two serial publications last named I gleaned a mass of factual matter relating directly to Major Hathorne, his brother John Hathorne, and his brother-in-law Richard Davenport. I also gleaned considerable definite information on the Major and his relatives from the histories by Winthrop, Felt, Perley, and Phillips. The genealogical tables in Perley were specially helpful. It was with them and the *New England Historical and Genealogical Register*, and *Vital Records of Salem*, that I was able to determine the Hathorne genealogy in the seventeenth century. Though the Hathorne manuscripts belonging to the Essex Institute yielded little that had not been printed, they were of great aid to me:

such an item as the original of a letter written by Major Ha-thorne October 26, 1670, brought me close to my subject.

But my richest source of information on the early American Hathornes turned out to be the following compilations: *Records of the Governor and Company of the Massachusetts Bay in New England 1628–1686,* ed. Nathaniel B. Shurtleff (Boston, 1853–54); *Records of the Court of Assistants of the Colony of the Massachusetts Bay 1630–1692,* published by the County of Suffolk (Boston, 1901–28); *Records and Files of the Quarterly Courts of Essex County, Massachusetts, 1636–1683,* published by the Essex Institute (Salem, 1911–21); and *The Probate Records of Essex County 1635–1681,* published by the Essex Institute (Salem, 1916–20).

For the matter on Major Hathorne and the Quakers I supplemented the court records, Perley, and Phillips with the following works: Samuel Groome, *A Glass for the People of New England* (London, 1676); John Whiting, *Truth and Innocency Defended* (London, 1702); George Bishop, *New-England Judged by the Spirit of the Lord* (London, 1703); James Bowden, *History of the Society of Friends in America* (London, 1850–54); Henry Lawrence Southwick, *The Policy of the Early Colonists of Massachusetts towards Quakers* (Boston, 1885); Richard Price Hallowell, *The Quaker Invasion of Massachusetts* (Boston, 1887); Horatio Rogers, *Mary Dyer of Rhode Island* (Providence, 1896); and Rufus Matthew Jones, *The Quakers in the American Colonies* (London, 1911).

The matter on Major Hathorne's attitude toward royal authority after 1660 is from Hutchinson's *History;* Phillips' *Salem in the Seventeenth Century; Records of the Governor and Company of the Massachusetts Bay; Records of the Court of Assistants; Edward Randolph . . . His Letters and Official Papers,* ed. Robert Nixon and Alfred Thomas Scrope Goodrick, published by the Prince Society (Boston, 1898–1909); and Julian Hawthorne, *Nathaniel Hawthorne and His Wife* (Boston, 1884).

The information on the roles played by the Hathornes, Davenports, Gardners, and Captain Nicholas Manning in King

Philip's War was taken from Hutchinson and Phillips and also from *Soldiers of King Philip's War*, ed. George Madison Bodge (Boston, 1906) and *Narratives of the Indian Wars*, ed. Charles Henry Lincoln (New York, 1913).

Other facts relating to Captain Nicholas Manning and also the matter on his mother, brother, and sisters are from Felt, Perley, *Essex Institute Historical Collections, Essex Antiquarian*, and *Records and Files of the Quarterly Courts of Essex County*. In the court records the trial of the Manning sisters on the charge of incest with their brother Captain Nicholas is reported in detail. In establishing the identity of each of the early American Mannings I was aided by William Henry Manning, *The Genealogical and Biographical History of the Manning Families of New England* (Salem, 1902).

The matter on Major Hathorne's last days and death is from Perley's *History* and from *Diary of Samuel Sewall*, published by the Massachusetts Historical Society (Boston, 1878–82). The Major's will and the inventory of his estate were printed in *The Probate Records of Essex County 1635–1681*.

COLONEL JOHN HATHORNE

1641–1717

The sources which I used in giving the personal history of Major Hathorne I again used in building up the portrait of his son Colonel John Hathorne. For supplementary matter on the boy's religious and secular education I drew from the following books: Alice Morse Earle, *The Sabbath in New England* (New York, 1892); George Emery Littlefield, *Early Schools and School-Books of New England* (Boston, 1904); George Leroy Jackson, *The Development of School Support in Colonial Massachusetts* (New York, 1909); and Sanford Fleming, *Children and Puritanism* (New Haven, 1933).

The facts on Colonel Hathorne's activities from the death of his father to the outbreak of the witchcraft delusion were taken from *Records of the Court of Assistants, Edward Randolph*, Hutchinson's *History*, Felt's *Annals*, Perley's *History*, Phillips'

Salem in the Seventeenth Century, Essex Institute Historical Collections, and *Essex Antiquarian.*

My sources for the chapter on Colonel Hathorne's role in the witchcrafts are the following works (listed in order of date of composition): Increase Mather, *An Essay for the Recording of Illustrious Providences* (London, 1684); Cotton Mather, *Memorable Providences* (Boston, 1689); miscellaneous manuscripts in the Essex Institute library; *Records of Salem Witchcraft,* compiled by W. E. Woodward (Roxbury, Mass., 1864–65); *Diary of Samuel Sewall* (cited above) and also *Letter-Book of Samuel Sewall,* published by the Massachusetts Historical Society (Boston, 1886–88); Robert Calef, *The Wonders of the Invisible World Displayed* (London, 1700); *Salem Witchcraft,* ed. Samuel Page Fowler (Salem, 1861); *Narratives of the Witchcraft Cases,* ed. George Lincoln Burr (New York, 1914); Thomas Hutchinson, *History* (cited above) and also *The Witchcraft Delusion of 1692,* ed. William Frederick Poole (Boston, 1870); Samuel Gardner Drake, *The Witchcraft Delusion in New England* (Roxbury, Mass., 1866); Charles Wentworth Upham, *Salem Witchcraft* (Boston, 1867); John Fiske, *Witchcraft in Salem Village* (New York, 1923); W. N. Gemmill, *The Salem Witch Trials* (Chicago, 1924); Kenneth Ballard Murdock, *Increase Mather* (Cambridge, Mass., 1925); George Lyman Kittredge, *Witchcraft in Old and New England* (Cambridge, Mass., 1929); Charles Sutherland Tapley, *Rebecca Nurse* (Boston, 1930); and Marion Lena Starkey, *The Devil in Massachusetts* (New York, 1949).

My main guide in tracing Colonel Hathorne's movements and experiences after 1692 was Emory Washburn, *Sketches of the Judicial History of Massachusetts from 1630 to the Revolution in 1775* (Boston, 1840). I also made use of facts found in the *Essex Institute Historical Collections,* the *Essex Antiquarian,* Sewall, Felt, Perley, and Phillips. A photostatic copy of the Colonel's will and the inventory of his estate are on file in the archives of the Essex County Probate Court. The will (with numerous errors) was printed in Julian Hawthorne's *Nathaniel Hawthorne and His Wife,* cited above.

CAPTAIN JOSEPH HATHORNE

1692–1762

Works already named which supplied me with direct facts on Captain Joseph Hathorne and on his Hathorne, Gardner, Porter, Higginson, Derby, Putnam, Bowditch, Manning, English, Touzell, Becket, and Phelps contemporaries are as follows: *New England Historical and Genealogical Register, Vital Records of Salem, Essex Institute Historical Collections, Essex Antiquarian,* Felt's *Annals,* and Perley's *History.* Added facts relating directly to the eighteenth-century Hathornes were supplied by George Granville Putnam, *Salem Vessels and Their Voyages* (Salem, 1922–25); James Duncan Phillips, *Salem in the Eighteenth Century* (Boston, 1937); and Harriet Silverster Tapley, *St. Philip's Church in Salem, Massachusetts* (Salem, 1944).

For the background matter in the section on Captain Joseph I used details found in Felt's *Annals,* Phillips' *Salem in the Eighteenth Century,* and the following books: Charles E. Trow, *The Old Shipmasters of Salem* (New York, 1905); Ralph D. Paine, *The Ships and Sailors of Old Salem* (Boston, 1924); and James Duncan Phillips, *Life and Times of Richard Derby* (Cambridge, Mass., 1929).

I drew considerable miscellaneous detail from the will of Captain Joseph Hathorne and the inventory of his estate, both of which are on file in the archives of the Essex County Probate Court.

CAPTAIN DANIEL HATHORNE

1731–1796

The story of Daniel Hathorne and Mary Rondel is told in Julian Hawthorne's *Nathaniel Hawthorne and His Wife.* I gleaned other intimate details relating to Captain Daniel from the Essex Institute collection of Hawthorne scrapbooks (made up of hundreds of newspaper clippings, a number of which contain anecdotal matter on the Hathornes and Mannings of the two generations preceding the romancer). I also found allusions to Captain

Daniel in the following works: *Essex Institute Historical Collections; Essex Antiquarian;* Felt's *Annals;* Perley's *History;* Phillips' *Salem in the Eighteenth Century;* and Hildegarde Hawthorne, *Romantic Rebel: the Story of Nathaniel Hawthorne* (New York, 1932).

The matter on Captain Daniel's Hathorne, Bowditch, Ropes, and Cheever relatives is from Felt, Perley, Phillips, and *Essex Institute Historical Collections.* The matter on Captain Richard Manning is from *The Genealogical and Biographical History of the Manning Families of New England* and the Essex Institute collection of Hawthorne scrapbooks.

In my effort to picture the Salem which Captain Daniel knew, I used Felt, Perley, Phillips, Winwar, and the following compilations: *The Diary of William Pynchon of Salem,* ed. Fitch Edward Oliver (Boston, 1890) and *The Holyoke Diaries 1709–1856,* ed. George Francis Dow (Salem, 1911).

The matter on Captain Daniel's voyages and privateering expeditions is from Putnam's *Salem Vessels and Their Voyages,* Paine's *The Ships and Sailors of Old Salem,* Phillips' *Salem in the Eighteenth Century,* and the following books: *The Navy of the United States 1773 to 1853: To Which Is Added a List of Private Vessels Fitted Out Under the American Flag,* ed. George F. Emmons (Washington, 1853); Edgar Stanton Maclay, *A History of American Privateers* (New York, 1924); and Gardner Weld Allen, *Massachusetts Privateers in the Revolution* (Boston, 1927). The ballad "Bold Hathorne" (it was reprinted in George Parsons Lathrop, *A Study of Hawthorne,* Boston, 1876) is given as it appeared in *Poets and Poetry of America,* ed. Rufus Wilmot Griswold (Philadelphia, 1842).

The matter on Simon Forrester and his rise to great fortune is from *The Diary of William Bentley,* published by the Essex Institute (Salem, 1905–14); Robert Ephraim Peabody, *Merchant Venturers of Old Salem* (Boston, 1912); and Henry Wyckoff Belknap, "Simon Forrester of Salem and His Descendants," *Essex Institute Historical Collections,* LXXI (1935), 17–64.

CAPTAIN NATHANIEL HATHORNE

1775–1808

The matter on Salem history during Captain Nathaniel Hathorne's lifetime is from the Salem *Gazette, The Diary of William Bentley, The Holyoke Diaries,* Felt's *Annals,* Perley's *History,* Phillips' *Salem in the Eighteenth Century,* Winwar's *Puritan City, Visitor's Guide to Salem,* and the following articles: Theodore Bolton, "John Hazlitt, Portrait Painter," *Essex Institute Historical Collections,* LVI (1920), 293–295, and "Presidential Visits to Salem," made up largely of a reprint from the Salem *Gazette* of November 3, 1789, *Essex Institute Historical Collections,* LXXXII (1946), 343–349.

The facts on Captain Nathaniel's mother, brother, and sisters were taken from Felt, Perley, Phillips, Belknap's "Simon Forrester of Salem and His Descendants," the Essex Institute collection of Hawthorne scrapbooks, and from records in the archives of the Essex County Probate Court. In assembling the data on the Mannings, I was guided by *The Genealogical and Biographical History of the Manning Families of New England.*

Julian Hawthorne's *Nathaniel Hawthorne and His Wife* and Hildegarde Hawthorne's *Romantic Rebel* were of value to me in building up the character of Captain Nathaniel.

On such voyages as he made to the Orient I found full treatment in Peabody's *Merchant Venturers;* in Edwin B. Hewes, "Nathaniel Bowditch, Supercargo and Mariner," *Essex Institute Historical Collections,* LXX (1934), 209–226; and in the two most recent books by James Duncan Phillips: *Salem and the Indies* (Boston, 1947) and *Pepper and Pirates* (Boston, 1949). But most of the matter on Captain Nathaniel's voyages was taken from the Essex Institute collection of Hathorne manuscripts, which includes logbooks.

It was in these manuscripts that I found the details relating to Captain Nathaniel's death. For the facts and figures relating to the settlement of his estate I relied also upon Essex County Probate Court records.

NATHANIEL HAWTHORNE

1804–1864

The diaries and local histories used in describing the Salem with which Captain Nathaniel Hathorne was familiar were again used when I set about picturing the Salem of which his son the romancer was a part. Particularly helpful were the files of Salem newspapers owned by the Essex Institute. I also gleaned details from the following works: Eleanor Putnam, *Old Salem*, ed. Arlo Bates (Boston, 1886); Marianne Cabot Devereaux Silsbee, *A Half Century in Salem* (Boston, 1887); Mary Harrod Northend, *Memories of Old Salem Drawn from the Letters of a Great-Grandmother* (New York, 1917); S. F. Kimball, *The Elias Hasket Derby Mansion in Salem* (Salem, 1924); *Catalogue of Portraits in the Essex Institute*, compiled under the auspices of the Salem Institute (Salem, 1936); Caroline Howard King, *When I Lived in Salem 1822–1866* (Brattleboro, Vt., 1937); Samuel Chamberlain, *Historic Salem in Four Seasons: a Camera Impression* (New York, 1938); *Portraits of Shipmasters and Merchants in the Peabody Museum*, compiled under the auspices of the Peabody Museum (Salem, 1939); and George Batchelder, "The Salem of Hawthorne's Time," *Essex Institute Historical Collections*, LXXXIV (1948), 64–74.

In collecting details for the portraits of Hawthorne and his mother and sisters I depended most upon his letters and autobiographical writings. The earliest of these is *Hawthorne's First Diary*, ed. Samuel T. Pickard (Boston, 1897). Though this little book was withdrawn from circulation when the editor discovered that it was not wholly authentic, I drew from it details which fit into the pattern of what is definitely known concerning Hawthorne's boyhood. The other autobiographical and epistolary publications, listed roughly according to time of composition, are as follows: *The American Notebooks*, ed. Randall Stewart (New Haven, 1932); *Love Letters of Nathaniel Hawthorne*, published by the Society of the Dofobs (Chicago, 1907); "The Old Manse," introduction to *Mosses from an Old Manse* (New York, 1846); "The Custom House," introduction to *The Scarlet Letter* (Boston, 1850); *The English Notebooks*, ed. Randall Stewart (New York, 1941); *Our Old Home* (Boston, 1863); *Passages from the French and Italian Note-Books*, ed. Sophia Peabody Hawthorne (New York, 1870); and *Letters of Hawthorne to William D. Ticknor 1851–1864*, published by the Carteret Book Club of Newark, New Jersey, 1910 (reprinted in Caroline Ticknor's *Hawthorne and His Publisher*, cited below).

Much more revealing to me were the letters found in many of the following biographical books and articles on Hawthorne, listed according to date of publication: James T. Fields, the section on Hawthorne in *Yesterdays with Authors* (Boston, 1871); George Parsons Lathrop, *A Study of Hawthorne* (Boston, 1876); Henry James, *Hawthorne* (New York, 1880); Julian Hawthorne, *Nathaniel Hawthorne and His Wife* (Boston, 1884); Moncure D. Conway, *Life of Nathaniel Hawthorne* (London, 1890); Elizabeth Manning, "The Boyhood of Hawthorne," *Wide Awake*, XXXIII (1891), 500–518; Horatio Bridge, *Personal Recollections of Nathaniel Hawthorne* (New York, 1893); Rose Hawthorne Lathrop, *Memories of Hawthorne* (Boston, 1897); Annie Fields, *Nathaniel Hawthorne* (Boston, 1899); George E. Woodberry, *Nathaniel Hawthorne* (Boston, 1902); Julian Hawthorne, *Hawthorne and His Circle* (New York, 1903); Frank A. Stearns, *The Life and Genius of Nathaniel Hawthorne* (Philadelphia, 1906); Frank B. Sanborn, *Hawthorne and His Friends* (Cedar Rapids, Ia., 1908); Caroline Ticknor, *Hawthorne and His Publisher* (Boston, 1913); Lloyd Morris, *The Rebellious Puritan: Portrait of Mr. Hawthorne* (New York, 1927); Herbert Gorman, *Hawthorne: a Study in Solitude* (New York, 1927); Newton Arvin, *Hawthorne* (Boston, 1929); Hildegarde Hawthorne, *Romantic Rebel: the Story of Nathaniel Hawthorne* (New York, 1932); Edward B. Hungerford, "Hawthorne Gossips about Salem," *New England Quarterly*, VI (1933), 445–469; Manning Hawthorne, "Hawthorne's Early Years," *Essex Institute Historical Collections*, LXXIV (1938), 1–21; Manning Hawthorne, "Hawthorne Prepares for College," *New England Quarterly*, XI

(1938), 66–89; Manning Hawthorne, "Mary Louisa Hawthorne," *Essex Institute Historical Collections*, LXXV (1939), 103–134; Manning Hawthorne, "Nathaniel and Elizabeth Hawthorne, Editors," *Colophon*, New Graphic Series, III (1939), 36–38; Manning Hawthorne, "Parental and Family Influences on Hawthorne," *Essex Institute Historical Collections*, LXXVI (1940), 1–13; Edward Mather, *Nathaniel Hawthorne: a Modest Man* (New York, 1940); Randall Stewart, "Recollections of Hawthorne by His Sister Ebe," *American Literature*, XVI (1945), 316–331; Manning Hawthorne, "A Glimpse of Hawthorne's Boyhood," *Essex Institute Historical Collections*, LXXXIII (1947), 178–185; Manning Hawthorne, "Aunt Ebe: Some Letters of Elizabeth M. Hawthorne," *New England Quarterly*, XX (1947), 209–231; Randall Stewart, *Hawthorne: a Biography* (New Haven, 1948); Robert Cantwell, *Nathaniel Hawthorne: the American Years* (New York, 1948); and Mark Van Doren, *Nathaniel Hawthorne* (New York, 1949).

The Essex Institute collection of Hawthorne scrapbooks provided me with anecdotal details not found in any of the biographical treatises.

The matter on the romancer's grandparents, uncles, aunts, and cousins not found in the sources listed above is from the following sources: Perley's *History; Essex Institute Historical Collections; Essex Antiquarian;* obituaries and miscellaneous notices in Salem newspapers; the article on Robert Manning in the *Dictionary of American Biography;* the article on Rebecca Manning (Robert Manning's daughter) in the Salem *Evening News* for July 25, 1933; the Essex Institute Hathorne manuscripts; the Essex Institute Hawthorne scrapbooks; miscellaneous manuscript material in the Essex Institute library, such as health records; and wills, inventories, and papers on the settlement of estates in the archives of the Essex County Probate Court.

The most complete and most trustworthy account of the murder of Captain Joseph White was written by Judge Benjamin Merrill, who was living in Salem at the time of the tragedy. His account, entitled "The White Murder," is to be found in the eleventh volume of *The Writings and Speeches of Daniel Webster*, National Edition (Boston, 1903). Much which I have on the tragedy was taken from Merrill. Much came also from the Salem *Gazette* for 1830, especially the matter relating to Richard Crowninshield. Of aid to me in tracing the relationship of Hawthorne to the Crowninshield family were the unprinted Crowninshield genealogical papers in the library of the Essex Institute. A source from which I took minor details is "Letters of Mary Boardman Crowninshield," *Essex Institute Historical Collections*, LXXXIII (1947), 112–143.

The Hawthorne correspondence supplied a good deal of the matter which I have on Horace Conolly. I also took details from the following sources: report of an interview with Conolly printed in the Salem *Evening News* for August 7, 1893, a few months before his death; "Hawthorne and *Evangeline*," an article compiled from manuscripts (including a letter from Hawthorne) left by Conolly, published in the Boston *Globe*, July 3, 1904; Manning Hawthorne, "Hawthorne and the Man of God," *Colophon*, new series, II (1937), 262–282; and Manning Hawthorne and H. W. L. Dana, *The Origin and Development of Longfellow's Evangeline* (Portland, Me., 1947).

The matter on the Peabodys was culled from the Hawthorne biographies; the Salem *Gazette* from 1820 to 1842; *Essex Institute Historical Collections;* Mary Tyler Mann, *Life of Horace Mann* (Boston, 1865); Sophia Peabody Hawthorne, *Notes on England and Italy* (New York, 1870); and Louise H. Tharp, *The Peabody Sisters of Salem* (Boston, 1950).

The facts on Pierce were taken either from the Hawthorne biographies or from Roy Franklin Nichols, *Franklin Pierce* (Philadelphia, 1931).

The biographers of Hawthorne are not the only critics to whom I am indebted. In arriving at my conclusions regarding *The Scarlet Letter* and other works I was in one way or another affected by each of the following treatises (listed according to date of publication): L. Dhaleine, *N. Hawthorne, sa vie et son oeuvre* (Paris, 1905); the section on Hawthorne in William

Crary Brownell, *American Prose Masters* (New York, 1909); the section on Hawthorne in Henry Augustin Beers, *Four Americans* (New York, 1919); Elizabeth L. Chandler, *A Study of the Sources of the Tales and Romances Written by Nathaniel Hawthorne before 1853* (Northampton, Mass., 1926); Julien Green, *Un puritain homme de lettres* (Toulouse, 1928); L. E. Chrétien, *La Pensée morale de Nathaniel Hawthorne* (Paris, 1932); "Books Read by Hawthorne 1828–1850: from the 'Charge Books' of the Salem Athenaeum," *Essex Institute Historical Collections*, LXVIII (1932), 65–87; Fannye N. Cherry, "The Sources of 'Young Goodman Brown,'" *American Literature*, V (1934), 342–348; Elisabeth Réti, *Hawthorne's Verhältnis zur Neu-Englandtradition* (Rüstringen, 1935); Austin Warren, "Hawthorne's Reading," *New England Quarterly*, VIII (1935), 480–497; Arlin Turner, "Hawthorne's Literary Borrowings," *Publications of the Modern Language Association*, LI (1936), 543–562; Edward Barker Dawson, *Hawthorne's Knowledge and Use of New England History* (Nashville, 1939); Bertha Faust, *Hawthorne's Contemporaneous Reputation: a Study of Literary Opinion in America 1828–1864* (Philadelphia, 1939); the section on Hawthorne in F. O. Matthiessen, *American Renaissance* (London, 1941); Arlin Turner, *Hawthorne as Editor: Selections from His Writings in the American Magazine of Useful and Entertaining Knowledge* (University, La., 1941); Dorothy Waples, "Suggestions for Interpreting *The Marble Faun*," *American Literature*, XIII (1941), 224–239; Lawrence Sargent Hall, *Hawthorne: Critic of Society* (New Haven, 1944); Leland Schubert, *Hawthorne the Artist* (Chapel Hill, 1944); Jane Lundblad, *Nathaniel Hawthorne and European Literary Tradition* (Cambridge, Mass., 1947); and Edward H. Davidson, *Hawthorne's Last Phase* (New Haven, 1949).

MOTHER ALPHONSA
1851–1926

For the facts on Elizabeth Manning Hawthorne after the death of her brother I relied upon Essex County Probate Court records; manuscripts and scrapbooks in the Essex Institute library; Julian Hawthorne's *Nathaniel Hawthorne and His Wife;* Randall Stewart's "Recollections of Hawthorne by His Sister Ebe"; Manning Hawthorne's "Aunt Ebe: Some Letters of Elizabeth M. Hawthorne"; and the following biographies of Mother Alphonsa: James J. Walsh, *Mother Alphonsa: Rose Hawthorne Lathrop* (New York, 1930); Katherine Burton, *Sorrow Built a Bridge: a Daughter of Hawthorne* (New York, 1930); and Theodore Maynard, *A Fire Was Lighted: the Life of Rose Hawthorne Lathrop* (Milwaukee, 1948). Facts from all these sources were supplemented by the obituary on Elizabeth Manning Hawthorne in the Salem *Evening News* for January 2, 1883.

Salem newspapers together with Essex County Probate Court records supplied the information on the less important Hawthornes and Mannings who survived the romancer.

The matter on his widow and elder daughter after 1864 is from Julian Hawthorne's *Nathaniel Hawthorne and His Wife;* Thomas Wentworth Higginson, "Una Hawthorne," *Outlook*, LXXVII (1904), 594–606; Julian Hawthorne, *Shapes That Pass: Memories of Old Days* (Boston, 1928); Randall Stewart, "Mrs. Hawthorne's Financial Difficulties: Selections from Her Letters to James T. Fields 1865–1868," *More Books*, XXII (1946), 45–53; and Theodore Maynard's *A Fire Was Lighted*.

From the admirable work last named and from various New York, Boston, and Salem newspapers I drew the material on Mother Alphonsa and George Parsons Lathrop.

Newspapers also supplied me with many facts relating to Julian Hawthorne between 1864 and 1912. Other facts relating to his career as a man of letters are from his *Nathaniel Hawthorne and His Wife, Hawthorne and His Circle*, and *Shapes That Pass*.

The matter on his trial and imprisonment is from his book, *The Subterranean Brotherhood* (New York, 1914); the New York *Times, World*, and *Sun;* and a collection of newspaper clippings in the Essex Institute library.

Obituaries on file in "the morgue" of the Journalism Library of Columbia University supplied the details on the last days of

Mother Alphonsa, Julian Hawthorne, and Edith Garrigues Hawthorne.

The account of the unveiling of the Nathaniel Hawthorne statue in Salem is based on the report printed in the Salem *Evening News* for December 24, 1925.

INDEX